THE JEWISH GHETTO AND THE VISUAL IMAGINATION OF EARLY MODERN VENICE

Dana E. Katz examines the Jewish ghetto of Venice as a paradox of urban space. In 1516, the Senate established the ghetto on the periphery of the city and legislated nocturnal curfews to reduce the Jews' visibility in Venice. Katz argues that it was precisely this practice of marginalization that put the ghetto on display for Christian and Jewish eyes. According to her research, early modern Venetians grounded their conceptions of the ghetto in discourses of sight. Katz's unique approach demonstrates how the Jewish ghetto engaged the sensory imagination of its inhabitants in complex and contradictory ways that both shaped urban space and reshaped Christian-Jewish relations.

Dana E. Katz is Joshua C. Taylor Associate Professor of Art History and Humanities at Reed College. Her research explores representations of religious difference in early modern Italy, with a particular focus on Jewish-Christian relations. Katz is the author of *The Jew in the Art of the Italian Renaissance* (2008), as well as articles in *The Art Bulletin*, *Art History*, and *Jewish History*.

THE JEWISH GHETTO AND THE VISUAL IMAGINATION OF EARLY MODERN VENICE

DANA E. KATZ
Reed College

CAMBRIDGE
UNIVERSITY PRESS

CAMBRIDGE
UNIVERSITY PRESS

One Liberty Plaza, New York, NY 10006, USA

Cambridge University Press is part of the University of Cambridge.

It furthers the University's mission by disseminating knowledge in the pursuit of education, learning, and research at the highest international levels of excellence.

www.cambridge.org
Information on this title: www.cambridge.org/9781107165144
10.1017/9781316691526

First published 2017

Printed in the United States of America by Sheridan Books, Inc.

A catalog record for this publication is available from the British Library.

ISBN 978-1-107-16514-4 Hardback

To my son

CONTENTS

ILLUSTRATIONS

ACKNOWLEDGMENTS

For the past ten years, I have had the pleasure of collaborating with colleagues at Reed College in an early modern humanities course that has motivated me to think between and through disciplinary boundaries, to draw from the disparate approaches of cognate disciplines in analyzing early modernity. Mark Bedau, Michael Breen, Ariadna García-Bryce, David Garrett, Kambiz GhaneaBassiri, Ray Kierstead, Robert Knapp, Mary Ashburn Miller, David Sacks, and Lisa Steinman have delivered lectures in the course that reaffirm my scholarly commitment to and pedagogical interest in interdisciplinarity. Such methodological richness has inspired me beyond the pages of this book. I have also profited greatly from my students at Reed, who read primary sources as well as contemporary and current theoretical texts with care to ignite dynamic classroom discussion.

Support for this project has come in many forms, most notably the institutions that provided me the resources to conduct extensive research in the Archivio di Stato di Venezia and beyond: the Gladys Krieble Delmas Foundation, the Michael E. and Carol S. Levine Foundation, the Andrew W. Mellon Foundation, the Renaissance Society of America, the Memorial Foundation for Jewish Culture, and Reed College. In addition, I received a generous publication subvention from the Samuel H. Kress Foundation and the Renaissance Society of America. I am also grateful to Edward and Sue Cooley as well as John and Betty Gray for their ongoing support of my research. The responses I received at the annual conferences of the American Association of Italian Studies, the Association for Jewish Studies, the College Art Association, the Renaissance Society of America, and the Sixteenth Century Society and Conference helped shape this book, as did the audiences at Brandeis University, the Centre for Reformation and Renaissance Studies, the College of Idaho, the Institute for Judaic Studies of the Pacific Northwest, Johns Hopkins University, the Museum of Fine Arts Houston, the Portland Art Museum, the University of California Santa Cruz, Western Washington University, Yale University, and York University.

In 2006 and 2008, I participated in the five-week National Endowment for the Humanities Summer Institute, "Venice, the Jews, and Italian Culture: Historical Eras and Cultural Representations," which allowed me to study the ghetto in situ with colleagues from different institutions and different disciplines. For their conversations and questions, I am deeply indebted to the Institute's participants and especially its organizers, Shaul Bassi and Murray Baumgarten. I am also thankful to the staff of the Archivio di Stato di Venezia who taught me how to navigate the archive's extensive holdings. Earlier versions of this research have appeared in *Jewish History* 24, no. 2 (2010); *Judaism and Christian Art: Aesthetic Anxieties from the Catacombs to Colonialism*, edited by Herbert L. Kessler and David Nirenberg (Philadelphia: University of Pennsylvania Press, 2011); and *Sensational Religion: Sensory Cultures in Material Practice*, edited by Sally M. Promey (New Haven, CT: Yale University Press, 2014).

The thoughtful interventions of the following art historians, architectural historians, urban planners, historians, literary critics, and religionists have informed my work: Karen-edis Barzman, Stephen J. Campbell, Charles E. Cohen, Federica Francesconi, Erin Hazard, Matthew C. Hunter, Herbert Kessler, Rabbi David Kosak, Guisela Latorre, Laura Leibman, Stephanie Leitch, Sara Lipton, Lia Markey, Marina Del Negro Karem, David Nirenberg, Dawn Odell, Lisa Pon, Sally M. Promey, Laurence Qamar, Benjamin Ravid, Michael Shapiro, Kenneth Stow, Steven M. Wasserstrom, and Diane Wolfthal. Their comments and criticisms will always be warmly received. The anonymous readers of my manuscript were equally instrumental in strengthening this book, as were the suggestions made throughout the publishing process by Cambridge University Press editors Anastasia Graf and Beatrice Rehl as well as Content Manager Katherine Tengco. For the care he took in editing these pages, I thank Michael W. Phillips Jr. For his assistance with the visual material, I am grateful to Akihiko Miyoshi. I am also grateful to Amyrose McCue Gill and Lisa Regan of TextFormations for compiling the index.

Mark Jurdjevic, Kathryn Lofton, and Meredith K. Ray read and, in many cases, reread each of these chapters. Their feedback has been indispensable, as their friendship will always be. For distracting me from my research with walks and quilts, I thank my colleague in the Mathematics Department, Irena Swanson. Our friendship first blossomed while standing around a Reed College printer discussing Renaissance perspective. Above all, I would like to thank my family for their continued support as I made my way through this project. I owe such gratitude to Lois Katz, Steven Katz, Debbie Katz, David Katz, Fleurette Katz, James Carter, Linda Carter, Andrew Carter, and Nicole Carter, who avidly listened to my ideas for this book and played with my son hour after hour while I wrote in the next room. Many vacations have been spent this way.

Among all those who supported me throughout these past years, E. J. Carter, my husband, and Simon Katz Carter, our son, remain my most cherished advocates. They have studied the ghetto beside me in the heat of the Venetian sun (with gelato), attended my public lectures, and worked around my writing schedule for many years. I dedicate this book to my son who now fills the blank page with his own research on Rubik's Cubes, Japanese spider crabs, World War II, and Neil Armstrong, topics that stimulate our dinner conversations.

INTRODUCTION

IN "A SCENE FROM THE VENICE GHETTO," THE TWENTIETH-century poet Rainer Maria Rilke vividly describes the architectonics of Jewish life in Venice: "[The Venetians] reduced the area of the Ghetto … so that its [Jewish] families … were forced to build their houses in the vertical dimension, one on the roof of another. And their city, which did not lie on the sea, grew slowly into the space of heaven as though it were another sea; and all around the square where the well was, buildings rose in dizzy perpendicularity like the walls of some giant's tower."[1] For Rilke, the tiny houses constituting the Venetian ghetto, "jammed in countless stories one on top of the other," created Babel-like towers from which the Jews viewed the Palazzo Foscari, a domed church, the silvery seascape, and the "quivering sky."[2] From this vantage point, the attenuated tenements offered their Jewish inhabitants a unique view of the city's complex rooflines. The ghetto created an architecture of vision that situated the Jews in a unique spatial relationship with the city. Ghetto heights made Venice legible from the city's edge.

Rilke's tales of ghetto gazing belong not to the twentieth century, however. The story of these multistoried buildings, which remain largely extant today, begins in the Renaissance.[3] In Rilke's spiritual narrative, looking heavenward may have inspired the Jews' humility, but in early modernity their ghetto views represented to the Christian majority the Jews' temerity. An era of ghettoization began in sixteenth-century Venice when authorities reduced Jews to objects of surveillance and supervision.[4] For Venetians, the Jews' social and religious marginality marked them as executors of a defiant, and at times perverse, will that required compulsory and confining accommodations. In other words, Venetian authorities forced Jews into the ghetto to survey their actions and interactions, to make the Jews objects of the Venetian gaze.[5] Yet Venetians were confronted with the reciprocity of that gaze when, as we will see, the Jews returned their look. Ghetto architecture, rising high above the horizon line, placed Jews in the position of urban onlookers whose viewing point did not necessarily degrade them to passive objects but rather animated the Jews' status as observing subjects. Through its vertical ascendancy, the Venice ghetto inadvertently granted its Jewish inhabitants visual recognition in a city that required their marginalization.

In *The Jewish Ghetto and the Visual Imagination of Early Modern Venice*, I study the ghetto as a paradox of urban space.[6] The ghetto marginalized Jews to the periphery to denote their civic subordination; yet it was precisely this practice of peripheralization that put the ghetto on display for Christian and Jewish eyes. Venice's oligarchic government differentiated land use to organize the city's constituent neighborhoods, zoning the ghetto to the northernmost district at a far distance from the political center of the city at the Piazza San Marco and the economic center at the Rialto Bridge (Figure 1). Pushed to the periphery to minimize their visual presence, Jews erected towering tenements that made that marginal community highly visible (Figure 2). The verticality of ghetto architecture deviated from conventions in Venetian urban planning to yield sites of visual disturbance that disrupted the well-ordered social fabric of Venice. Ghetto urbanism, marked by its exaggerated elevations and architectural asymmetries, created a crisis of visuality in that its singularity drew attention from Christians and Jews alike. The ghetto became an imposing monument that heightened the Jews' visibility both from within its walls and from without.

Ghettoization began in Venice on March 29, 1516, when the Senate ordered all Jews residing in the city to move behind the walls of the Ghetto Nuovo (Figure 3).[7] The decree stipulated that the Jews would be locked into the ghetto at night behind gates and would undergo continual surveillance (Figures 4–6). Jews could not own ghetto property; therefore, they rented their high-rent apartments in perpetuity.[8] According to the senatorial decree, ghetto enclosure was necessary to avoid the improprieties and illegalities that surfaced when Jews spread throughout the city:

> Given the urgent needs of the present times, the said Jews have been permitted to come and live in Venice, and the main purpose of this concession was to preserve the property of Christians which was in their hands. But no godfearing subject of our state would have wished them, after their arrival, to disperse throughout the city, sharing houses with Christians and going wherever they choose by day and night, perpetrating all those misdemeanours and detestable and abominable acts which are generally known and shameful to describe, with grave offence to the Majesty of God and uncommon notoriety on the part of this well-ordered Republic.[9]

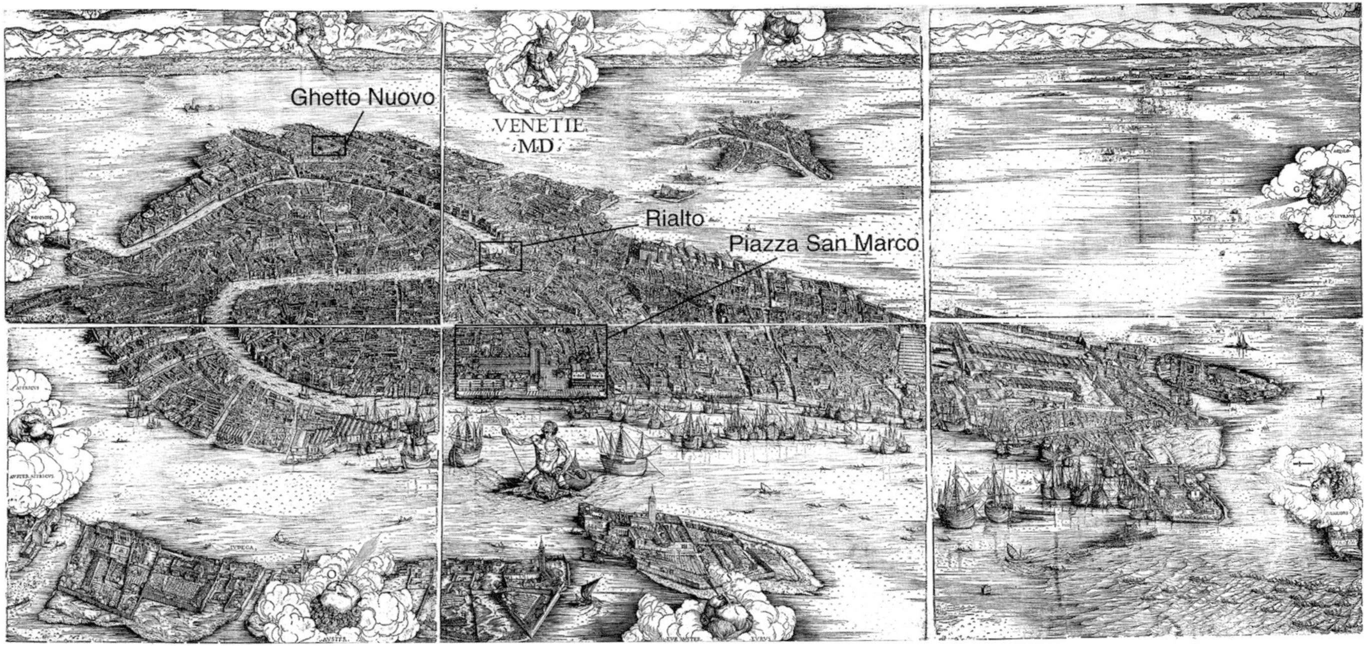

1. Jacopo de' Barbari, *Venetie*, 1500, monument indications added to original by author. Photo courtesy Novacco Collection, The Newberry Library, Chicago.

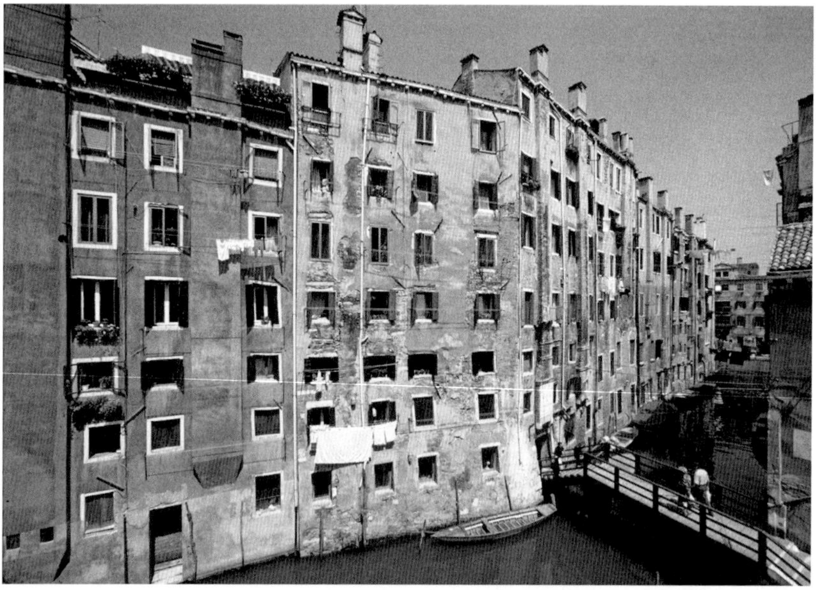

2. Ghetto Nuovo, established in Venice in 1516. Photo courtesy Graziano Arici.

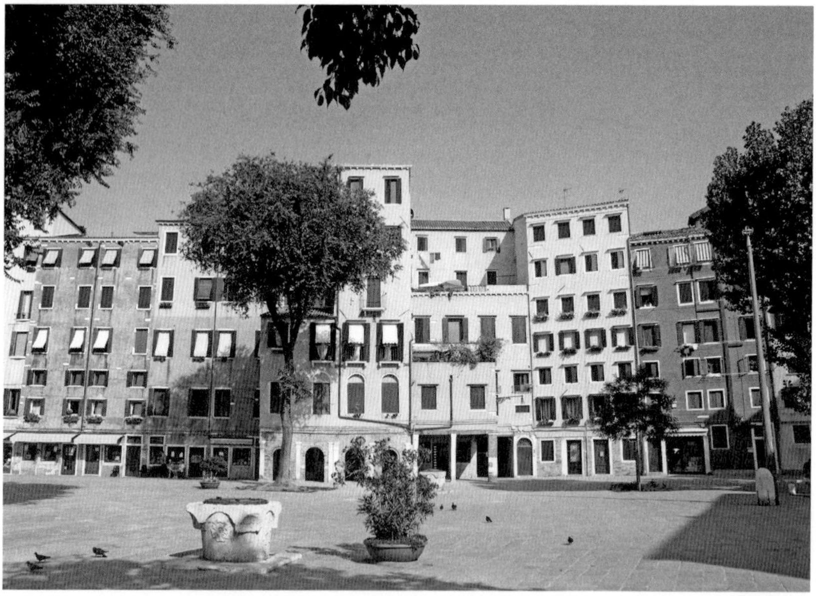

3. Ghetto Nuovo, view from the Campo del Ghetto Nuovo, Venice. Photo: author.

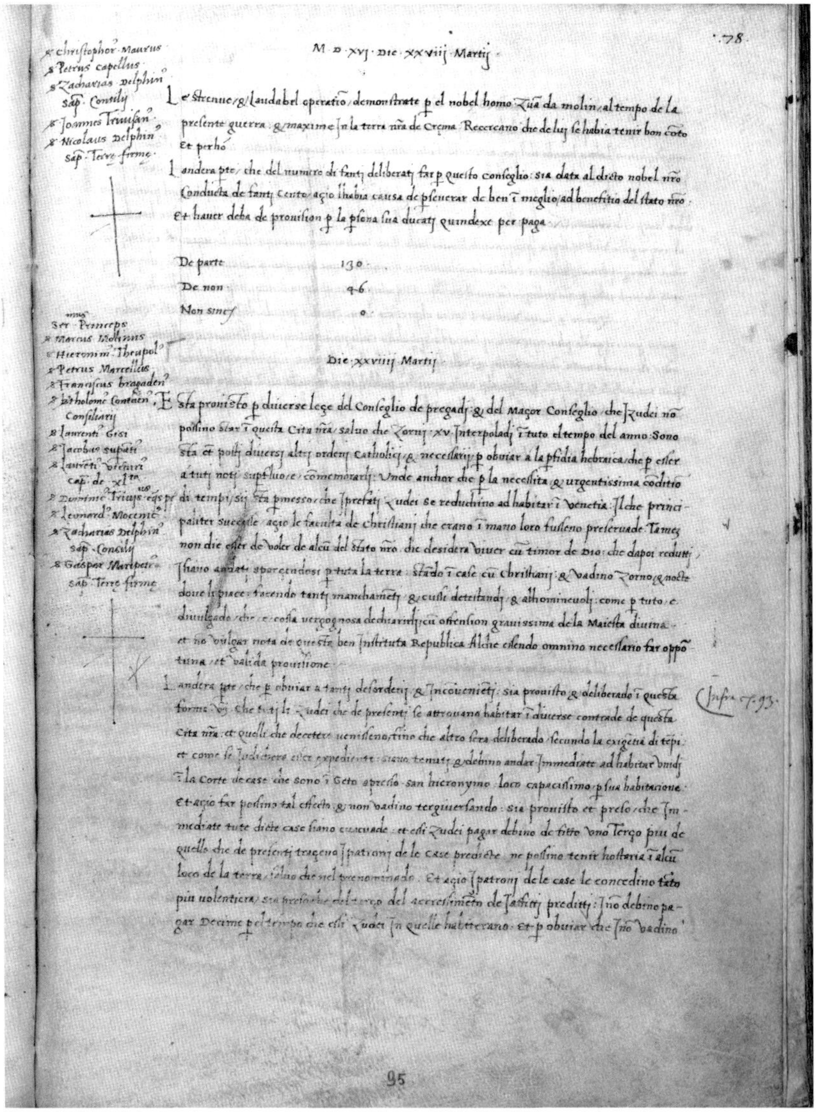

4. Senate decree establishing the Ghetto Nuovo in Venice, March 29, 1516. Archivio di Stato di Venezia, Senato, Terra, registro 19, fol. 78r. Photo courtesy Ministero per i Beni e le Attività Culturali, n. 30/2016.

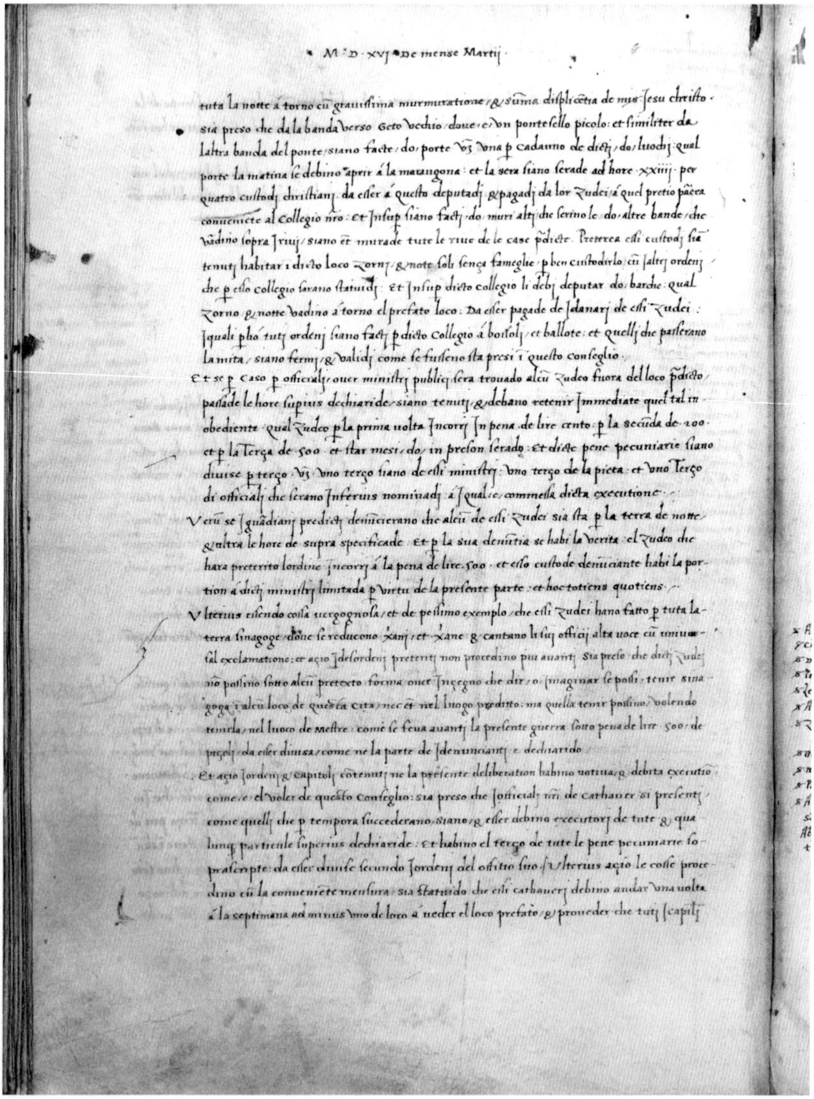
M·D·XVJ De mense Martij

5. Senate decree establishing the Ghetto Nuovo in Venice, March 29, 1516. Archivio di Stato di Venezia, Senato, Terra, registro 19, fol. 78v. Photo courtesy Ministero per i Beni e le Attività Culturali, n. 30/2016.

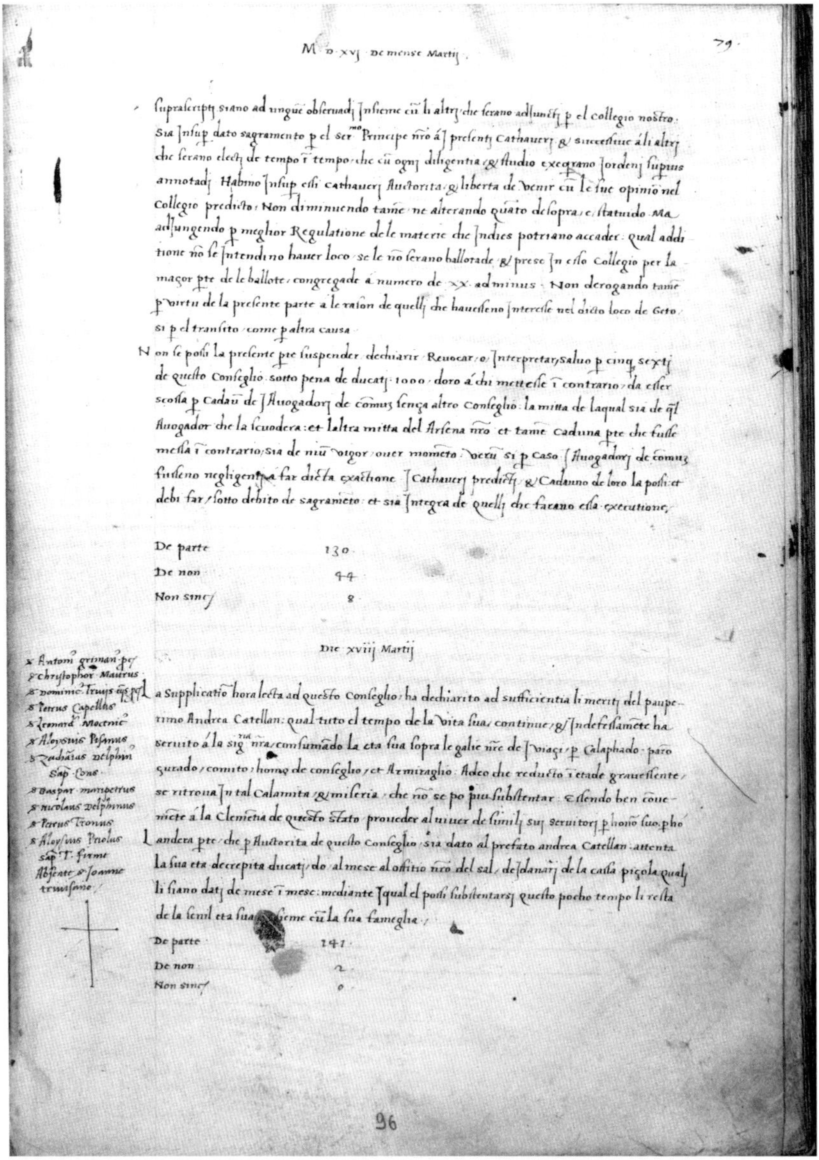

6. Senate decree establishing the Ghetto Nuovo in Venice, March 29, 1516. Archivio di Stato di Venezia, Senato, Terra, registro 19, fol. 79r. Photo courtesy Ministero per i Beni e le Attività Culturali, n. 30/2016.

Although previously permitted to visit Venice for a maximum of fifteen days a year, Jews settled permanently in the city following the Venetian Republic's military defeat by the League of Cambrai in 1509. The economic opportunities of Jewish settlement benefited the republic by replenishing the treasury depleted from the war and promoting the development of private credit markets and public finance.[10] William Thomas, writing the first English book on Italy in 1549, briefly describes the economic presence of the Jews in Venice: "It is almost incredible what gain the Venetians receive by the usury of the Jews, both privately and in common."[11] Authorities never embraced Jews as full members of the community but as traders in money and merchandise, occupations that induced economic prosperity in the early modern city.[12] Jews thus were tolerated for their *utilitas*, as they, in the words of Jacques Le Goff, helped "to propel the economy and society ... ahead toward capitalism."[13]

The economic motives for Jewish settlement in Venice often clashed with concerns over religious difference. Following their arrival in Venice, Jews settled in the parishes of San Cassiano, Sant'Agostino, San Polo, and Santa Maria Mater Domini, which, writes the Venetian noble and diarist Marin Sanudo in April 1515, "is a very bad thing. No one says anything to them because, with these wars, they need them; thus they do what they want."[14] As allegations circulated of ongoing Jewish misconduct and blasphemy, the Senate decree of March 29, 1516 tightened restrictions on the Jews: "that all the Jews who are at present living in different parishes within our city, and all others who may come here ... shall be obliged to go at once to dwell together in the houses in the court within the Geto at San Hieronimo, where there is plenty of room for them to live. ... The Jews may not keep an inn in any part of the city, save the Geto."[15] The Senate further mandated that the Jews, who would come to reside in the ghetto for nearly three hundred years, would be responsible for paying the salaries of their Christians guards, four of whom would live inside the ghetto and two would patrol the surrounding canals by boat.[16] The spatial practices of community in Venice disenfranchised Jews with the perpetual gaze of surveillance embedded in the Jews' enclosure.

The material effects of the ghetto changed the urban physiognomy of Venice when authorities legislated the Jews' compulsory residence.[17] Restoration of the buildings was continually necessary because of the poor quality of ghetto construction. Bricks were the principal building material used in the ghetto, as elsewhere in the city. Brick, together with a soft mortar of lime, could withstand the structural movement typical of Venice.[18] Istrian stone, a white limestone significantly lighter than marble, was used for the sills, gutters, and doorframes. To avoid excessive loads, Jews constructed all public stairways, ceilings, and partitions separating rooms of timber (Figure 7).[19]

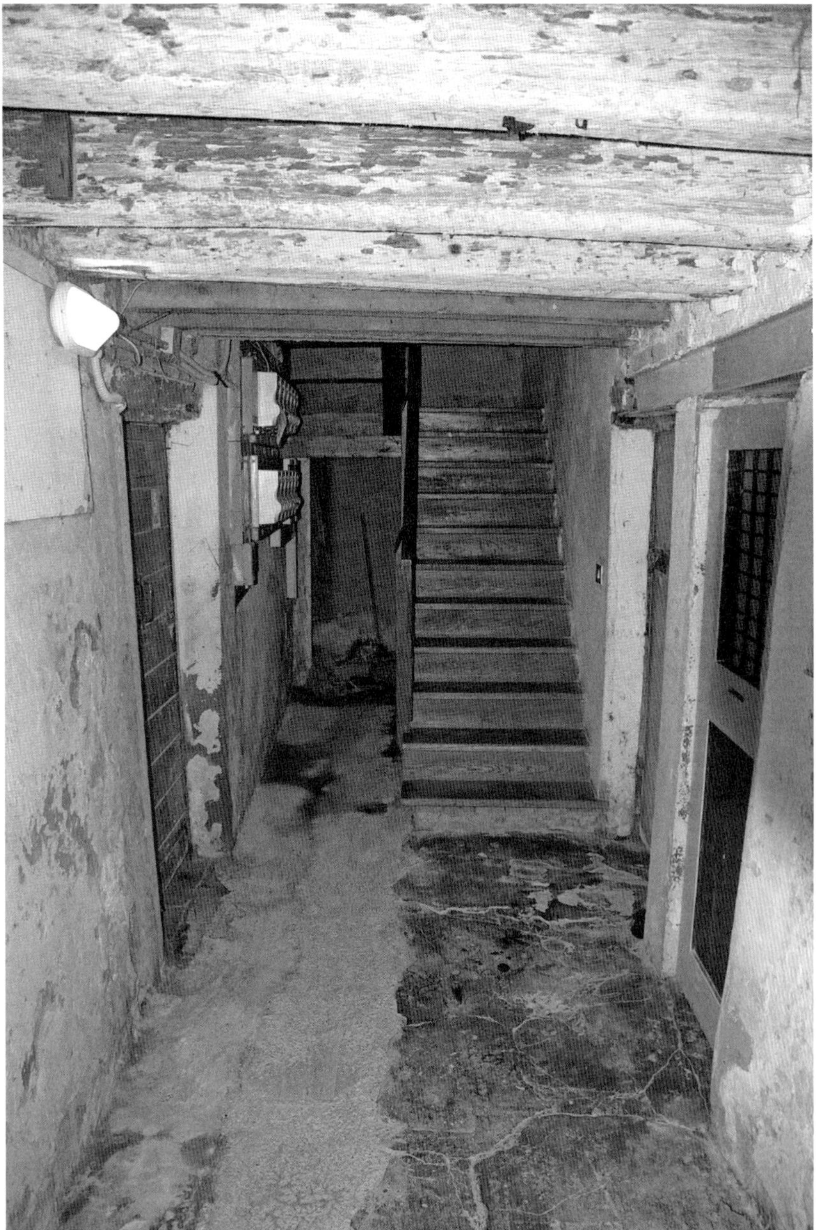

7. Stairwell in the Venetian ghetto complex, Ghetto Vecchio, Venice. Photo: author.

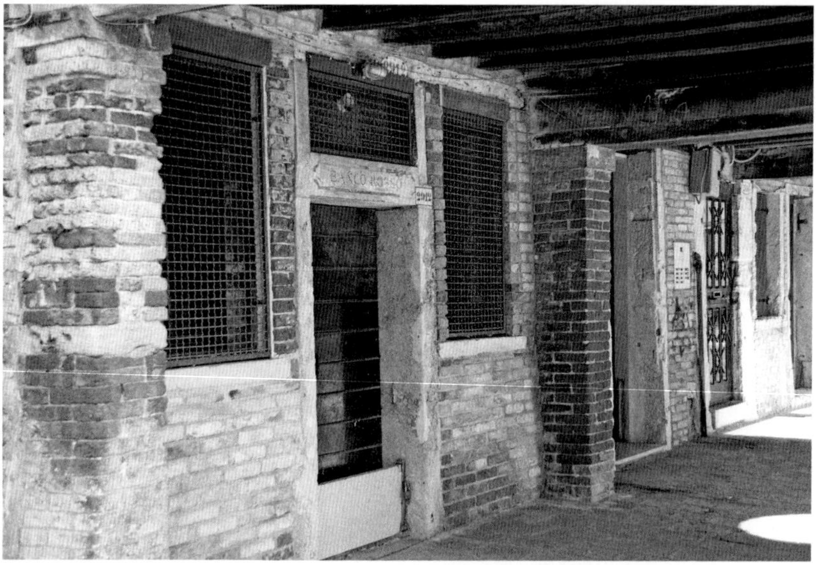

8. Banco Rosso pawnshop in the Ghetto Nuovo, Venice. Photo: author.

Shops, stores, and lending institutions occupied the ghetto's ground floor (Figure 8). To maximize space, this floor was often divided horizontally into two, creating an extra floor with ceilings just under six feet that could be used for storerooms, kitchens, or servant quarters.[20] The elevation of ghetto structures further compounded the buildings' fragility. Overcrowding, resulting from natural population growth and immigration, caused the Jews to expand their tenements vertically, constructing buildings up to nine stories around the central *campo* (public square). Ghetto elevations, anomalous in Venice given the fragility of the soft lagoonal terrain, produced architectural instability. Venice was a city founded on a pliable substructure of silt, sand, and clay that could not easily accommodate multistory structures. Jews, therefore, could not trust the load-bearing strength of their vertical structures, built, in the words of Rilke, "with such flimsy stones that the wind no longer seemed to take notice of the walls."[21] These poorly constructed hovels present the structural debilities inhering in Venice's ghettoized space, the conspicuous architecture exposing the Christian preoccupation with Jewish difference.

Authorities expanded the ghetto complex in 1541 and 1633 with the establishment of the Ghetto Vecchio and Ghetto Nuovissimo on land adjacent to the Ghetto Nuovo (Figures 9–10). These extensions to the ghetto complex sought to accommodate the residential needs of Levantine and

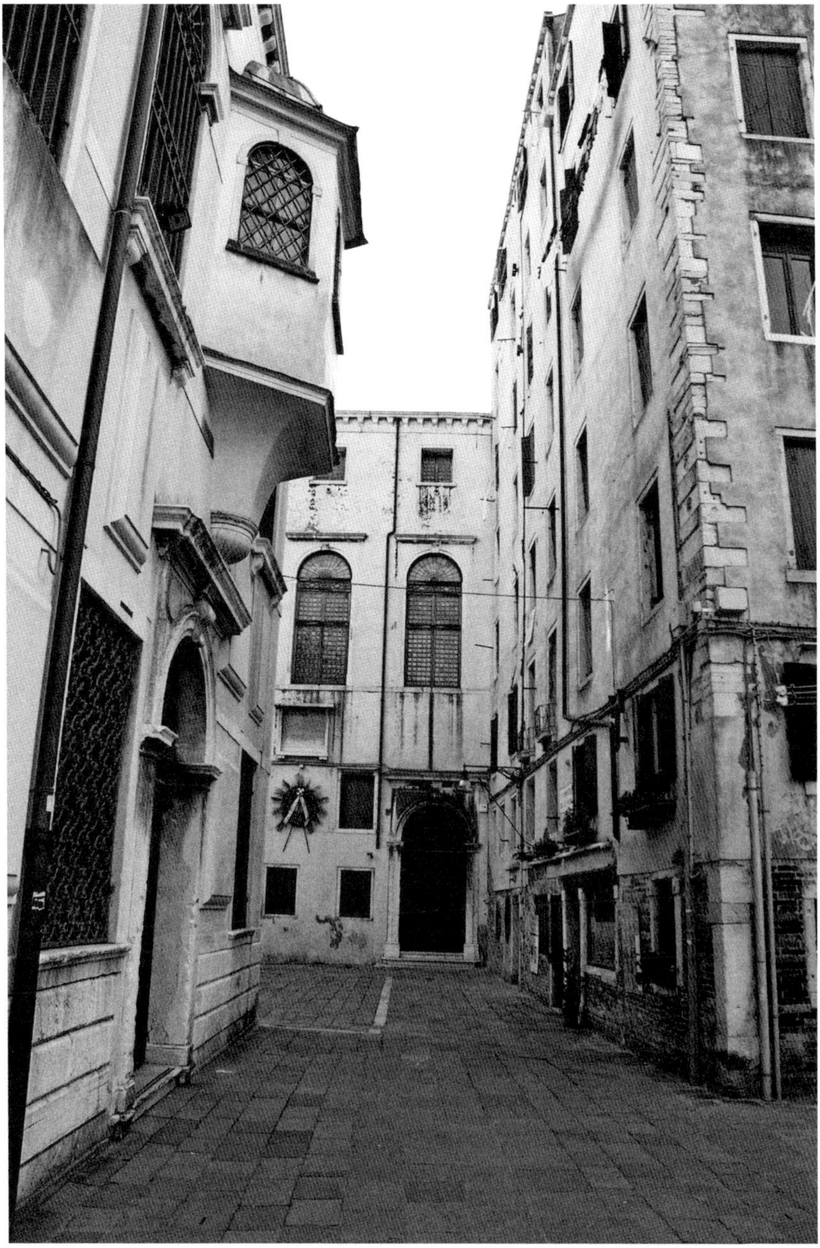

9. Ghetto Vecchio, established in Venice in 1541. Photo: author.

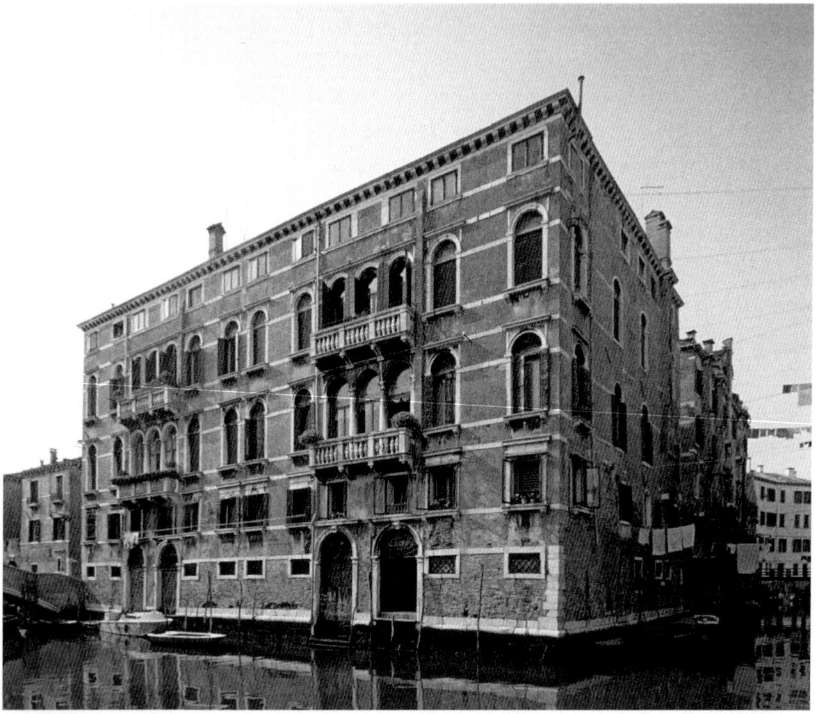

10. Ghetto Nuovissimo, established in Venice in 1633. Photo courtesy Graziano Arici.

Ponentine Jewish merchants, descendants of Jews formerly exiled from Spain and Portugal, whose engagement in "pure mercantile activity" the Venetian government sought to promote.[22] A symbiotic relationship formed between Jews and the Venetian government: Tedeschi (German or Ashkenazi) and Italian Jews in the Ghetto Nuovo earned compensation by working as moneylenders primarily for the urban poor, selling goods secondhand, and serving as physicians; Levantine and Ponentine Jewish merchants in the Ghetto Vecchio and Ghetto Nuovissimo engaged in wholesale maritime trade via the Mediterranean; while Venice profited from the growth of its commercial activities and increased revenue exacted from the Jews as taxes. Tedeschi Jews remained the most marginalized in the ghetto, as their work did not curry the political and economic favor of the Venetians as did the Levantini, whose direct trade between Venetian and Ottoman territories provided them tax concessions and other privileges. Zoning the mass housing projects of Venice's ghetto complex thus represented the social stratification of its inhabitants and their economic utility.[23] The urban residential areas of the Venetian ghetto segregated living quarters by ethnicity, class, and trade, at least until the early years of the seventeenth century when Jews moved more freely between ghetto spaces.[24] Venetian authorities partitioned the ghetto complex into three distinct spaces; nevertheless, ghettoization for all Jewish residents required curfews and compulsory confinement from 1516 to 1797 with the final collapse of the Venetian Republic.[25]

The formation of the Venice ghetto was an architectural manifestation of the city's republican values. The construction of the ghetto complex perpetuated the mythologizing of Venice as the harmonious, stable, just, and tolerant republic, one that protected within its walls a well-established political and social order.[26] Francesco Sansovino emphasized this toleration when writing in 1581 that Jews "prefer to live in Venice rather than in any other part of Italy. Since they are not subject to violence or tyranny here as they are elsewhere ... reposing in most singular peace, they enjoy this city almost like a true promised land."[27] As Sansovino suggests, the ghetto offered Jews the opportunity to settle in Venice without the fear of physical violence. Although not the land of biblical promise, Venice provided Jews a sequestered space to dwell with relative security.[28] Indeed, Leon Modena, rabbi of Venice and one of the most prominent Jews of the seventeenth century, describes how he preferred living in Venice to other Italian cities. In his autobiographical *The Life of Judah* (compiled between 1617 and 1648), he explains that, after moving to Ferrara in 1604, he longed to return to Venice:

> [In Ferrara] I was received with great affection and was honored and welcome in that household like a lord benefactor. Unbelievable as it is to tell, that entire holy community, great and humble alike, loves me dearly to this day. They appointed me their regular Sabbath preacher in the Great Synagogue and loved and praised my words. Some young men organized an academy and [study] society, and to fill my pockets, I would teach them each weekday, and on the Sabbath [give them] words of Torah and a sermon. In this way I accumulated more than 260 scudi a year.... [B]ut despite this, I was overcome by depression and did not live there willingly, due to my great longing and love for Venice, the city of my birth.[29]

His success in Ferrara notwithstanding, with its forty-eight percent increase in annual salary, Leon Modena returned to Venice's cramped ghetto space.[30] The distinctive architecture of the ghetto, established to provide physical form to the subordination of Jews and Judaism in Venice, paradoxically reveals that its enclosing walls and gates attracted a growing Jewish population. Ghetto architecture offered the proximities of religious difference in

Venice to mark out the boundaries of Jewish settlement and spatialize alterity within the *Corpus Christianum*. The ghetto segregated Jews as a means of urban classification and social organization; however, the architectural configuration of that enclosure provoked a disordering of Venetian social order.

Renaissance architectural theorists, including Leon Battista Alberti, Sebastiano Serlio, and Andrea Palladio, treat the built environment as a space predicated on symmetry and uniformity, as such unity bespeaks a community governed by social order. As historian Edward Muir states, the Neoplatonic dictum that outward beauty signifies inward virtue inspired humanist theorists to conjoin rationally ordered architecture with civic stability and harmony.[31] Alberti, for instance, in his *De re aedificatoria* of c. 1452, consigns the regularized and well-proportioned Florentine loggia to the elders of society, who, enjoying the salubrious air and protected from the heat of the central Italian sun, were to monitor and control the city's boisterous young men.[32] Here the Renaissance portico and its accompanying piazza serve as a site for social conviviality among the community's senior members, while also functioning didactically to teach proper civic comportment to the city's youth. Architectural monuments educate civil society through their reciprocal sight lines, public buildings exposing the city's inhabitants "to the eyes of so many curious observers."[33] In this mid-fifteenth-century architectural treatise, Alberti assigns the urban environment the powers of social control to promote civic order. The sights produced by the spaces of urban life become central to the formation of the city's social structure and political order.

Later commentators repeated the trends of this socioaesthetic assessment. In *I quattro libri dell'architettura* (first published in Venice in 1570), Andrea Palladio similarly invests the spatial expression of Venetian architecture with social resonance. Palladian design promoted symmetry and proportion through the traditions of classical architecture. For instance, he describes the union of measure and proportion as requisite criteria in church construction in order to venerate God properly, writing: "we are bound to include in them [churches] all the embellishments we can, and build them in such a way and with such proportions that together all the parts convey to the eyes of onlookers a sweet harmony and each church fulfills properly the use for which it is intended."[34] According to Palladian theory, stimulating viewing with harmonious architectural proportion allies form with function. Architects, past and present, are at blame when "they have failed to make every effort to build … in as excellent and noble a form as human circumstances allow."[35] In Palladio's Venice, architecture is prescriptive in that it creates a social contract dependent on accepted conventions of proportion and positioning.[36] Visual harmony defines the rhythmic symmetry of building design to create apposite settings for Venetian social life. Indeed, Venetian building with its decorative columns, capitals, and cornices became a marker of civic pride, a source of admiration among the city's residents and tourists.

The Venice ghetto did not fulfill the terms of this social contract. If it is true that architectural symmetry and harmony are associated with social order, as Alberti and Palladio observe, and that the "stunning [Venetian] cityscape alone gave proof of a well-arranged political and social order," as Muir describes in his study of Venetian historiography, then the opposite must also be true.[37] That is, the disharmonious, asymmetrical, unstable, and even dangerous Venetian ghetto can be interpreted as a subversion of Venice's political and social order. Thus the ghetto is not merely an expression of Venetian tolerance, but also a visual remonstration against the traditional "myth of Venice." The irregular fenestration patterns, uneven building heights, and unsystematic projection of structures extending into the ghetto *campo* create a space visually charged with discord. Renaissance harmony and uniformity do not characterize these structures. Rather, the ghetto appears organic, evolving and growing (upward and outward) with the increasing demographic pressures of its inhabitants. It was precisely the haphazard form of the ghetto that indelibly marked Venetian urbanism with architectural anomaly. The exterior articulation of ghetto buildings accentuates their pronounced verticality and demonstrates the axial social hierarchy of ghetto life with wealthier Jews residing on the upper floors because they were able to pay the city an annual tax for the privilege of adding balconies or rooftop belvederes to their apartments. Whereas the Christian patrician class resided on the *piano nobile*, or the second story of a residential palazzo, wealthy Jews often chose to live on the higher floors. The way of life for the ghetto Jews, even those with significant financial means, did not parallel Christian life. For Jews to obtain more space, they climbed the long stairways to the tops of ghetto tenements with their panoramic views of Venice.

Such views did not give the Jews the right to look. Their roaming eyes vexed Venetian officials since visuality's authority ostensibly resided with the Christians filling the city's administrative buildings, palaces, and churches.[38] With the construction of the ghetto, the Senate instituted barriers on visibility. The government granted Jews the privilege to settle in the city, but compelled them to reside in buildings that walled up specific windows, quays, doors, and other architectural apertures to obstruct the Jews' views. It was precisely this politics of invisibility that created new sight lines in ghettoized Venice. Authorities sited the ghetto on the city's margin to reduce the Jewish presence in Venice, and legislated nighttime curfews and architectural containment to restrict optical transmission *to* and *from* ghetto apartments. However, such restructuring of the city's urban plan provided the Jews with a wide-angled lens to Venice vis-à-vis the ghetto's tall towers. Venetian officials founded an apparatus of looking when classifying socio-religious distinction through processes of urban planning and policies of architectural confinement. The ghetto that immured Jews on the city's edge placed their ghettoscapes in direct opposition to their right to look.

Archival documents, governmental and ecclesiastical, overwhelmingly reveal how early modern inhabitants of Venice grounded their conceptions of the ghetto in discourses of sight. Vision repeatedly punctuates contemporary records because the ghetto's enclosing walls could not regulate the Jews' claims on looking. Ghetto elevations conjured vistas above and beyond that which Venetian authorities could control or conceal. "Visualization demonstrates authority," writes Nicholas Mirzoeff, and Venetian ghettoscapes repeatedly put pressure on that authority.[39] Mirzoeff's work, as well as that of the other proponents of visual culture, informs my investigation of the Venice ghetto. The 1990s debates on visual culture, chronicled in the *October* questionnaire, document architecture's fraught relationship with the nascent subfield.[40] It would appear, as Sylvia Lavin proposes, that architectural theorists should want to embrace visual culture given architecture's adjunct position in the field of art history. She remarks on the analytical possibilities visual culture could bring the built environment, writing: "[T]he inter- or even antidisciplinary framework of visual culture would seem to provide architecture with a way into new intellectual possibilities and beyond its own difficulties with things such as the vernacular, the commercial, and the everyday."[41] Despite this methodological potential, Lavin remains concerned by visual culture's reductionist treatment of architecture in relegating the three-dimensional structure to "the economy of the image."[42] The materiality, utility, and habitability of architecture are distinctive qualities not found in the other images visual culture examines; thus, it cannot adequately account for architecture's eccentricities.[43] Architecture invokes a phenomenal experience that draws not exclusively on vision but on all the senses.

The experiential intimacy of architecture is multisensorial. Sight is yoked to the other senses, as eyes, ears, noses, hands, and mouths unite within the embodied spaces of the built landscape. Yet, as Henri Lefebvre remarks, space "presupposes and implies a logic of visualization."[44] The act of seeing is foundational to studies of the built environment in that vision situates the spectator-cum-tenant within a complex field of spatial relations. Visual culture does not seek to segregate vision from the tactile, auditory, gustatory, or olfactory in those matrices of space. Instead, it inquires into the nature of visual processes to problematize and historicize the practices of sensing. As W. J. T. Mitchell writes, "Visual culture is the field of study that refuses to take vision for granted."[45] While art historian Michael Baxandall in the 1970s advanced notions of the "period eye" in the pictorial practice of fifteenth-century Florence to reveal the cultural constructedness of vision, theorists of the built landscape have only recently turned to visual theory in their investigations of the built form.[46] Dianne Harris and D. Fairchild Ruggles, in their revisionist work on vision, implore historians of architecture and landscape to engage sight as "a prism for understanding (and misunderstanding) space."[47] They stress that such examinations do not "entail removing vision from the other senses or denying their impact. The study of landscape may be, as some have claimed, ocularcentric; however, visual theory itself remains little explored and underutilized in the field."[48] In the pages that follow, I take my cue from Harris's and Ruggles's appeal to study the built landscape as a site yet unseen. Sight actualizes architecture and the spaces between and beyond building to orient the onlooker and stage scenes of everyday life. Sight functions to locate and dislocate the viewer, to activate space and memorialize experience. I follow the motions of the eye to expose the visual limits of urban enclosure and to tease out its particularities in the early modern ghetto.

To that end, I begin in Chapter 1 on the Cannaregio margins where Venetian authorities sited the ghetto. Specifically, I turn to the ghetto's placement within the urban landscape of Venice, comparing the location of the Venetian ghetto on the city's periphery to the disposition of the ghettos in Rome and Florence in the city center. This comparative analysis, in Italy and elsewhere, seeks to define the contours of ghettoization and to elucidate the principles of urban planning in the Venetian context. Here I interrogate the margins of marginality as a site of urban consolidation. I explore the ghetto as an architecture of confinement in which issues of centrality and marginality were constantly negotiated. Chapter 2 narrows the lens on the Venetian urban form to examine the parcelized space of the ghetto. I investigate the disparate topographies of early modern Venetian enclosure to localize the Jews' *clausura*. Enclosure compels study because it striates space to re-envision the landscape. Enclosure, marked by incongruity in and through a pronounced process of division, produces antagonistic spaces that offer a fractured picture of the world while simultaneously promising visions of a new spatial order. In this chapter, I differentiate enclosure in the Venice ghetto from conventual urbanism that nourished nuns spiritually by barricading them in. Post-Tridentine cloistration sought to seal off the nun permanently from social contact, whereas *clausura* in the Jewish ghetto instead limited the Jews' contact with the city to the daytime hours. As I seek to demonstrate, ghetto enclosure, in modifying Jewish movement through space, actualized new ways of seeing that transformed the habits of the eye.

In *Skyline: The Narcissistic City*, Hubert Damisch meditates on the window as an opening to the spectacles of the street. For Damisch, the window stages scenes of urbanity: "The city (the 'street') is there, it unceremoniously forces upon him [the window observer] its indiscreet, even 'chthonic' presence."[49] In Chapter 3, I look through ghetto windows to study Venice's urban indiscretions, as such windows produced sights that disturbed the sovereign eye of the republic. In particular, I examine the archival voice of Venetian authorities to analyze interfaith interactions at ghetto windows and the city's ongoing claims to obstruct them in the early modern period. In 1560, the Cinque Savi alla Mercanzia required Jews in the Ghetto Vecchio to wall up certain windows, balconies, and doors when Christians accused Jews of committing profane acts from their ghetto casements. The architectural aperture of the window frustrated the strict segregation of ghetto urbanism. To enrich my examination of ghettoized Venice, this chapter offers a comparison with Shakespeare's London. As Shylock in *The Merchant of Venice* instructs Jessica to avoid taking in views from their home's casements, so Elizabethan London regulated alien subjects through window restrictions. The spatial practices associated with social marginality in Venice and London orient us to the early modern window.

The final chapter scrutinizes the senatorial directives to contain the Jews in the ghetto at night and to conceal them from sight. Whereas the transparency of the window afforded sensory access to sight, the opacity of the wall challenged sight's supremacy and, I argue, motivated the desire to touch. I analyze the social relations that congregated on both sides of Venice's ghetto walls to suggest that architectural reception conjoins both the visual and the tactile. Walter Benjamin observes that architecture participates in a complex network of sensory information related to sight and touch.[50] For Benjamin, architecture relies on the sensory complexity of the optical and the tactile to stimulate the senses of space. In this chapter, I investigate the materiality of ghetto walls that colonized the eye and incited the tactile engagement of Jews and Christians. Here I pursue how the walls of the Venice ghetto emblemized the city and the senses that sustained it.

The Jewish Ghetto and the Visual Imagination of Early Modern Venice is not a diachronic study of the ghetto's architectural development or a microhistory of the masons who erected its tenements. Instead, this is a book about how the built landscape makes, in the words of Mitchell, "seeing show itself."[51] I focus on everyday architectural elements in order to call attention to the vernacular vision of early modern Venice. I am interested in the exchange of gazes framed by ghetto architecture that exposes how visuality shapes sociality. That is, I am interested in ways of seeing windows, walls, and gates that look through them to see how they actively inform society. Through a dissection of the ghetto's architectural anatomy, I parse its constituent elements to interrogate seeing as a mediator of urban experience. I analyze the details of construction and design to deconstruct how the ghetto's fenestration patterns, building heights, and enclosure walls stimulate the senses of space and engage lines of sight.

The application of visual and spatial theory to the study of the ghetto alters our perceptions of the Venetian social world. To date, the scholarship on the Venetian ghetto provides historical surveys of the ghetto's foundation and critical discussions of Christian-Jewish relations. This literature, however rich in its social, religious, and political history, does not consider ghettoization in sensory terms. There has been no book to investigate the culturally conditioned ways in which ghetto architecture confronted sensorial politics. There has been no monograph that probes the spatial and sensory significance of ghetto urbanism. Yet such an approach is essential to understanding the impact of the ghetto and its effect on Venetian culture. If we shift the focus from historical statements about the purpose of the ghetto to the ways in which Venetians perceived it, we see that the impact of the ghetto ran counter to the purposes for which it was constructed. As I discuss in these pages, the Venetian Senate established the ghetto to reduce the Jews' visibility in the city by relegating them to compulsory residences on the city margins. Yet the Jewish presence in Venice became more prominent when the ghetto complex reached such heights. Architectural ideology sought to control social difference through an elaborate configuration of spatial relations that distinguished Christian from Jew; nevertheless, the formation of the ghetto created a space in which Jews visually commanded a marked presence in Venice.

We remain blind to such fundamental conclusions when privileging archive over architecture, word over sense. Recognizing the impact of Italy's first Jewish ghetto and its proliferation throughout Christian Europe requires us to heighten our own senses. As noted in Stuart Clark's *Vanities of the Eye*, religion set certain visual protocols that censured sight and punished visual oversights.[52] A balanced examination of the extant visual and verbal documents pertaining to the ghetto engages not only Jewish historiography but also early modern religious culture more broadly, for the Venetian ghetto played a critical role in the sociopolitical and religious infrastructure of early modern Italy. The vernacular spaces of ghetto life similarly offer a unique contribution to art and architectural history, the Jews' tall tenements promising visions of a new *imago urbis*. Sight structures the city in these pages. Indeed, this book sees Venice with ghetto eyes. Visuality serves as an analytical approach to urban experience that exposes the negotiations of Jewish-Christian relations in the early modern spaces of ghettoized Venice.

1

MARGINS AS LABORATORIES OF URBAN PLANNING

MAPS TELL SPATIAL STORIES. IN THE SECOND HALF OF THE seventeenth century, Giovanni Merlo completed a view of Venice that conveys cartographic tales of urban life (Figure 11). This monumental print, first published in 1660 by Stefano Scolari, chronicles the authority of landscape over the edges of the lagoon; the integration of serpentine canals and ancillary streets into a well-ordered topography; and the incorporation of individual parishes into a unified community.[1] Indeed, the mapmaker treats Venice as a majestic city floating on the adjacent waters of the northern Adriatic and protected by the Lion of Saint Mark. Although a flourishing city, Venice nonetheless remains unpopulated in this imagined landscape. Early modern artists typically render panoramic city views as uninhabited, and Merlo's Venice is no exception. Oarsmen perhaps pepper the lagoon waters, but the city's streets and squares await signs of life. The mapped Venice presents a totalizing view of the city, a utopian portrait of an inhabited city that is emptied of its residents.[2] Gondoliers dot the canals and a few figurines stand enclosed within the piazza, yet their spatial significance diminishes among the expanse of terrain. The oblique angle of the map, rendered in perspectival lines and decorative flourishes, combines the Euclidean measure of geometry with the pictorial observation of chorography to create a view from on high.[3] Modeled after Jacopo de' Barbari's celebrated woodcut plan of 1500, Merlo's bird's-eye view presents a framed vision of town and territory that reproduces, as specified in the title, the "true and magnificent design of the illustrious city of Venice" (Figure 12).

This is a map, as all maps are, of bounded space. The artist literally carved Venice out from its watery surroundings to denote the characteristic contours of a Renaissance city: its churches, its palaces, its bridges, its streets. The city, emptied of its citizenry, remains a repository for its monuments. Here the architectural density of the city is on display. At first glance, no specific building

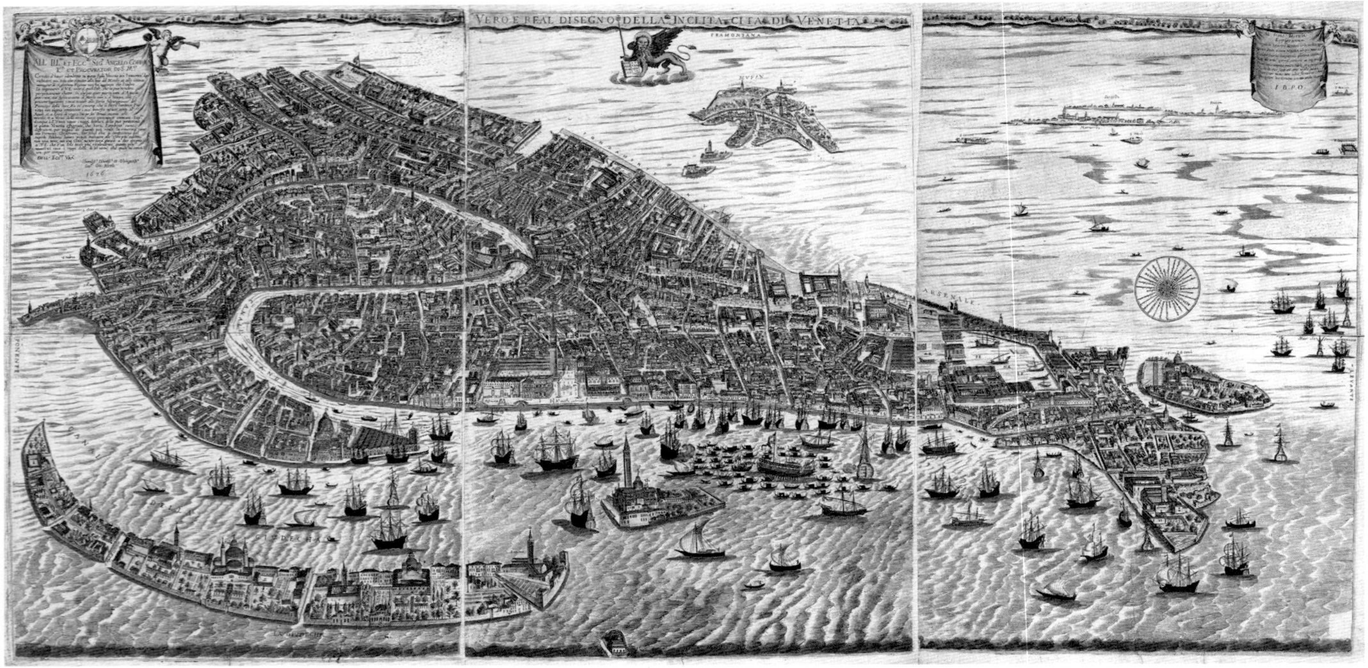

11. Giovanni Merlo, *Vero e real disegno della inclita cita di Venetia*, 1676. Photo courtesy Novacco Collection, The Newberry Library, Chicago.

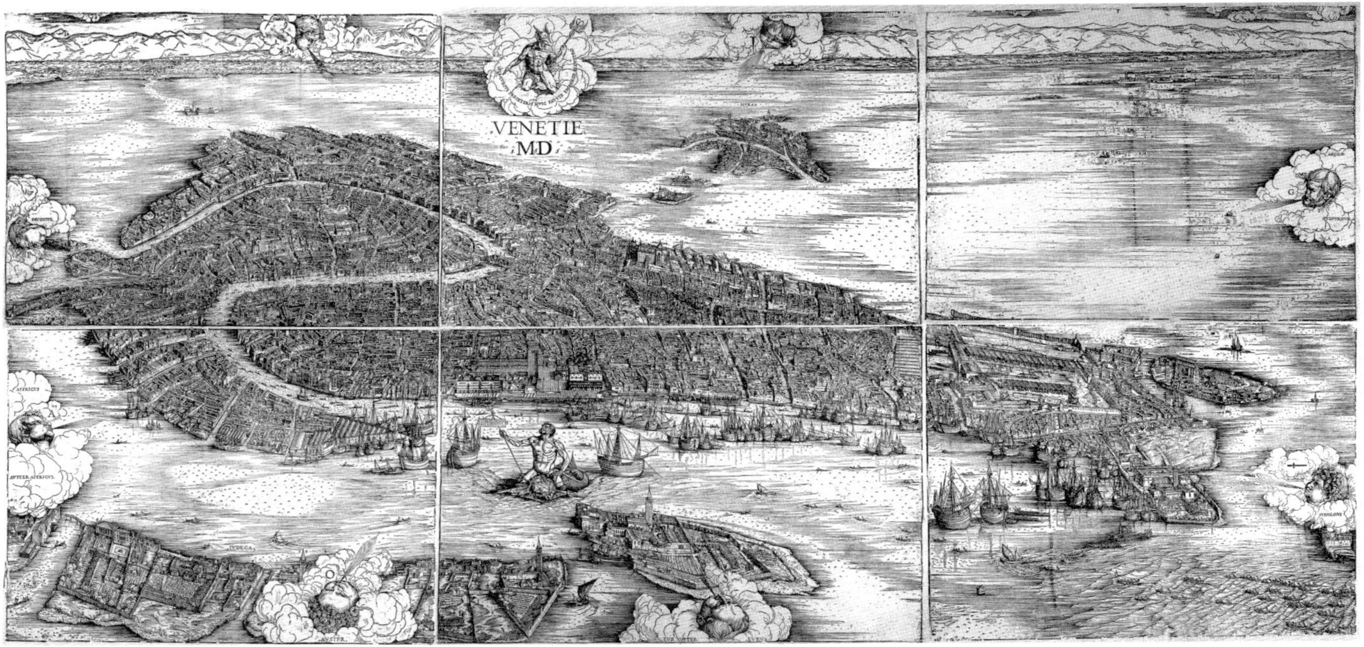

12. Jacopo de' Barbari, *Venetie*, 1500. Photo courtesy Novacco Collection, The Newberry Library, Chicago.

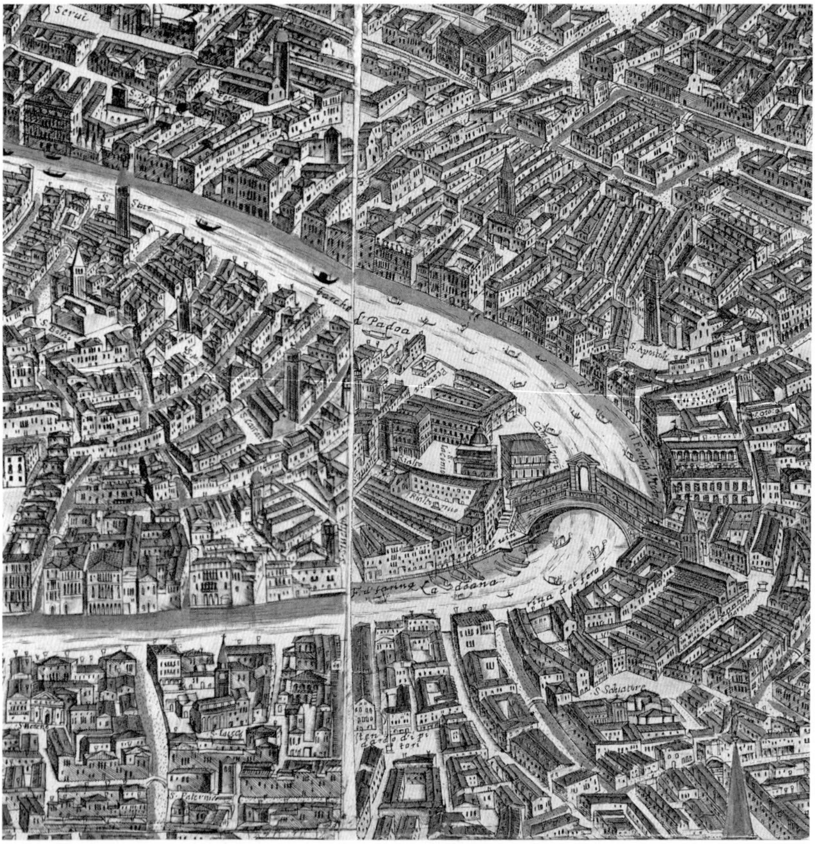

13. Giovanni Merlo, *Vero e real disegno della inclita cita di Venetia*, 1676, detail of the Rialto. Photo courtesy Novacco Collection, The Newberry Library, Chicago.

catches the viewer's eye. Instead, Merlo harmonizes the Vitruvian and the vernacular, the sacred and the secular, the public and the private. The map offers a way of seeing the urban landscape as a collective architectural experience. The descriptive visual (and textual) details provided in the map also call for closer inspection, with certain distinguished sites slowly coming into view. The Rialto, the bridge spanning the Grand Canal, serves as the engraving's nucleus.[4] Venice, a prominent Mediterranean entrepôt, relied on the Rialto as the commercial core of the city, and Merlo symbolizes its socioeconomic centrality with pictorial parity (Figure 13). The artist similarly provides visual distinction to Venice's civic center at the Piazza San Marco (Figure 14). The piazza features a large swathe of space housing the Doge's Palace, the

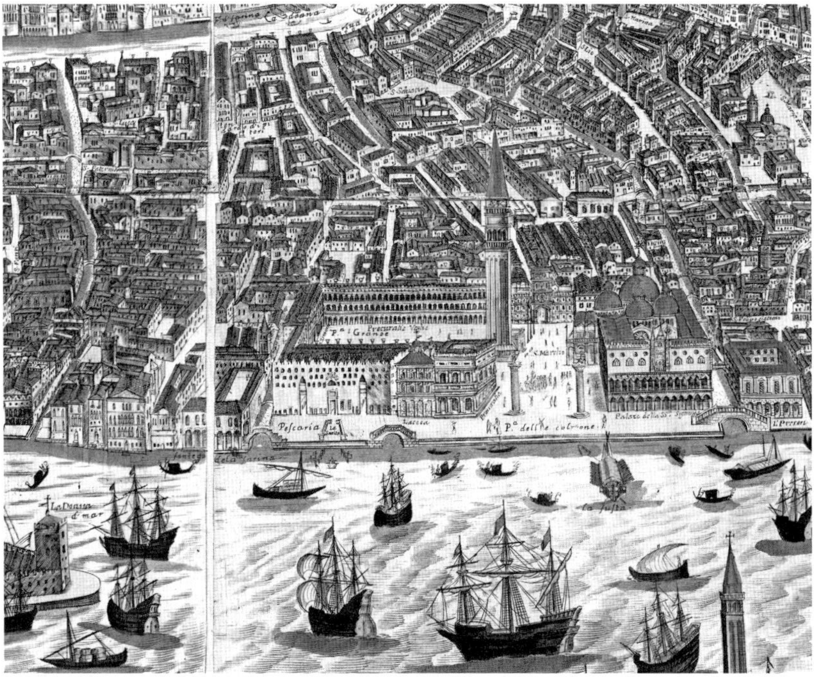

14. Giovanni Merlo, *Vero e real disegno della inclita cita di Venetia*, 1676, detail of the Piazza San Marco. Photo courtesy Novacco Collection, The Newberry Library, Chicago.

Basilica of San Marco, the Columns of Justice, the bell and clock towers, and the administrative buildings of the Procuratie. Merlo offers minute details of the city center as well as Venice's margins. For instance, on the eastern periphery of the city in the Castello district is the Arsenale, where the city engineered naval and mercantile ships to promote its power and wealth (Figure 15). The map articulates its geopolitical position with ramparts that fortify its perimeters and toponyms that spatialize in text. This map envisions the constructed spaces of Venice, from center to periphery, with equal detail. Visual description synchronizes the various vistas of the cartographic Venice to forge an organic unity. Bronwen Wilson writes of Jacopo de' Barbari's view of Venice that his map "avoid[s] privileging sites … to present instead a homogenous republican fabric."[5] Merlo's revised vision likewise arranges Venetian topography with spatial homogeneity at the city center and on the edges of urban life. Representation conjoins with urbanity to erect the palaces, churches, and state buildings at the city's core as well as to draw urban attention to peripheral development.

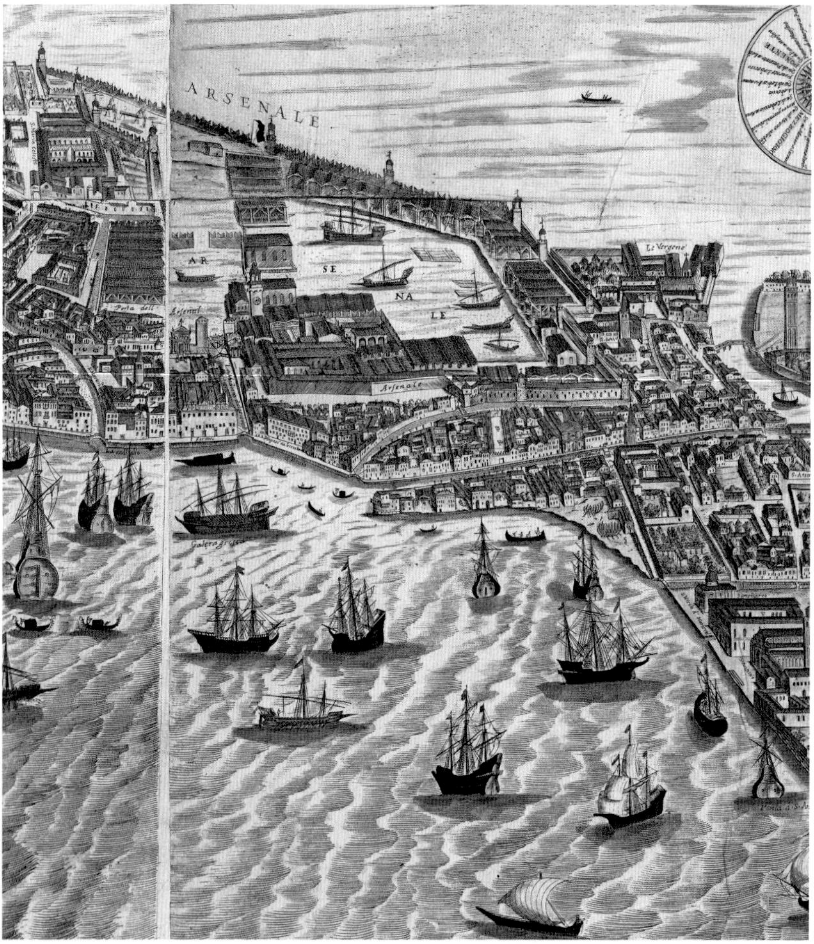

15. Giovanni Merlo, *Vero e real disegno della inclita cita di Venetia*, 1676, detail of the Arsenale. Photo courtesy Novacco Collection, The Newberry Library, Chicago.

Merlo's way of seeing may relate to Venice's built reality, but it aestheticizes that reality in favor of a unified order that screens out difference. The map occludes incongruities. It standardizes spatial networks to create mythic narratives of scenic play. For example, the depiction of the Ghetto Nuovo in the northernmost district of Cannaregio, here labeled "Il Ghetto," takes on the architectural qualities of neighboring buildings (Figure 16). Beginning in 1516, the Ghetto Nuovo was a compulsory housing complex for the Jews of Venice situated on the city's old foundries (Figure 17). Authorities submitted Jews to pecuniary fines and a prison term if found outside the ghetto enclosures after

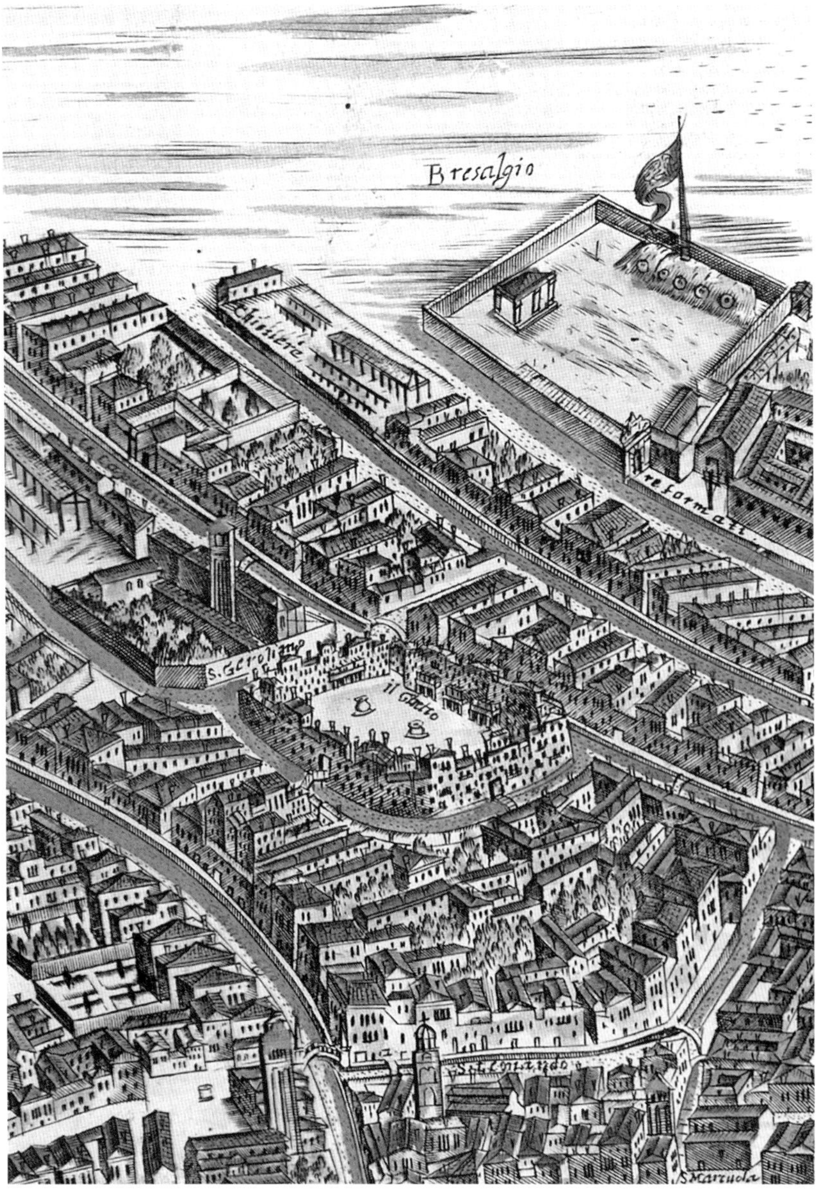

16. Giovanni Merlo, *Vero e real disegno della inclita cita di Venetia*, 1676, detail of the ghetto. Photo courtesy Novacco Collection, The Newberry Library, Chicago.

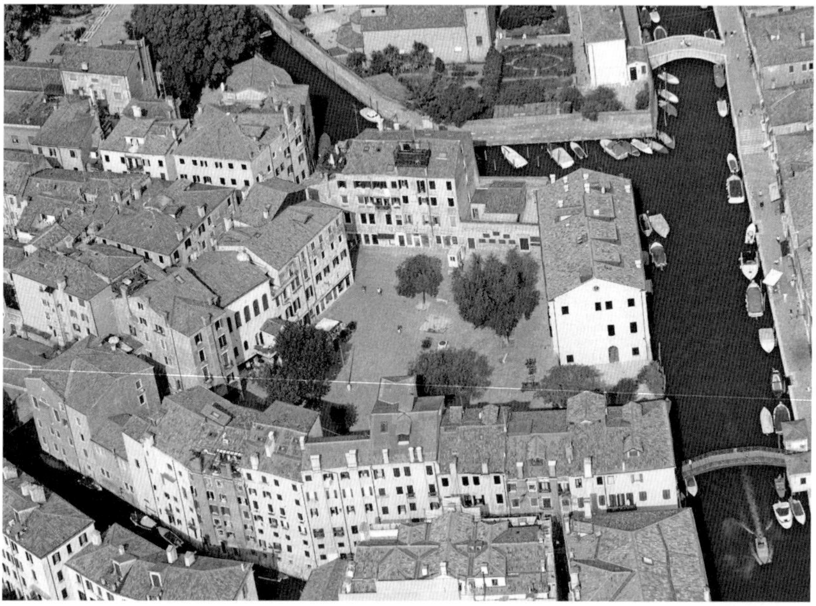

17. Aerial view of the Venetian ghetto complex, as it appears today. From 1516 to 1797, walls enclosed the ghettos of Venice. Photo courtesy Davide Calimani.

nightfall. Overcrowding was an endemic problem in the ghetto. Jews were forced to build vertically in Venice, as ghetto tenements ascended up to nine stories. Such soaring heights are not evident in Merlo's pictorial rendition. Although the artist conveys congestion through the ghetto's dense fenestration, he does not accentuate the buildings' vertical expansion. Rather, Merlo portrays buildings of three to four floors that regularize ghetto elevations to correspond to their Christian environs. Moreover, he reduces the ghetto, composed of three building complexes, to the first of its structures. That is, he labels as "Il Ghetto" only the Ghetto Nuovo that housed Jews of German and Italian descent, despite the fact that Venetian authorities had ghettoized Levantine and Ponentine Jews in the Ghetto Vecchio and later in the Ghetto Nuovissimo.[6] Merlo marks the ghetto as a site of cartographic inquiry, but his map simplifies the ghetto's disparate geographies within a congruous urban form.

But center and periphery were never so equally inscribable topographically. Difference played a critical role in Venice's built environment. In this chapter, I situate Jewish difference on the city's edge to put marginality's displacement in full view. Margin – from its classical Latin etymon *margo, marginis*, meaning brink, border, boundary – suggests relations geographical and ideological. Margins lie immediately within the boundaries of a surface to designate their outer edges and to denote their distinction. Here I probe these distinctive limits to analyze marginality as both a physical space and a social identity disenfranchised from privilege and power. As Bryan Palmer remarks in his histories of transgression: "Marginality is simultaneously an identity/consciousness and a structure/place. It is a construction both social and concrete, removed from power's centers in displacements physical and discursive. As such it is often related to the oppositional dualisms and polarizations within which difference is articulated. . . . How such difference is perceived and lived, however, is never ultimately 'set.'"[7] Inherent in the concept of marginality are the dichotomous spatial relations it provokes, the strict dividing line of urban segregation and the stratifications of social status. Marginality is a lived experience of social and geographical displacement marked by negotiations of position. Rigid spatial polarities between inside and outside, center and periphery, are never securely fixed; instead, marginality is constantly redefined by instability and transmutation. If, as Edward Muir aptly notes, travelers "experienced Venice from the center outward," I propose to concentrate on Venetian space from its ghettoized margins.[8] Examining architecture from the outside affords views of urban innovation that present new perspectives of the inside.[9] This chapter turns to the edges of Venice to explore the ghetto as a peripheral site that offered a new design in urban planning. The ghetto created a laboratory of the periphery that forged a site not always out of center. Instead, I examine the ghetto as it works through and between issues of centrality and marginality, visibility and invisibility, siting and sighting.

Spatial interstices constituted Venice's civic infrastructure. Politically, the imperial interests of the seafaring city broke through the structures of republicanism to complicate relations of center and periphery. The centralized vision of the Venetian Empire at times clashed with the compromises and alliances it forged with the oligarchies of its subject cities. Venice endeavored to pursue a program of mediation that respected the autonomous statutes of subject territories to stave off local conflicts while attempting to erode the political power left in the periphery.[10] Venice saw its colonial status as one of succession, often employing the legal system of the former regime in the administration of its overseas territories.[11] A division of power, situated in the gaps between center and periphery, functioned as the capstone of this maritime republic. Economically, Venice relied on negotiations of spatial boundaries to strengthen the trading networks operating the city's mercantilism. Trade flourished in Venice during the fifteenth and early sixteenth centuries. A prolonged recession, however, threatened the economic stability of the city in the late sixteenth and seventeenth centuries when the

Ottoman Empire expanded maritime control over the Mediterranean. The merchant companies of the Atlantic seaboard – the English, the Dutch, and the French – challenged Venice with additional commercial competition that further weakened the Venetian economy.[12] Merlo's revision of Jacopo de' Barbari's Venice obfuscates the city's economic fragilities. De' Barbari executed his cinquecento map, the largest and most comprehensive plan of its time, during the heyday of Venetian economic growth. His image exemplifies the impact of republican mythmaking in that it institutionalizes narratives of civic unity and communal belonging.

Similar to de' Barbari's plan, Merlo's map of the seventeenth century reinforces the city's political and economic institution building through its topographical detail and emphasis on collective homogeneity. Merlo's cartographic *communitas*, however, conceals the effects of market loss. Its fleet of ships floating atop the lagoonal waters suggests Mediterranean competition is of no consequence to Venice's trade emporium, despite the fifty percent reduction in Venetian shipping with the increased presence of foreign vessels.[13] Merlo, moreover, makes little allusion to the world outside Venice. He stylizes the depiction of the *terraferma* on the map's uppermost boundary with renderings of schematic trees to demonstrate the territorial reach of the Venetian Empire. Merlo's map may isolate Venice, but Venice's isolation is not isolationist. The city occupies a very crowded corner of the Mediterranean yet retains its independence. Merlo's Venice is a utopian frontier located on the boundless sea and limited only by the imagination. It occupies the space between nature and culture, water and land, representation and reality. Merlo's isolation-making project bespeaks the affective power by which Venice is viewed as the center of the world. Wilson writes, "By the beginning of the seventeenth century, the image of Venice was redefined; no longer a capital of an empire – a model that radiates from the core to the periphery – Venice was transmuted into a metropole, an image of the city in which all the world could be seen."[14] The world is visible in Merlo's Venice with chorographical precision. This seventeenth-century prospect is synecdochic; it conjoins the edges of the world by routes of travel that always lead back to Venice.

Navigating the boundaries between center and periphery is not an easy task in Venice given the competing characteristics of the city's most notable features: its insular environment and its demographic diversity. Venice offered a city simultaneously inside and outside, open and closed. On the one hand, its settlement on the marshy lagoon islands of the northern Adriatic protected the city from the outside world. Urban planning evolved in Venice as a process of drainage and reclamation that shaped the landscape, while shallow waters and sandbars defended it against foreign invasion. In this way, the inside was protected geographically from what lay beyond. Such geographic isolation, on the other hand, prompted contact with the outside world since Venice lacked natural resources. Therefore, its citizens were compelled to cultivate long-distance trade relations and welcome foreigners to its shores. In early modernity, Venice teemed with the non-Venetian. Merchants, lacemakers, clothing sellers, bankers, tourists, doctors, and diplomats visited the city. Foreign sojourners and settlers alike, attracted to Venice's real and imagined landscape, traveled to the lagoon in search of new market opportunities and a glimpse at the city of the sea.

The Flemish-born French ambassador Philippe de Commynes was one of the city's many visitors to leave a written account of his Venetian journey. In 1494, Commynes accompanied King Charles VIII to Italy on a diplomatic mission. While the king conducted business in Naples, Commynes set sail for Venice to experience the city firsthand. In an entry to his *Mémoires* dated October 2, 1494, he describes his Venetian peregrination as a spectacle for the eye: "And I marveled greatly to see the placement of this city [Venice] and to see so many church towers and monasteries, and such large buildings, and all in the water.... It is the most sumptuous city which I have ever seen."[15] This French diplomat records not only the city's architectural sights sited on the water, but he also provides his royal readers a brief lesson in military history when comparing Venice's naval battles to the landlocked skirmishes of ancient Rome. Commynes's memoir is more than a travelogue. It is a *speculum principis* ("mirror for princes"), a literary genre that advises the prince in his quest for honor, glory, and fame.[16] These instructional manuals, most notably Machiavelli's *The Prince*, operated on the ancient conceit of inviting the prince to gaze into a mirror, seeing in his reflection an image of the ideal ruler. The mirror-for-princes theorists argued that the achievement of *virtù* was the most essential quality to the prince's administration of justice and peacekeeping, "the key to 'maintaining his state' and enabling him to fight off his enemies."[17] Commynes finds Venice's watery surroundings breathtaking. However, he praises Venice first and foremost for its governance, emphasizing that "they [the Venetians] do not have civil strife in the city, and this is the greatest wealth that I can see that they have.... Moreover, most of their people are foreigners."[18] For Commynes, the wealth of the city could not be measured monetarily. Rather, he quantifies Venetian abundance based on displays of civil obedience in a community defined by the foreigner. Venice's *virtù* was its ability to fight off military enemies from abroad while permitting outsiders to reside within. Early modern travelers often remarked in written accounts on

Venice's singularity through a discussion of its demographic diversity.[19] In Venice, alienness became a form of familiarity.

In fact, the barrier between inside and outside was a threshold Venice's *forestieri* (foreigners) continually traversed throughout the medieval and early modern periods. "The Germans and Bavarians, French and Lombards, Tuscans and Hungarians, and all the people who live from trade came directly to Venice to buy goods, and to take them back to their countries," wrote Martino da Canal in the mid-thirteenth century.[20] Not all foreigners, however, journeyed home. Greeks, Turks, Germans, Albanians, Dalmatians, Armenians, Jews, and Flemish, among others, resided as immigrant communities in Venice.[21] In 1468, Cardinal Bessarion donated hundreds of Greek and Latin manuscripts to Venice, which Bessarion referred to as "another Byzantium," in gratitude for the hospitality the city provided nearly four thousand Greeks.[22] These Greek émigrés, the majority migrating from Venice's colonies, lived primarily in the Castello district and worked in the Arsenale as designers, carpenters, or rowers for the Venetian galleys.[23] Dalmatians likewise concentrated in Castello. The Slavs of Dalmatia served the Adriatic empire as sailors for the Venetian navy.[24] Whereas Greeks and Slavs resided primarily near the Arsenale, all German merchants, "whether from Upper or Lower Germany, and whether they are subjects of the Emperor or of any other German ruler, and likewise Poles, Hungarians and Bohemians," moved to the Fondaco dei Tedeschi on the Grand Canal near the Rialto Bridge.[25] The Fondaco dei Tedeschi remained compulsory housing for German merchants, who could not "on any pretext take lodgings in any place outside the exchange house."[26]

Unlike the various German-speaking merchants, textile entrepreneur Ludovico Talenti was not restricted by residence. Ludovico came from an immigrant family that hailed from Florence; his father Zuanne Talenti was a Florentine merchant who moved to Venice in the fifteenth century and obtained the legal status of *cittadinanza de intus et extra*, after twenty-five consecutive years of mandatory residence.[27] As naturalized Venetian citizens, Talenti and his heirs received all the privileges that came from full citizenship. Ludovico used these financial and social benefits to purchase *botteghe* at the Rialto market and a nearby palace (completed around 1535) on the Grand Canal. Martino d'Anna (né Van den Haanen), a wealthy Flemish merchant turned naturalized Venetian, purchased Talenti's palace in 1538 and, according to tax records, also opened three *botteghe* at the Rialto.[28] Proximity to the Rialto represented the powerful trading interests of immigrant entrepreneurs and provided wealthy émigrés the possibility of social mobility.

The spatial economics of Venice relied on these clusters of foreign settlement to promote effective trade relations. The commercial interests of

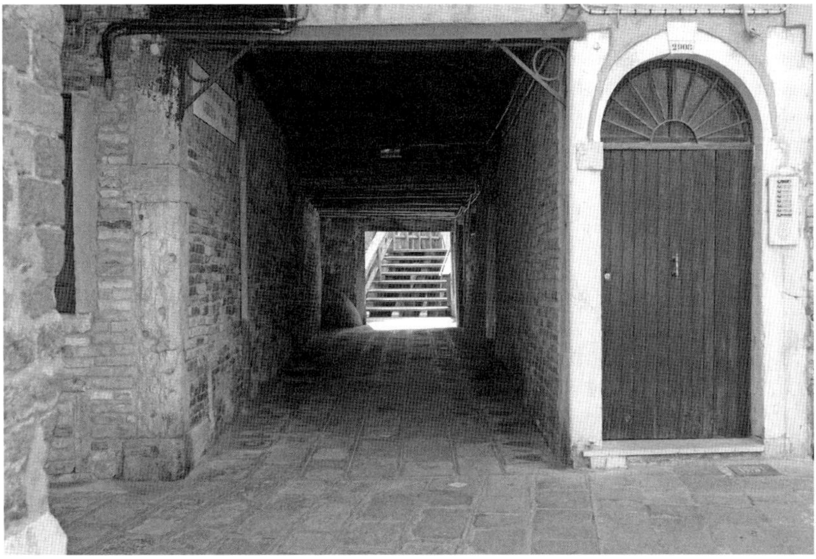

18. Former gated entrance to the Ghetto Nuovo, Venice. Photo: author.

Venice overlapped in its imbricated spaces. For instance, Richard Goy classifies the Rialto, the Arsenale, and the Piazza San Marco as nuclei of the city.[29] There is nothing arbitrary about this grouping. Venice relied on several nucleated centers around which the city's aggregate activities of commerce, defense, and politics were grouped, around which its homogenizing identities as "most loyal servants of this most holy State" were collected.[30] In addition to these prominent institutions, Goy categorizes the Jewish ghetto as the remaining urban nucleus.[31] If the ghetto was central to the built environment of Venice, it was a center of Jewish life decentered from the larger Christian community. On March 29, 1516, the Senate ordered all Jews residing in the city to move to the Ghetto Nuovo. Following their arrival in Venice after the Venetian Republic's loss to the League of Cambrai at the Battle of Agnadello in May 1509, Jews settled in various parishes throughout the city. The 1516 legislation prohibited the Jews' residential dispersion, instead compelling them to consolidate their presence on the Cannaregio margins in the newly founded ghetto. The senatorial decree also stipulated that the Jews would be watched by Christian guards twenty-four hours a day and locked into the ghetto at night behind gates (Figure 18).

Neither exterminating nor exiling local Jews, the Senate displaced them to the margins of the city. Displacement serves as a site of inquiry precisely because it unsettles notions of place. Authorities permitted Jews safe conducts to dwell in Venice, renewable every five to ten years, with the stipulation that they move behind ghetto walls.[32] In this way, displacement played an operative role in the construction of Jewish life in Venice, as officials relocated the Jews elsewhere. Such deracination conjures images of the wandering Jew, the exilic figure of suffering and homelessness cursed by Christ when taunting him en route to the Crucifixion and punished to wander eternally, only to find rest with the Second Coming.[33] This tropic traveler, with antecedents in the medieval past, came to position the Jew on the margins as a symbol of peripatetic consequence and geographic alienation. In the case of the Venice ghetto, officials displaced the Jews not to banish them from city limits but to reallocate them to a new home. The ghetto served as a physical embodiment of the diasporic condition in that, in the words of Jean-François Lyotard, "They [the Jews] are … always away from home when they are at home."[34] The establishment of the ghetto preserved the Jews' position as a legally constituted community; however, the politics of place in Venice required their subordinated status. That is, the divisions of society inscribed in the urban fabric secured the Jews' place through destabilizing policies of displacement. The incorporation of the ghetto into the built environment created an urban matrix of shifting borders and delimiting places of private life that draws attention to the unstable divide between center and periphery. Officials advocated the foundation of the ghetto to protect the boundaries within city limits by designating in Venice the outside of the inside.

Place matters. The siting of buildings makes sociospatial claims on the community. The disposition of the Venice ghetto on the northern margins of the city identified and institutionalized Jews as/in margin.[35] The ghetto acted metonymically for the Jews' marginality, aligning architecture with the bodies it housed. As Piero Camporesi explains in his study of medieval and early modern religion and folklore, "People's fears were exorcised by dumping them on those who inhabited the edges of the known world, who were lesser in some sense. . . . The centre . . . could not tolerate the thought that the object of horror might not take root like nasty infection in the ghettos of the more distant suburbs of the world. . . . [T]he outskirts are felt to be infected zones, where all kinds of monstrosities are possible, and where a different man is born, an aberrant from the prototype who inhabits the centre of things."[36] Here Camporesi inserts social hierarchies into *mappaemundi* to create dichotomous spatial relations. Fears are assuaged when ordering urban topographies into distinct social units of center and periphery. The ghetto in this equation becomes a metaphor for infection and abjection, a state of nature that subsumes the fears of the world into the aberrant margins. But the historical ghetto offers a multiplicity of margins and marginalities. The historical ghetto offers an archetypal housing form that maps power moving betwixt and between the edges of the city.

The orientation of Europe's Jewish ghettos speaks to the design of early modern marginalization. North of the Italian peninsula in the Germanic city of Frankfurt am Main, a significant Jewish population arose from the expulsions in certain cities in the Holy Roman Empire such as Cologne, Nuremberg, and Ulm, as well as elsewhere in Europe. In 1462, Frankfurt's city council required Jews to move from the center of town, where the city's oldest synagogue stood near the cathedral, to the newly constructed *Judengasse* (Figure 19). Located on the eastern edge of Frankfurt outside the old city wall known as the Staufenmauer, the *Judengasse* consisted of timber-frame gabled houses facing and flanking the street for nearly a quarter mile. As residency in the *Judengasse* surged, new dwellings were built behind the streetfront houses and stories were added to existing homes.[37] The *Judengasse*, sited on what was formally a desolate area of this growing commercial city, became a dark and crowded corner with inexpensive housing overtaking green space.[38] The compulsory housing of Frankfurt's *Judengasse*, which predates the establishment of the Venice ghetto by over fifty years, reveals the relationship between Jewish marginality and early modern urbanity. The city council of Frankfurt designated the Jews as outsiders, displacing their living spaces outside the medieval city wall.[39] Such displacement has symbolic implications. City walls are an architectural signifier of physical separation, a barrier constructed within the urban landscape to distinguish outside from inside. Relocating the Jews and their architectural imprint (homes, synagogue, yeshiva, ritual bathhouse, bakery, hospital, dance hall, hostel) beyond the sacred and civic core of Frankfurt reveals how the currents of power moved spatially to demarcate jurisdiction. Difference "could only be defined by establishing what lay outside."[40]

The outside is not a stable spatial condition with definite edges, however. As Gilles Deleuze suggests, "The outside is not a fixed limit but a moving matter animated by peristaltic movements, folds and foldings that together make up an inside."[41] This peristalsis contributes to the singular status of ghetto architecture, which inhabits an infinite crossroads of outside/inside coordinates. The ring of densely populated tenements constituting the Venice ghetto was, as Donatella Calabi observes, an "organizing principle of settlement ... for [a] collective Jewish identity."[42] Venice was the first Italian city to ghettoize Jews, and the formal qualities of Venetian ghetto architecture informed ghetto designs in cities such as Padua in 1603 and Modena in 1638.[43] The Venice

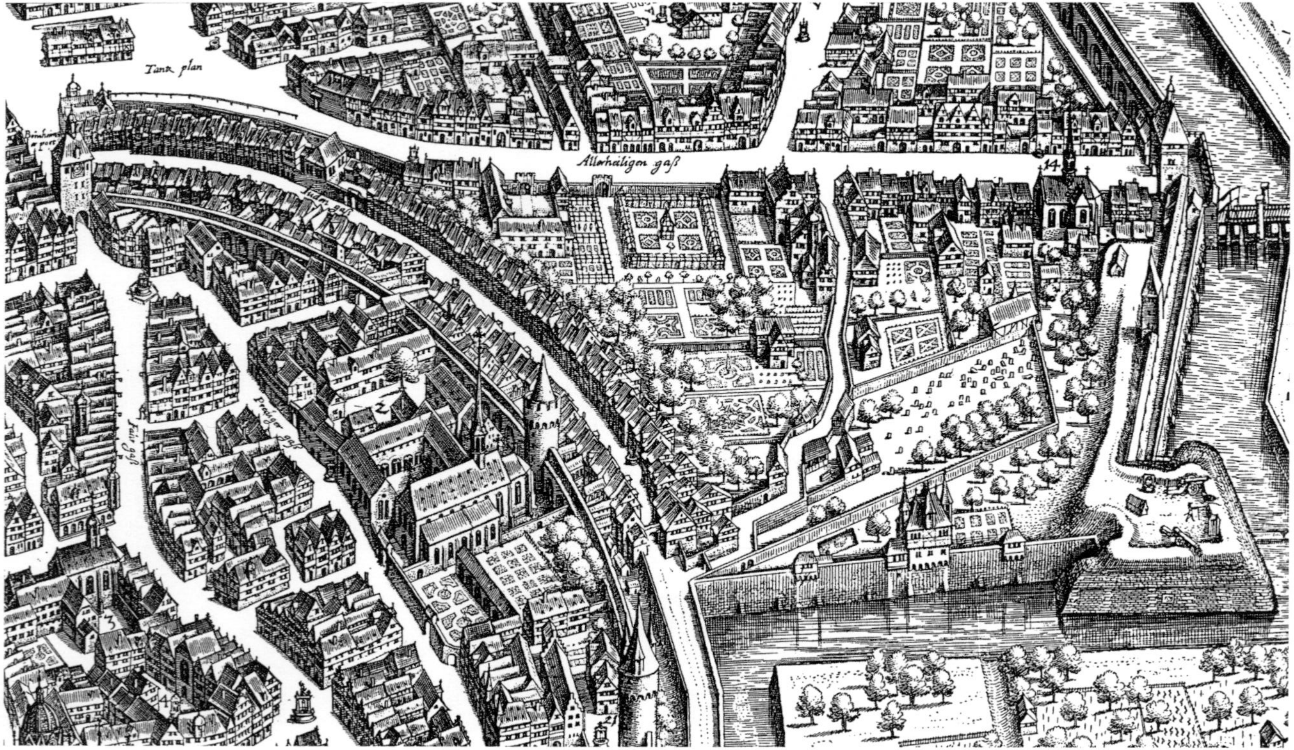

19. Matthäus Merian, *Frankfurt am Main*, 1628, detail of the *Judengasse*. Photo courtesy Private Collection / Bridgeman Images.

ghetto may have been cited elsewhere, yet how such cities sited their ghettos offers alternative views of marginal living. The subordination of Jews did not always require movement to the periphery; the outside architecture of ghettoization could dwell in the heart of the city.

As noted in the ghettos of Rome and Florence, the contours of ghettoization complicate relations of outside and inside to underscore their transmutability. Rome, the Eternal City, constructed its ghetto complex in the Rione Sant'Angelo, a district located along the Tiber River about a mile from St. Peter's Basilica. In July 1555, Pope Paul IV ordered the construction of ghetto walls following the promulgation of *Cum nimis absurdum*, the papal bull that segregated Roman Jews to motivate their conversion to Christianity.[44] In Counter-Reformation Rome, the conversionary aspirations of the pope prompted the residential segregation of local Jews.[45] For over three centuries, the Jews remained walled in the ghetto with its subsidiary stories and annex constructions that housed the swelling Jewish population of Rome. Two main streets and three principal piazzas filled the seven-acre area that regularly received the Tiber's floodwaters (Figure 20). In the mid-nineteenth century, Ferdinand Gregorovius described the arduous living conditions of Rome's Jews:

> What a melancholy spectacle to see the wretched Jews' quarter sunk in the dreary inundation of the Tiber! Each year Israel in Rome has to undergo a new Deluge, and like Noah's Ark the ghetto is tossed on the waves with man and beast. When the Tiber, swollen with mountain snow and torrents of rain, and driven back by the west wind from the sea, goes into flood misery is multiplied. Those who live beneath take refuge in the upper floors, which are intolerably crowded and tainted by pestilential atmosphere. The stoppage of food supply and of work increase the misfortune, and the flood ruins everything that cannot be removed.[46]

Despite its centralized location, the Roman ghetto marked the Jews' marginality through the site's insalubrity. The city of Rome acknowledged the intolerable conditions when, in 1885, following the unification of Italy, city officials initiated a public works program to beautify the city. Authorities sought to raze entire districts of Rome, and began with the *risanamento* of the ghetto. L. Scott Lerner analyzes this bureaucratic term, "risanamento" connoting a return to health, as "a symbolic as well as a practical cure not only for the Jewish quarter but also for the city and the nation."[47] The urban clearance of the ghetto released Jews from their compulsory residences and cleansed Rome, now the capital of the Kingdom of Italy, of pestilence and dishonor, the residual consequence of Jewish enclosure. Nothing remains today of the

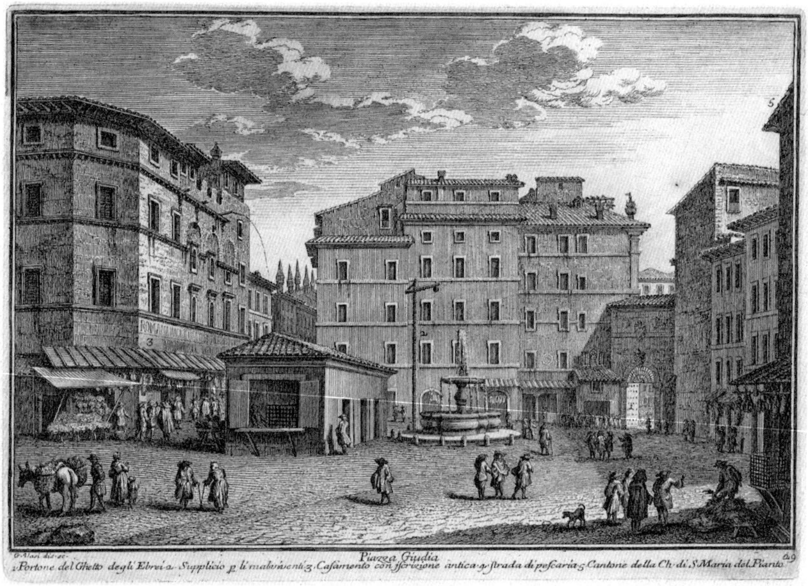

20. *Piazza Giudia*, engraving from Giuseppe Vasi's *Delle magnificenze di Roma antica e moderna: Libro II, Le piazze principali di Roma con obelischi, colonne, ed altri ornamenti.* Rome: Stamperia di Apollo, presso gli Eredi Barbiellini, 1752. William A. Rosenthal Judaica Collection, Special Collections, College of Charleston. Photo courtesy College of Charleston Library.

early modern ghetto of Rome. Lerner writes that its complete demolition functioned as a topographical *tabula rasa* on which the Jewish community in 1904 erected the Great Synagogue (Figure 21).[48] Adaptations to the built environment in Rome entailed converting the former ghetto businesses and residences of sixteenth-century squalor to the centrally planned, domed synagogue of twentieth-century regeneration. This purgation process required the building of monumental sacred architecture to sanitize the physical and symbolic spaces of Jewish Rome. The politics of place transformed the Jews' distinct space in Rome, mapping the volatility and variability of marginality to the center of urban life.

The spatial practices of early modern Florence similarly positioned Jews in the city center. In October 1570, Duke Cosimo I de' Medici issued an expulsion order requiring all Jews living in the city and countryside of his Tuscan dominion to move to the walled and gated ghetto of Florence. Located in the city center near the Mercato Vecchio, on a portion of land now occupied by the Piazza della Repubblica, the ghetto transformed

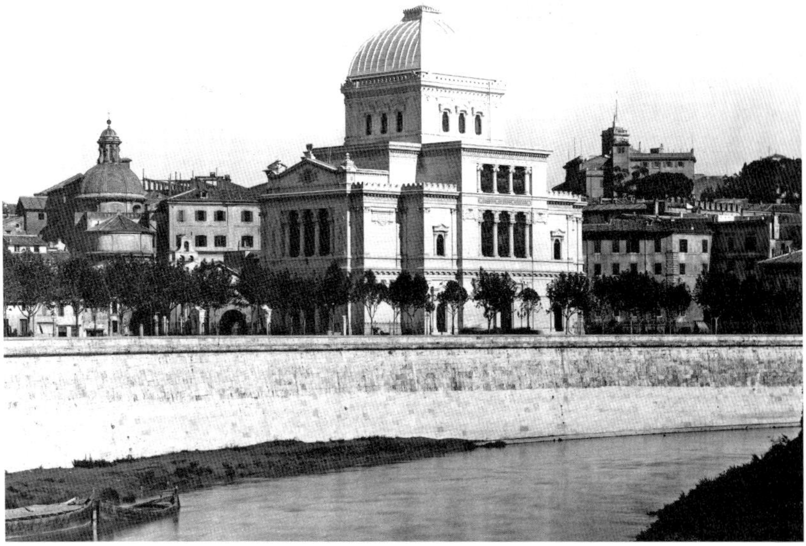

21. Vincenzo Costa and Osvaldo Armanni, Great Synagogue, Rome, completed 1904. Photo courtesy Alinari / Art Resource, New York.

a derelict area in the heart of the city into ghettoized housing of profitable rental property. Stefanie Siegmund studies the construction of the Florentine ghetto in 1571 as an act of Medicean institution building.[49] In Florence, Siegmund argues, the origins of the ghetto went beyond the history of Christian anti-Jewish policies to exploit religious difference as a method of statecraft and urban redevelopment. The siting of the ghetto in Florence oriented Jews to an area of the city center between via de' Succhelinai and via de' Rigattieri on land previously occupied by prostitutes.[50] In 1403, the Ufficio dell'Onestà (Office of Decency) institutionalized prostitution in Florence when opening its first public brothel on the Mercato Vecchio site. The Onestà had planned to build two other brothels on the eastern and southern periphery of the city, but these Onestà bordellos were never built since the more centralized brothel at the Mercato Vecchio attracted a growing constituency from all parts of town. Nicholas Terpstra remarks on the location's convenience, "It was easily reached by wool workers along the Arno, cabinetmakers around S. Croce, soldiers in the pay of the duke or in the company of some visiting noble, and domestic servants from across the city – anybody with good eyes, a sense of humor, and some handle on Florentine slang could find this area where taverns had names like The Pussy, The Little Whore House, The Cunt, and The Depraved."[51] Accessibility to the brothel in early modern Florence was indispensable to civic honor given that sacred and secular authorities believed prostitution protected chaste girls from potential illicit behavior and provided men an alternative to sodomy.

Yet prostitutes were not contained within the civic brothel. The Onestà also issued licenses to sex workers to work the streets surrounding their homes. Prostitution thus spilled into the city's well-trodden thoroughfares and hidden alleys. Because prostitution was everywhere in Florence (even the Medici leased space to prostitutes), Siegmund disallows any spatial association between prostitutes and Jews in favor of the cultural connections that joined their social inferiority.[52] Indeed, Florentine magistrates regulated prostitution within the urban form without concentrating that regulation in a single structure, as they did when ghettoizing Jews. Urban planners may not have collected prostitution into the Old Market site, but they did inscribe this disreputable space with deviance when locating the ghetto on the site of the old civic brothel. The space came to embody relations of domesticated difference. The space became a locale that built social marginality into the city center. To localize the Jewish presence in Florence requires a study of the intertwined spatial relations built between inside and outside. Those relations point to particular places on the Florentine map where spatial stories of reprobate practice found a home in the heart of the city.

Whereas Frankfurt displaced Jews outside the old city walls and city officials in Rome and Florence allocated Jews to the urban core, Venice positioned its Jewish population within city limits on the northern periphery. The siting of the Venice ghetto was a question of debate among the city's powerful politicians. According to the diaries of Marin Sanudo, on April 23, 1515, Giorgio Emo recommended to the Collegio "that the Jews, many of whom living in this land are in various houses and quarters setting a bad example for all Christians, [should] be sent to live on the island of the Giudecca."[53] The Jewish community met Emo's proposal with fierce resistance, and wealthy bankers Asher Meshullam and his brother Chaim, who rented the resplendent Ca' Bernardo palace in the parish of San Polo, were able to forestall the Jews' relocation.[54] However, in March 1516, the Venetian Senate passed legislation requiring the Jews' rehousing on the Cannaregio margins. Sanudo does not specify why the Senate selected this new location, but he indicates that Jewish community leaders feared for their safety on the remote islet of the Giudecca. It seems that in the construction of the Venice ghetto what constitutes the outside came with certain geographical restrictions. The placement of the ghetto was an act of shifting boundaries in Venice's urban form, an architectonic rethinking of outsider status that marginalized the Jews without recondite seclusion. Displacement in Venice compelled the Jews' separation from the center of the city, but it did not oblige isolation on the Giudecca. Ghettoization in Venice engenders a complex articulation of spatial conditions in which outside architecture could not be located too far outside. Instead, the Venetian Senate folded the Jews within city limits with contiguous contact to the city center.

Although ghettoization in Venice precluded lagoonal seclusion on the Giudecca, the Senate founded the ghetto complex on a remote area of Cannaregio in the parish of San Girolamo on terrain circumscribed on all sides by narrow canals with no churches or grand palaces. In this way, the Jews were physically relegated to the city margins on land that was not highly valued because of its distance from the Rialto and San Marco, nor was it inscribed with Christian iconography through prominent churches. Rose Marie San Juan concludes in her study of early modern Rome that urban space requires erasure of any ambiguity of identity.[55] There was no room for ambiguity in the distinctive buildings housing the Jews' marginality. Ghetto architecture changed the urban physiognomy of Venice with its unusual design. The strict boundaries surrounding the ghetto enclosure required Jews to build vertically, as the walls within which they were immured grew to soaring heights. Jacopo de' Barbari's map of Venice suggests that in 1500 the foundry, which in 1516 would become the site of the first ghetto structures, originally housed buildings of two stories (Figure 22). Archival records document how the architectural configuration of the site changed dramatically as Jews built atop the low-profile property in the Ghetto Nuovo and Ghetto Vecchio, owned respectively by the Christian proprietors of the da Brolo and Minotto families.[56] Ghettoization created multistory and multifamily Jewish structures in the Venetian cityscape in which concepts of striated space and recognized marginality shaped peripheral boundaries.

In Venice, city officials pushed Jews to the periphery; however, that periphery offers more than the inevitable spaces of marginality. The spatial conditions of the Jews' locality produced a new form of urbanity in which high-density living produced high-rise architecture. As the disposition of the ghettos in Rome and Florence demonstrate how periphery transcends geography to situate marginality in the city center, so too the siting of the Venice ghetto on the periphery reveals how its architecture offered an alternative form of urban living. Verticality defined ghetto urbanism. The word ghetto, now

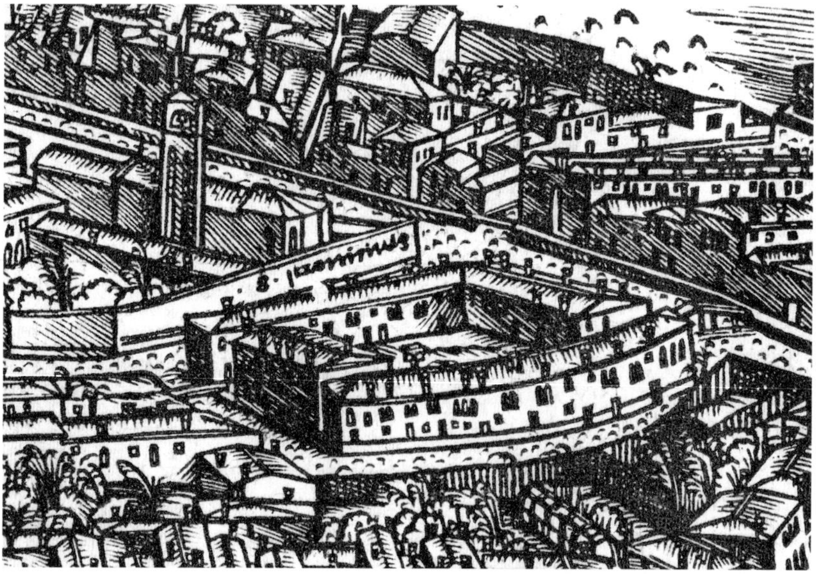

22. Jacopo de' Barbari, *Venetie*, 1500, detail of the area in which the Senate founded the Ghetto Nuovo. Photo courtesy Novacco Collection, The Newberry Library, Chicago.

referring to a densely populated slum area inhabited primarily by minorities, has its origin in sixteenth-century Venice. Its etymology recalls the foundry (*getto* in Italian) on the outskirts of Venice where authorities established the Jewish ghetto complex.[57] In form, modern ghettos such as Cabrini-Green in Chicago, Illinois or Pruitt-Igoe in St. Louis, Missouri may recall the Venice ghetto with their high-rise tenement buildings punctuating the urban skyline, but the early modern ghetto tenement differs markedly in meanings architectural and ideological. The myths surrounding twentieth-century ghettos profess the achievements of High Modernism. The minimalist slab complexes constructed for high-density living were designed, following the tenets of Le Corbusier, as iconic modernist monuments filled with "sun, space and greenery."[58] These high-density, inner-city projects failed to promote these "three essential joys of urbanism" when – in the case of Pruitt-Igoe, completed in 1954 – the elevators with stops on alternating floors and internal galleries intending to foster a community of vertical neighborhoods instead proved "opportune environments for violent crime" (Figure 23).[59] Housing reformers conclude from Pruitt-Igoe, demolished in 1972, that public housing projects require development of the urban periphery so as to eliminate the need for high-density, high-rise buildings (Figure 24). In the construction of the modern ghetto, the city center gave rise to towering tenements.

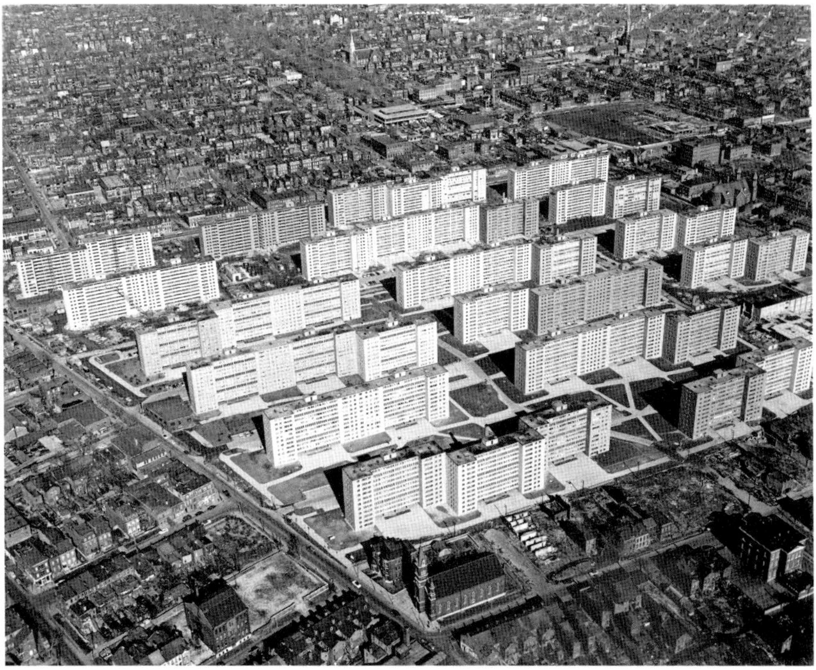

23. Leinweber, Yamasaki & Hellmuth, Pruitt-Igoe, St. Louis, Missouri, 1954. Photo courtesy Ted McCrea / Missouri History Museum, St. Louis.

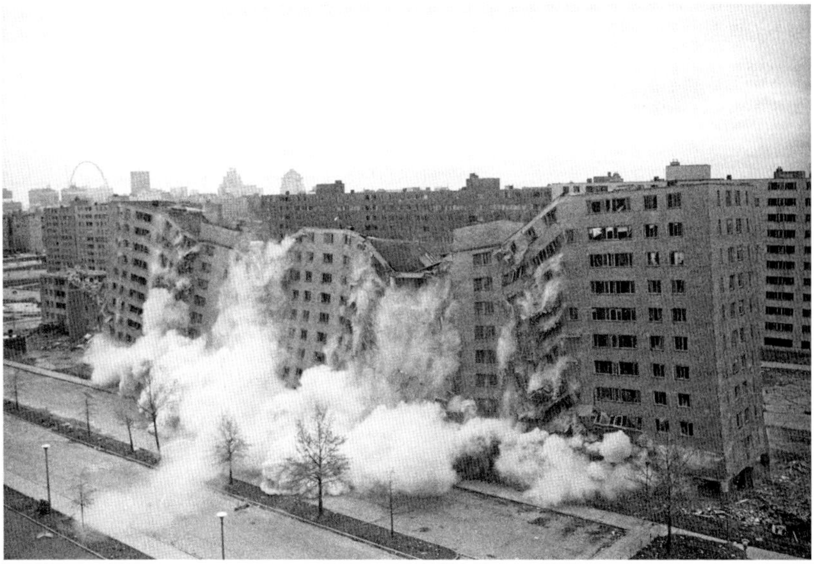

24. Demolition of Pruitt-Igoe, St. Louis, Missouri, 1972. Photo courtesy Bettmann Photography / Bettmann Collection / Getty Images.

In early modern Venice, authorities instead positioned high-density living on the Cannaregio margins. But it was this peripheralization that gave rise to the high-rise in Venice. After propositions failed to relocate the Jews to the Giudecca, the government "obliged [them] to go at once to dwell together in … the Geto at San Hieronimo, where there is plenty of room for them to live."[60] Ghetto accommodations were never so capacious; therefore, Jews built up (Figure 25). The height of the ghetto buildings were even more exaggerated during the sixteenth century because there were fewer buildings in this area, which was dominated primarily by gardens and one- or two-story structures.[61] The ghetto complex in fact was anomalous in the urban form, as Venetian residences beginning in the late fifteenth century traditionally rose only three or four floors.[62] Even the exchange houses inhabited by Protestant Germans or Muslim Turks, situated in the city center along the Grand Canal, did not exceed conventional building heights. Ghetto architecture was singular in that its attenuated apartments constructed a new vision of urbanity. Not only did Venetian urbanism designate the spatial dimensions of segregation horizontally through topographical coordinates of center and periphery, but patterns of spatial segregation in Venice also shifted vertically with the ghetto's ascendancy (Figure 26).[63] Jews built upward against the drag of gravity and the weakness of the soil they were forced to build upon. The Serenissima, the Most Serene Republic of Venice, subjected Jews to their cramped and confined conditions on the city's periphery to separate Jew from Christian and to minimize the Jewish presence. The conspicuousness of the buildings instead visualized, both physically and symbolically, the Jews' urban presence.

The ghetto marked Jews with the material signs of difference mapped spatially onto the Venetian cityscape. The restrictions of the ghetto mirror the Venetian regulation first established by the Fourth Lateran Council in 1215 mandating Jews to wear distinguishing garb; both residential and sartorial restrictions visually differentiated Jew from Christian and controlled social intercourse. The indelible mark of difference blazoned on the Jews' bodies, the special colored Jewish head cover in Venice or the yellow badge in other Italian cities, denoted their nonnegotiable visual identity. Jews were to be "distinct and diversified from Christians in dress as they are in faith."[64] If the bright yellow and red head coverings served to identify and draw attention to the Jew within the Christian crowd in Venice, the ghetto, by contrast, functioned to minimize the Jews' appearance by relegating them to compulsory residences on the city margins.[65] Ghettoization in Venice became an early modern spatialization of power that evolved outside the ghetto by dominating Christian forces that sought to minimize the Jews' presence behind ghetto walls.

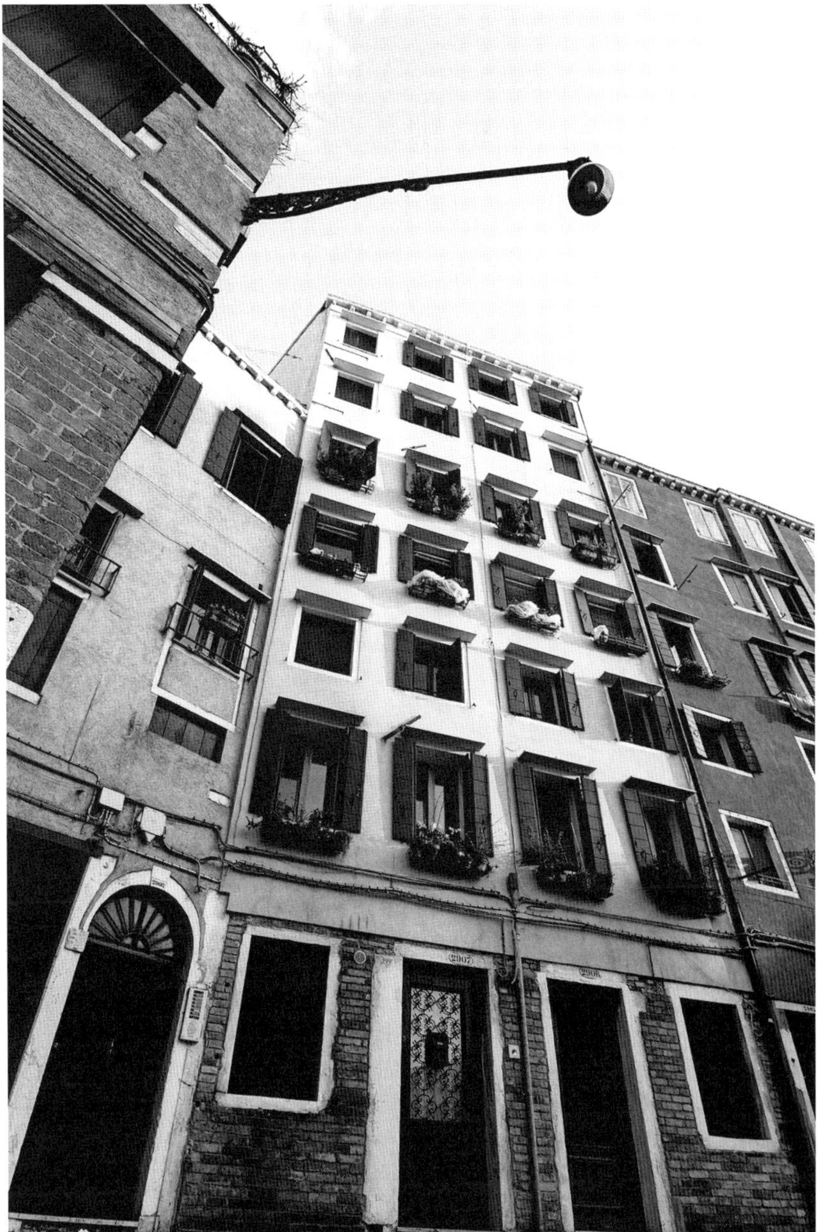

25. Ghetto Nuovo elevations, Venice. Photo courtesy Gabriele Gomiero.

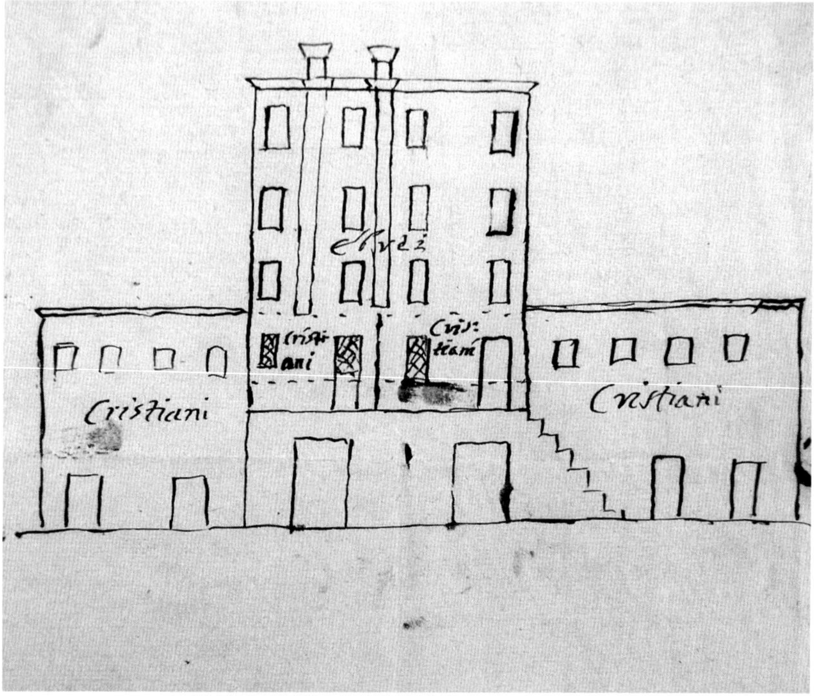

26. Eighteenth-century drawing of the Venetian ghetto, distinguishing Christian space (*Cristiani*) from the elevations of Jewish space (*Ebrei*) in the Ghetto Nuovissimo. Archivio di Stato di Venezia, Ufficiali al Cattaver, busta 278, c.n.n. Photo: author, with the consent of the Ministero per i Beni e le Attività Culturali, n. 30/2016.

As Jews erected those irregular and attenuated walls, the Jewish presence in Venice became more prominent – more visible – when the ghetto reached extraordinary heights. The verticality of the ghetto that lifted the Jews above the city caught the attention of Christians who lived outside its walls. In fact, the elevated structures that constituted the ghetto became a highly dynamic housing environment that drew attention from afar. One example of the ghetto's urban attraction is noted in the writings of the English visitor Thomas Coryat. In 1611, Coryat dedicated a lengthy portion of his travelogue to the "place where the whole fraternity of the Jews dwelleth together, which is called the Ghetto, being an Iland: for it is inclosed round about with water."[66] *Coryat's Crudities* emphasizes the form and content of the ghetto through ethnographic examinations of Jews and their rituals. Coryat, for example, includes a rich discussion of the layout of the Venetian synagogues and their decor, while also reporting on a religious service in which a "Levite ... pronounce[d] before the congregation not by a sober, distinct, and orderly reading, but by an exceeding loud yaling, undecent roaring, and as it were a beastly bellowing of it forth."[67] The Englishman's ghetto excursion elicited both fascination and frustration toward the "unchristian miscreants," ending with an altercation with a rabbi. Coryat's accounts provide a compelling look at the ghetto from the gaze of a Christian foreigner.[68] His travelogue defines the geographical identity of the ghetto by localizing the compound and its residents' cultural practices along Venice's margins. The fortified walls enclosing the ghetto perhaps served to neutralize Jewish difference, but Coryat demonstrates how the prominence of those walls in effect exposed the difference housed within. In other words, the attenuated tenements of the ghetto never cast space as neutral. Instead, the ghetto revealed the specificity of that difference. City planning indeed sought to control social difference through the residential segregation of Jews on the Cannaregio margins; nevertheless, the volatility of ghetto verticality unsettled Venice's urban design to offer Jews a commanding presence in Venice.

2

ENCLOSURES AS TOPOGRAPHIES OF VISION

IN HIS 1889 PUBLICATION *DER STÄDTEBAU NACH SEINEN KÜNSTLERISCHEN GRUNDSÄTZEN*, Viennese architect Camillo Sitte examines the production and reception of urban space. Classical antiquity informs the way Sitte's theories of city planning locate the viewer within the built environment. Inspired by Aristotelian thought, Sitte remarks: "a city must be so designed as to make its people at once secure *and happy*. In order to realize this, city planning should not be merely a technical matter, but should in the truest and most elevated sense be an artistic enterprise."[1] Sitte found the medieval and early modern piazza of northern Italy the apotheosis of this artistic urban expression. According to his analysis, the closed design of the Italian piazza creates a picturesque ideal unique to the history of urbanism.[2] Surrounding buildings tightly enclose the piazza's open form to create "an overpowering effect" on residents.[3] The irregularities in its design do not detract from its powerful presence. Sitte argues, "we are not annoyed by any obtrusive little tailor shop, by the confusion of a café, or by the shouts of drivers and porters. Peace prevails, and the totality of effect assists our spirit to enjoy and comprehend the works of art accumulated in this place."[4] The artistic effects of the Italian piazza assist proprioception to construct a *genius loci* in the material spaces of the urban landscape.

Writing at the end of the nineteenth century, Sitte criticized the gridiron plans of the modern city. He maintains that the expansive open plazas with accompanying axial streets produce excessive traffic that merely passes through the space. No longer does the modern square serve as a physical setting of civic celebration. People do not congregate in the plaza since public life has moved indoors.[5] Only the historic city confers an indelible quality on the urban environment, and the Italian piazza marks that indelibility through its enclosure. Sitte observes: "The main requirement for a plaza, as for a room, is the enclosed character of its space. Modern city planners are unaware of this most important and really essential prerequisite of any artistic effect. In olden times, on the other hand, a variety of means were employed to achieve, under the most diverse conditions, a decidedly enclosed quality of space."[6] The Italian piazza becomes a paradigmatic space of urban enclosure in Sittesque town planning. The piazza harmonizes its constituent parts to balance the site with the surrounding structures. The piazza frames prominent buildings through the intersection of terminated vistas and cultivates connections between structures and pedestrian observers. In his comparative analysis, Sitte condemns the vast plazas of the modern metropolis "with their yawning emptiness and oppressive ennui" because they have the potential to induce agoraphobia.[7] Agoraphobia, literally "fear of the marketplace," was first diagnosed in 1871 by Austrian psychiatrist Carl Friedrich Otto Westphal who used the term to refer to the fear of unbounded spaces.[8] Sitte, writing in response to the demolition of Vienna's city walls for the construction of the expansive Ringstrasse, advocated the enclosure of public spaces. He argued that enclosure keeps anxiety at bay since it fosters spatial intimacy. According to Sitte, only through the close quarters of enclosure can urban design contain the collective identity of *civitas*.

Sittesque boundaries provide protection from overexposure to open spaces. Plazas may be clustered together; however, architectural surrounds enfold the urban onlooker within this grouped space. In *Der Städtebau*, Sitte lingers over the plaza grouping of the Piazza San Marco and the Piazzetta in the heart of Venice as an archetype of urban design, writing: "So much beauty is united on this unique little patch of earth, that no painter has ever dreamt up anything surpassing it in his architectural backgrounds; in no theater has there ever been seen anything more sense-beguiling than was able to arise here in reality."[9] For Sitte, the Piazza and the Piazzetta represent an aesthetic beauty unsurpassed (or unsurpassable) in two-dimensional representation, for such beauty can only be found in the real world (Figure 27). Particular to Sitte's architectural admiration is the irregularity of Venice's piazzas. He delights in the offset placement of the Campanile at the nexus of the two squares because it facilitates movement between the adjoining spaces. The offset orientation of the bell tower does not undermine the piazzas' orderliness. Orthogonals are not needed to create urban order. The Piazza San Marco harmonizes the built and the somatic through the circumscription of architectural boundaries and the asymmetrical positioning of monuments in space. Order ensues from the negotiation of spatial irregularities.

As Sitte promoted historic urban planning over the geometrization of industrialized societies, so too English critic John Ruskin championed traditional Italian architecture in opposition to modern building. In his

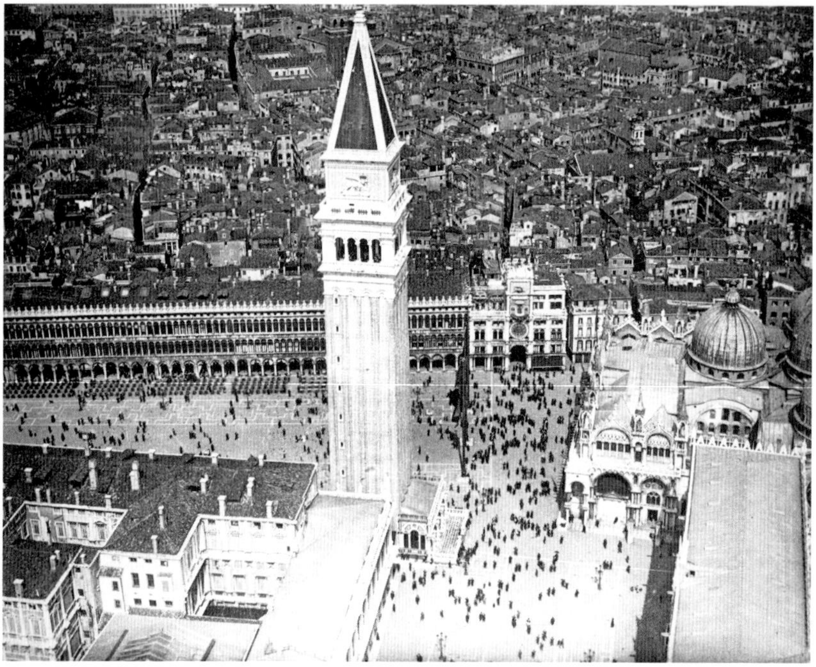

27. Aerial view of the Piazza San Marco and the Piazzetta, Venice. Photo courtesy Alinari / Art Resource, New York.

mid-nineteenth-century *The Stones of Venice*, Ruskin presents architecture in three volumes as a system of beliefs for those who constructed its walls. While he composed the first book as an architectural treatise codifying specific building tenets, the remaining volumes study individual structures in the city of Venice. Among the spaces under consideration is the Piazza San Marco, which Ruskin, like Sitte, extols for its urban enclosure and social order. Indeed, he describes the optical harmony of the long arms of colonnaded structures that flank the Piazza San Marco as a metaphor for the city's virtue and as a visual demonstration of the republic's stability (Figure 28). Ruskin notes:

> for between those pillars [at the end of the Piazza] there opens a great light, and, in the midst of it, as we advance slowly, the vast tower of St. Mark seems to lift itself visibly forth from the level field of chequered stones: and, on each side, the countless arches prolong themselves into ranged symmetry, as if the rugged and irregular houses that pressed together above us in the dark alley had been struck back into sudden obedience and lovely order.[10]

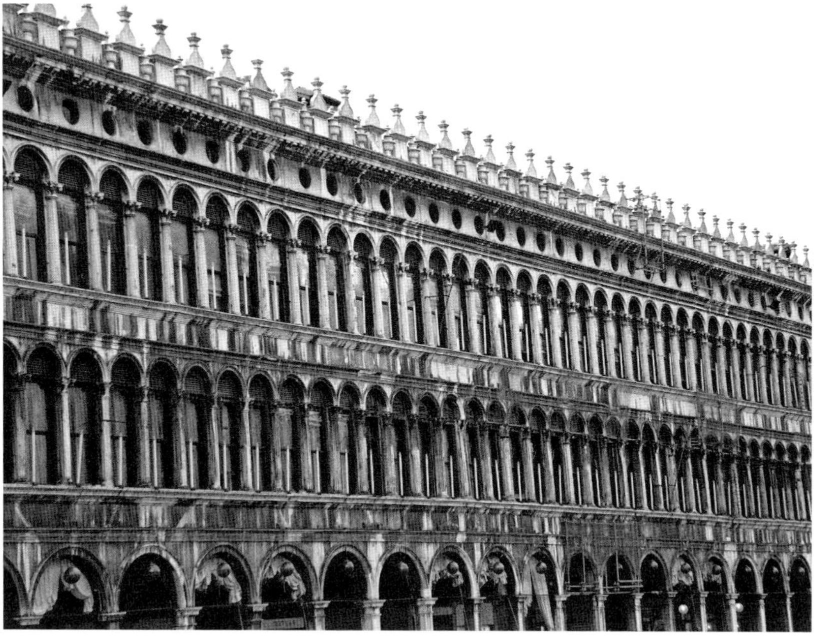

28. Procuratie Vecchie, Piazza San Marco, Venice, begun c. 1500. Photo: author.

The rhythmic design of the porticos framing the Piazza San Marco constructs a space replete with artistic effect. Such symmetry dominates the city's vistas to deflect views of architectural discord. Ruskin conjoins congruence in architecture with civic stability and order.[11] For Ruskin and Sitte, exponents of late medieval Italian urbanism, such stability and order were bound together through projects of enclosure.

In this chapter, I explore the topographies of enclosure in the Venetian urban form. Enclosure is a spatial condition predicated on the construction of boundaries to segment space. As Martin Heidegger writes, "A boundary is not that at which something stops but, as the Greeks recognized, the boundary is that from which something *begins its presencing*."[12] Here I investigate enclosure for its boundaries that produce a distinctive urban presence. I argue that urban enclosure animates the lives inhabiting its restricted spaces to recast engagements with sight. Sitte's aesthetic judgments rely on terminology such as "line of sight" and "angle of vision" since he understands beauty as a framed panorama for the spectator's eye. Spatial enclosure promotes cohesive vistas because it directs and restricts vision. The city becomes a site of controlled sighting. Yet the closed spaces of enclosure open new lines of sight that discipline the eye. The contraction of space may present a fractured and localized picture of the world, but it also offered visions of a new spatial order. In the case of the piazza, such enclosure is in fact premised on perforation. Arcaded passageways and corner streets remain open to incorporate the piazza within the larger urban form and, in the words of Sitte, to "expos[e] it to the eyes of all passersby."[13] The enclosed spaces of the piazza generate "well selected lines of vista" that promote physical connections between bodies and buildings.[14] For Sitte, urban enclosure serves as an effective background for the scenes of daily life. More importantly, enclosure builds communal relationships through the intersection of foreshortened horizontal structures and terminal streets that define the distinctive visuality of early modern Italy.

The properties of enclosure are determined by its openings. Venice's Piazza San Marco creates a built environment open to continual communal accessibility. Gateways demarcate the outside-inside relation in the form of arcades, streets, and embankments to promote admission. Contact with spatial extension thus defines the contours of the piazza's enclosure. However, Venice also constructed urban enclosures whose gates were impassable. Tensions between exposure and enclosure resided around such impermeable sites that limited mobility. The ghetto was certainly such a site. Guarded gates and high walls immobilized Jews during particular times of the day to delimit Jewish life in the early modern city. If the Piazza San Marco regulates collective identity through shared space in the city center, the Venetian ghetto pushes enclosure to the periphery to limit ingress and egress. If the Piazza San Marco consolidates *civitas* through open gateways and streets, the ghetto segregates space with guarded gates and nocturnal curfews to create a compulsory *civitas Judaeorum* in the city of Venice. That is, the ghetto defines enclosure through the marking off and walling up of space to classify and organize the limits of urbanity. These spaces marginalized Jews to the periphery and restricted their bodily movement. Yet the ghetto never blinded the Jews' peripheral vision. Instead, enclosure elevated the ghetto to a prominent position in the urban form, yielding new vistas. In fact, the ghetto put Venice on display for Christian and Jewish eyes, which ultimately prompted officials to restrict the sights of enclosure.

Segmented Spaces

Venice was a city that segmented the spaces of ethnic residence. The principles of urban planning in the Venetian context emphasized social unity through the strategic distribution of ethnic space. Jews were not the only social outgroup affected by segregation. Greeks, Turks, Germans, Albanians, Dalmatians, and Armenians preserved their own identities in separate districts of the city.[15] By granting different ethnic groups autonomous spaces, Venice presented itself in myth and practice as an equitably mapped republic. Neither persecuting nor banishing its minorities, Venetian civic ideology claimed to offer peace and security to various groups, cooperating politically and economically to form a perfect republic. The separation of foreigners into distinct ethnic enclaves became a physical expression of the republic's policy of tolerance. The early modern conception of tolerance, which circulated in the works of canon law and scholasticism, permitted Jews and other social outgroups to dwell among the communities in Latin Christendom provided their deviance proved no threat to Christianity. Tolerance offered limited social forbearance to Jews while opposing policies of expulsion and extermination.[16] The establishment of the ghetto gave urban form to Renaissance toleration, inviting Jews to the lagoon city with regulatory restrictions permeating the details of everyday life.

In early modern Venice, segregation and surveillance were often complicit in the politics of toleration. Certain foreign communities could settle in the city provided they comply with compulsory housing. For example, Venetian law penalized German merchants fifty ducats for taking lodging outside the German exchange house, known as the Fondaco dei Tedeschi (Figure 29).[17] First constructed in the thirteenth century, the Fondaco dei Tedeschi felt the impact of the Reformation by the 1520s when self-professed Protestants moved into it.[18] The spread of Lutheranism heightened papal concern in sixteenth-century Rome, but Venetian authorities permitted a German presence given that the Fondaco dei Tedeschi had been well entrenched within the socioeconomic life of Venice since the Middle Ages and its newly arriving Protestants performed their so-called heretical practices clandestinely.

By contrast, Venice's Fondaco dei Turchi was a seventeenth-century invention (Figure 30). City officials grew anxious about the Turks' presence for both their religious difference and the political and military strength of their emperor and navy. On May 27, 1621, the Cinque Savi alla Mercanzia drew up regulations governing fondaco life that required the enclosure and surveillance of Muslim Turks, which included "the Turks of Asia [Minor]

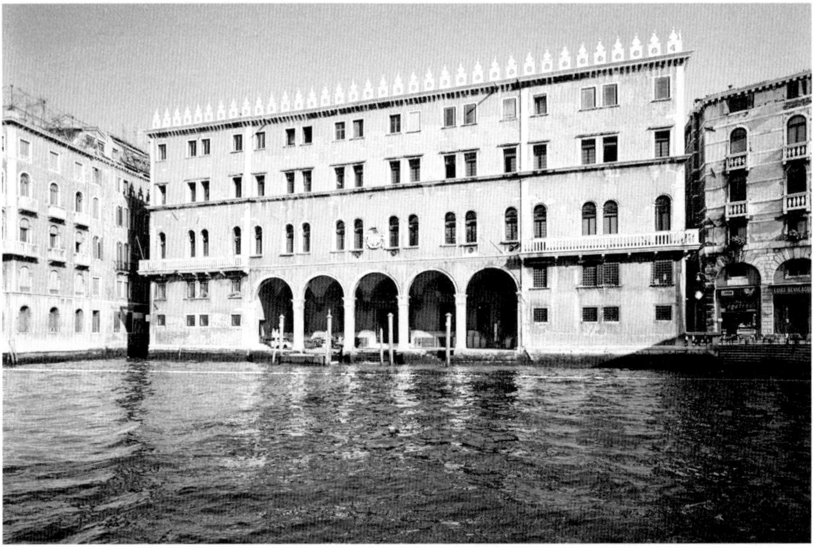

29. Fondaco dei Tedeschi, established in Venice in 1228 and reconstructed in the early sixteenth century. Photo courtesy Scala / Art Resource, New York.

and Constantinople" and "the Turks of Bosnia and Albania."[19] E. Natalie Rothman notes that such regulations functioned to limit the Turks' bodily mobility and restrict their viewing. She writes, "At least one-third of the thirty-three regulations [governing the Fondaco dei Turchi] were concerned with the obstruction of vision and movement, as well as the creation of internal barriers to prevent vision and movement among the three wings of the house."[20] Indeed, the confinement of Muslim Turks in the Fondaco dei Turchi followed the model of Jewish ghettoization. In 1621, the Venetian government required Turkish residence in an isolated area of the city, along the Grand Canal in the parish of San Giacomo dell'Orio, with house rules that mirrored those established in the early sixteenth century in the Jewish ghetto. The Cinque Savi mandated that the Turks, like the Jews, must have a guardian, who "shall be obliged to lock the doors, both to landward and to seaward, at dusk, and to open them again at sunrise, from the outside, with good and effective keys, which he must keep."[21] Venetian authorities did not differentiate among the heterogeneous worlds of Islam. To alleviate ambiguities emerging around the designation "Turchi," the Cinque Savi, in 1662, legislated the more comprehensive terminology of "Mohammedan Nations" to distinguish Muslim from Christian.[22] Occupancy in the fondaco thereby expanded to house Muslims of Turkish and Persian descent; however, the

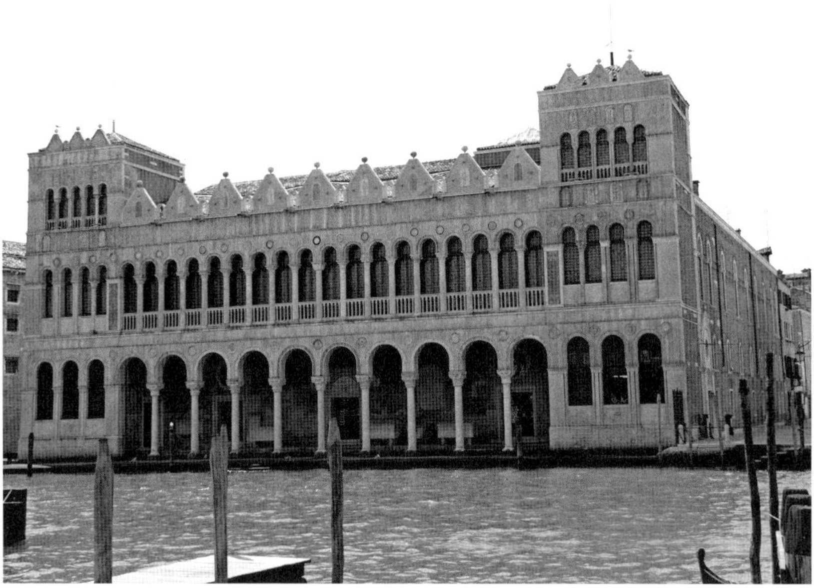

30. Fondaco dei Turchi, established in Venice in 1621. Photo: author.

Fondaco dei Turchi maintained its status as a warehouse and living quarters primarily for itinerant Muslim traders traveling between the Ottoman and Safavid empires and their posts in Venice. The ghetto, on the contrary, housed families of Jews who settled permanently in the Christian cityscape of Venice.[23] Segregation was not temporary for the Jews as it was for Muslims, but rather an ongoing condition of confinement and surveillance.

Contemporary diaries, decrees, and travelogues detail the structural hermeticism necessary in ghetto design to quiet concerns developing between state and faith. Diarist of Renaissance Venice Marin Sanudo, for example, likened the architectural form of the Ghetto Nuovo to "a castle," which is to "[be closed] off with a wall and drawbridges. They [the Jews] are to have only one gate, which is to be closed so that they remain within."[24] On March 29, 1516, the Senate institutionalized the organizing principles of ghetto confinement: "on the side towards the old Geto, where there is a little bridge, and likewise on the other side of the bridge, two doors shall be made, one for each of these two places. These doors must be opened in the morning at the sound of the *marangona* [the bell rung at sunrise], and in the evening they shall be shut at the twenty-fourth hour [sunset] by four Christian guards."[25] The containment of

Jews behind ghetto walls and gates implicates architecture in a system of binaries that mapped the boundaries of faith. The partitioning of space in Venice epitomized a paradoxical process of communal belonging. As Ania Loomba suggests, "the outsider is not safely 'outside' at all," to denote "the fragility as well as strength of the boundaries between communities."[26] Such boundaries were not in fact fixed. Instead, perimeters manifested a form of social production that was never securely set, "always in process, and always constituted within, not outside, representation."[27] Maintaining boundaries was a necessary practice of daily life; to exceed them made Jews potentially dangerous in the eyes of Christians. In Venice, boundary making came with a curfew, sunset signaling the temporal parameters of enclosure.

Ghetto walls may have contained the Jews by night, but enclosure within the ghetto multiplied when Venetian officials mandated the obstruction of the tenements' apertures. In 1560, the Cinque Savi alla Mercanzia required Jews to obstruct their canal-side view outside the newly constructed buildings in the Ghetto Vecchio by walling up windows, balconies, and doors to prevent ocular contact between Jew and Christian. Defining the forbidden views from the ghetto formed part of Venetian legislation with the founding of the Ghetto Vecchio in 1541 (Figure 9). At that time, the Venetian government prohibited the construction of balconies along the wall of the Ghetto Vecchio at Cannaregio without also installing iron grates to separate Jews and Christians.[28] This act of fortification, though later rejected, sought literally to bar Jews entry into Christian spaces, for Christians remained on portions of the land adjoining the Ghetto Vecchio. Although the proposed iron grates participated in a project of segregation, they did not necessarily preclude visual access to the Christian world, as did the recommendations of 1560. In this later mandate, the Cinque Savi sought not only to close off specific windows, balconies, doors, and quays, but they also requested the erection of new unpunctured walls to ensure complete enclosure (Figure 31).[29]

Legislative exemptions at times deferred the reality of a completely sequestered windowless space, but the idea of an idealized geography that occluded Jewish vision lingered in the legislation. Such directives indicate that Venetian magistrates sought not only to monitor Jewish movement through compulsory nocturnal enclosure but also to control the Jews' vistas during all times of the day. If, as Rothman writes, "familiarity and intimacy ... were believed to grow from physical proximity and the sharing of living space," then Venetian officials sought to dissolve that spatial amity through architectural obstruction.[30] Ghetto walls did not fully mitigate Christian concerns over Jewish cohabitation; instead, they enhanced anxieties around tenement

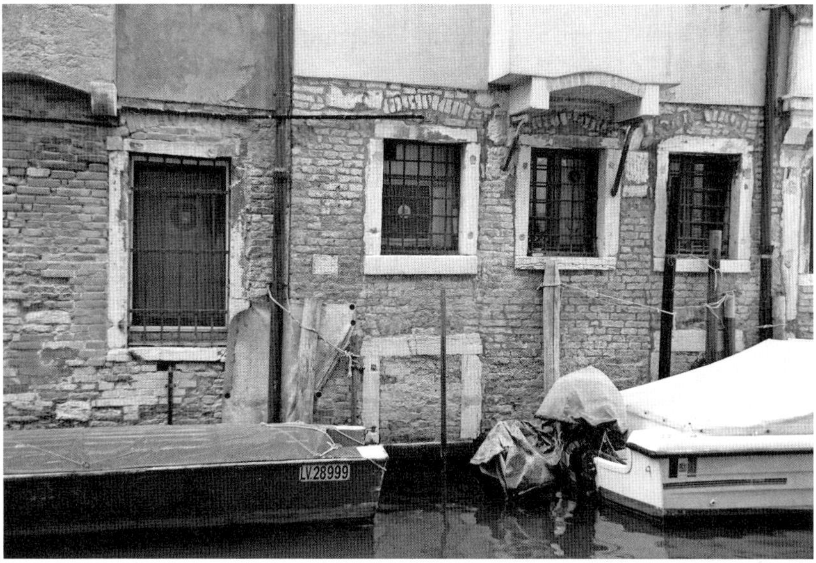

31. Bricked-up quays along the canal at the Ghetto Nuovo. Photo: author.

apertures from the unmediated views they produced.[31] Ghetto gazes that penetrated also alienated. As such, the Venetian government would not permit the Jews to experience the world outside the ghetto with autonomous eyes. The reciprocity of the urban gaze, the look and the look returned, engendered an encroachment of space explicitly identified as Christian that created an uneasy social instability. The establishment of the ghetto produced a space that visually defined the Jews' objecthood. Venetian authorities positioned Jews as objects on the periphery for continual observation. Built into this system of surveillance was the potential for Jews to conduct their own act of fenestral looking. This reciprocity of gazes and sight lines provoked social tensions precisely because Jews as objects, controlled and disciplined, transformed with their optical powers into subsidiary subjects. As Beatriz Colomina argues, "Architecture is not simply a platform that accommodates the viewing subject. It is a viewing mechanism that produces the subject. It precedes and frames its occupant."[32] The renegotiation of the Jews' visual access to Christians in the vicinity conveys the Venetian authorities' attempt to define the edges of urban space, to overcome the visual reciprocity, through the occluded views of the ghetto. Displaced within ghetto walls, the Jews were "caught in the act of seeing, entrapped in the very moment of control" that housed their illicit varieties of viewing.[33]

Fenestral Filtering

The restrictions placed on early modern windows were not unique to ghetto enclosures. The obstructed ghetto vistas are analogous to those found in other forms of architectural sequestering, particularly those that housed women.[34] As citizens festooned windows and balconies during civic celebrations with lavish garlands and tapestries, so too did they limit access to those ceremonies' viewership. For instance, on June 13, 1656, the College of Cardinals in Rome preempted the Santissimo Corpo di Christo procession with a *bando* (street poster) identifying the desired demographic for the solemn event: "on this day of the feast, from the sun rising till the entire procession has passed, no man dare to be at windows together with women of any sort, even if it is the most honest woman, who happens to be his own wife or sister, or parent or close relative, throughout the street where the procession passes."[35] Positioned at prime locations throughout Rome, street posters covering a broad range of civic issues made distinctions in economic class and social status visually legible for all passersby. As Rose Marie San Juan observes, printed *bandi* often impeded the movements of such social outgroups as vagabonds and Jews throughout the arterial streets of early modern Rome.[36] Mining the particulars of the Santissimo Corpo di Christo poster, the social marginality of women is cogently on display. Women neither participated actively in the public performance of sacred ceremony at street level, nor did they engage at times as private spectators in the passive act of fenestral looking. From Italian humanist Leon Battista Alberti to Dutch moralist Jacob Cats, early modern writers codified this custom by ensconcing the woman within the folds of the domestic interior, eschewing her from public reach.[37] Discursive practices documented in quotidian posters as well as in lofty books of manners spatially isolated women indoors and forbade them admission to their own household windows.[38] Diane Wolfthal attributes much of the woman's detachment from the window and other apertures to the economies of consumption.[39] She equates the alluring display windows of shopkeepers, dressed with sumptuous jewelry, textiles, or foodstuffs, with the windows that framed the prostitute's body for sale. In both cases, windows served to procure potential customers.

The gendered geographies of early modern Europe constructed spatial barriers that often restricted women to the domestic interior. Even prostitutes in Renaissance Ferrara were legally bound to the confines of their *chiuso* (small residence).[40] The urban topographies of early modernity enclosed women within in order to shield them from the outside patrilineal world, thereby defining and defending male *virtù*.[41] The window, with its proximity to public space, frustrated the woman's prized propriety. The potential to breach the barrier of the threshold, to enter, if even momentarily, the world outside, provoked anxiety. When Shakespeare's Jessica leaves Shylock's "sober house," she does so at night dressed as a page.[42] Only in the guise of a (Christian) male could a (Jewish) woman leave the confines of her confinement. Crossdressing was a peril for any city, both socially and spatially. Not only did it blur the distinctions between the sexes, but it also permitted the concealed woman to trespass on the spatial dominion of men.[43] Governance of the city demanded men's participation in the full spectrum of civic space. According to legislative and literary sources, women, by contrast, were to remain vigilantly out of sight.

This vigilance in Venice was at its highest in the spaces housing the city's cloistered celibates. It was imperative that windows, which in Renaissance brothels displayed the prostitute's body, defend the nun's body, her virginity, from immodesty or, worse, iniquity. To protect the purity and moral virtue of female monastics and to enhance their spiritual education, the convent segregated religious women from secular society within an architecture of *clausura*. The complete enclosure of nuns, advocated by the mid-sixteenth-century reforms of the Council of Trent (1545–1563), sought to regulate monastic behaviors through the built environment. Marilyn Dunn writes in her work on post-Tridentine convent architecture in early modern Rome that shaping the spiritual life of nuns required the erection of high walls that surrounded the convent complex to separate the sacred from the profane.[44] Problems arose when neighboring residents from nearby palaces or houses threatened the introverted conventual life with windows that overlooked the nuns' cloistered space and compromised the nuns' disciplined privacy. Dunn cites an example from 1666 implicating the Dominican religious from the convent of Santa Caterina a Magnanapoli in Rome when they threw stones at the masons working on an addition to the Buzi family palace. Fearing the Buzi would disturb the nuns' strict *clausura* with potentially dangerous stares and horrible noises from their windows that looked out over the convent, the nuns petitioned Pope Alexander VII to have the work on the Buzi palace halted immediately. The pontiff rejected the Dominicans' written appeal, although other communities, including the Discalced Carmelites at Santa Teresa, protected their cloistered sanctuary by purchasing the land adjacent to their convent.

Such monastic anecdotes related to conventual urbanism emphasize in this case the nuns' need for optical seclusion.[45] In a cramped early modern city where space was difficult to find and building projects required vertical expansion, these cloistered nuns sought male authorization to protect their sanctified space and their moral virtue from the outside gaze. Here *clausura*, defined by a complex negotiation of male supervision residing beyond the convent, was a positive accomplishment, a spatially desirable ideal, safeguarded by the female monastics housed within. As recent scholarship on convent culture demonstrates, the cloistered confines of early modern nuns were not in fact impregnable.[46] Nuns fought to defend their visual presence not only by terminating urban building projects that overlooked their cloisters, but also by improving their views within the convent itself. Prelates and noblemen often governed the convent and designed its walls – adorned with iron grilles and wooden shades covering windows and strong locks securing thick doors – to minimize contact between the nuns and outsiders. The strictures of *clausura* instituted a community of enclosure that nonetheless inspired some female monastics to pursue the convent's perforated points. Convent apertures, located at exposed places in the public church, sacristy, and garden, offered nuns a momentary look at men both clerical and lay performing duties related to the convent's spiritual and physical maintenance.[47] Despite ecclesiastical attempts to render female religious houses impenetrable with reinforced stone- and ironwork and enforced rules of isolation, nuns at times advocated for architectural alterations to their convents to enhance their views. For instance, in 1629, the abbess of San Francesco dell'Osservanza in Naples appealed to Cardinal Buoncompagno to increase the nuns' visual access to the convent church, among other sites.[48] After the Council of Trent, nuns no longer could enter conventual churches. Instead, they watched the mass performed at a distance from screened clerestory windows. The nuns of San Francesco dell'Osservanza exemplify how early modern female monastics attempted to defend and expand their visual contact within the convent's interior and to exercise their cloistered powers of sight.

Both the sequestration of nuns and the ghettoization of Jews engender a relationship of power and discipline that expresses how a spatially confined subgroup articulates politics and ideology.[49] In both examples, the gaze is spatially at play. As clerics feared the outsider's penetrating look on the virginal nun because it sought to sexualize her, so Venetians feared the sexuality of Jews and ghettoized them as a means of control. Such control was lost when Jews built their disproportionately tall tenements. The pronounced verticality of the ghetto structures became a prominent aspect of Venice's skyline; its conspicuousness within the Venetian cityscape demonstrated its symbolic powers. "Command of the city was epitomized vertically," writes Helen Hills in her study of seventeenth-century

Neapolitan convents.[50] Perhaps female monastics problematized the highly prized performance of seeing and being seen from their cloisters, but their quest to maintain visual dominance through the unrivaled elevation of their bell towers or unobstructed clerestory windows sought principally to heighten their spirituality rather than incorporate them within the larger secular society. Hills offers various examples whereby nuns from their convent belvederes refused a glimpse of the laity below during civic celebrations including Carnival. Invoking discourses of humility, the nuns protected themselves from the sights of the world around them.[51]

The spatial practices of early modern nuns, who repeatedly avoided their views from on high, differentiate the convent's claims to the urban fabric from that of the Venetian ghetto and its Jewish occupants. While female monastics often repudiated the panoramic view of the outside world and refused to return the look, Jews unequivocally directed their ocular attention to the world outside the ghetto. Such a distinction relates to conflicting conceptions of *clausura*. Convent walls nourished nuns spiritually through complete enclosure, as post-Tridentine cloistration sought to seal off the nun permanently from societal contact. *Clausura* in the Jewish ghetto instead came with a key. In fact, archival documents specify that two keys were to be placed "over each of the gates of the ghetto enclosure" (*dovendosi metter sopra ogn'una delle porte della clausura del'Ghetto due chiavi diverse*) to give Jews diurnal contact with Venice.[52] Access to these keys became an important element of statecraft, as demonstrated by the jurisdictional disputes between the Cattaveri and Cinque Savi alla Mercanzia over the Ghetto Vecchio keys. In 1516, the Senate authorized the Cattaveri to oversee the enclosure of the Ghetto Nuovo that housed the Tedeschi and Italiani Jews, while the Cinque Savi maintained control of the Ghetto Vecchio where, beginning in 1541, the Levantine (and later Ponentine) Jewish merchants resided. Over time the constituencies of the two ghettos blended (particularly as German Jews moved to the Ghetto Vecchio), which incited the two magistracies to wrangle for control over jurisdiction. In an unprecedented incident dated September 22, 1609, the Cattaveri ordered a locksmith to remove the locks on the Ghetto Vecchio gates, which the Cinque Savi administered, and forced the guards, on pain of imprisonment, to relinquish their keys.[53] Legislation passed by the Senate ultimately entrusted the enclosure of the Ghetto Vecchio and the custody of its keys (*la clausura et custodia delle chiave del Ghetto Vecchio*) to the Cinque Savi, but the conflict surrounding ghetto keys bespeaks the variability of ghetto enclosure.[54] *Clausura* in the ghetto required the systematic shifting of boundaries circumscribing the Jews' marginalization to uphold Venice's public interest. As the five patricians composing the

Board of Trade, the Cinque Savi had the expertise to manage the mercantile concerns of the Levantine and Ponentine Jews and provide them with the access to the seas they needed in plying their trade. *Clausura* of the Venetian ghetto endeavored to promote commercial interactions with Christians when the ghetto remained opened and to prohibit interfaith interrelations when guards closed the ghetto gates. Whereas the enclosure of the piazza remained open to promote civic accessibility and the convent remained closed to protect monastic values, ghetto enclosure was predicated on the deliberate movement of its gates. Closure and aperture of the Venetian ghetto complex were inseparable and mutually constitutive conditions of confinement, interconnected categories essential to the stabilization of Venice's social geography and economic prosperity. In Venice, the financial and residential needs of the city produced an anomalous place for the Jews within the Venetian skyline. Through the vertical ascendancy of the ghetto and its resultant rooftop vistas, the complex received power and recognition urbanistically, and from its heights sheds light on the new spatial relations built between Jews and Christians.

The Venice ghetto became an architectural apparatus predicated on confinement and surveillance in which spatial discourses of centrality and marginality, visibility and invisibility, were continuously negotiated. As such, the ghetto offers a compelling comparative to the modern conception of the Panopticon. The Panopticon, developed by Jeremy Bentham and examined in the work of Michel Foucault, is an annular building of light-flooded cellblocks that surround an opaque central inspection tower.[55] Situated within the tower is an unseen supervisor who has constant visibility of the cells' occupants. The arrangement offers the tower an axial visibility that conditions the occupants in their cells to monitor themselves for fear of the perpetual gaze of supervision. This built environment constructs a well-ordered mechanism of power that segregates, on the one hand, and disciplines, on the other. It is not my intention to align the complex institutional forms of disciplinary power in Bentham's blueprint for a Panopticon in the late eighteenth century to the establishment of the ghetto in cinquecento Venice, nor is it to question the historicity of the panoptical moment in the modern period. The Jewish ghetto in Venice was hardly an early modern precursor to Bentham's Panopticon. Rather, I am interested in the ways architectures of surveillance create social controls grounded in networks of stability and community that ensure the constant regulation of daily life. From the central tower in Bentham's design, the cellmates never exchanged gazes with their panoptical guard, who remained permanently out of sight. Similarly, the virginal nun in her conventual enclosures (and her male supervisors) sought an analogous system of invisibility to protect the nun "from her own (inappropriate) looking and especially from the looking of others."[56] The ghetto, however, offered a new architectonic system of visuality whereby the power of opticality resided with the marginalized Jews. While supervised enclosures secured the Jews' placement through urban policies of displacement, this contained world of protected topography was breached when Jews looked out from their windows. The ghetto, erected to minimize urban contact with Jewish difference, concomitantly transformed Jews to observing subjects.

The ghettoization of the Jews in Venice raises critical questions about how religious difference and agency came to dwell in early modern Venice, how Jews and Christians deployed the gaze in negotiating Venetian life. Ghettoization presented the Jews of Venice a structured visibility that allowed them access to a fluid exchange of gazes; that is, they could see and be seen, they could initiate the gaze and the look returned. The ghetto window consequently engendered a new form of social relations that provoked contestation and renegotiation. That the Serenissima sought to block the Jews' view from their windows and balconies suggests they attempted to impede the vertical prominence of the ghetto vistas and to deflect the Jews' powers of observation. By rendering the Jews' gaze impotent, the government acted to control ocular tensions between Christians and Jews, whose invitation to dwell in the lagoon city did not extend as far as their lines of sight. Hills writes in the conventual context of Naples that the "struggle over the optics of power sheds light on how new urban spatial relationships were forged and on the nature of … power itself."[57] Given the ghetto's visibility within the Venetian skyline, the Jews acquired an agency from their elevated optical placement that provoked a disordering of the Venetian order of things.

Archival records support such a claim, as authorities such as the Venetian Patriarch Lorenzo Priuli advocated for more rigorous enclosure regulations by obstructing the dangerous views of the Jews.[58] In the late sixteenth century, allegations circulated that Jews had committed indecent acts before the windows of the ghetto facing the nunnery of San Geronimo. Priuli recommended that the Venetian Senate modify the windows such that only light could be transmitted – not the defiling look of the Jews.[59] Separating Jews, supposed Christ-killers, from nuns, brides of Christ, was especially important in early modern Venice, where post-Tridentine efforts to enclose the nuns within the confines of *clausura* did not prevent them from maintaining social, and at times sexual, relations with members of secular society.[60] For instance, convent *parlatori* (parlors) in Venice evolved as a salon

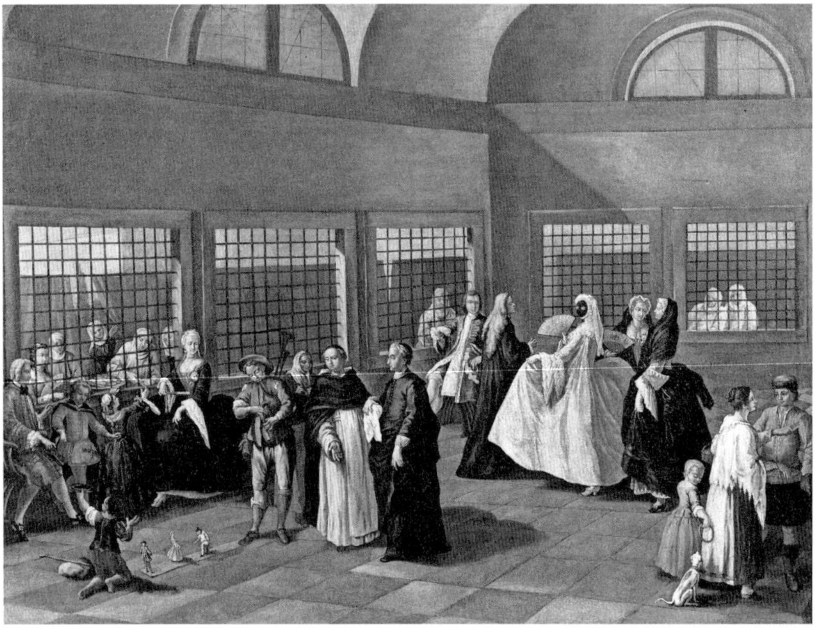

32. Pietro Longhi, *The Visiting Parlor in the Convent*, mid-eighteenth century. Venice, Ca' Rezzonico. Photo courtesy Alfredo Dagli Orti / The Art Archive at Art Resource, New York.

space that offered monastic women limited contact with outside visitors. Furnished with an iron screen and an overseeing chaperone, conventual *parlatori* partitioned the sisters from their callers through walls with window-like apertures, as exemplified in Pietro Longhi's mid-eighteenth-century genre painting now in Venice's Ca' Rezzonico (Figure 32).[61] The permeability of *parlatori* made them highly regulated fenestral sites since they cultivated relations with people from all social backgrounds including, according to a document from 1625, a converted Jew named Moisè Coppio, who was found having "noisy," "licentious," and "scandalous" discussions with multiple nuns from the convent of Santa Maria Maddalena.[62] Upon conversion, Moisè Coppio hebreo, "now Christian of appearance," became Francesco Zachia, thereby gaining him access to Christ and Christ's cloistered brides at parlor windows.[63] Testimony taken from Santa Maria Maddalena records the convert's salacious antics. Francesco (né Moisè) caused an uproar in the monastery when exchanging indecent conversation, letters, and gifts with Suor Querina Falier, Suor Serafina, Suor Clementina, and Suor Pulisena through the grilled parlor windows and

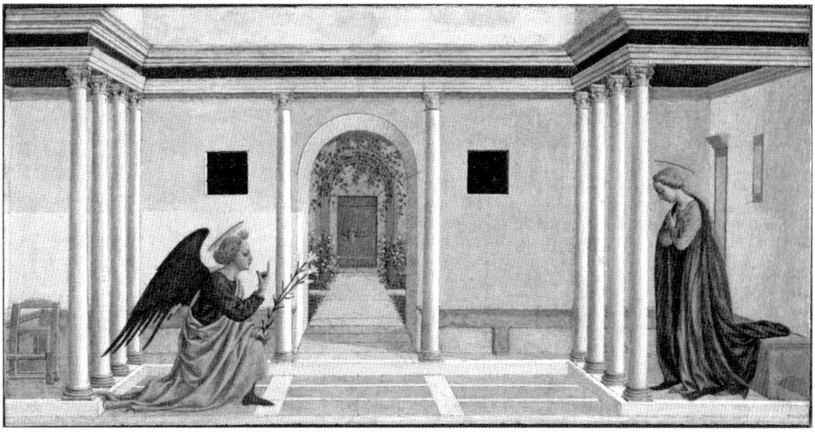

33. Domenico Veneziano, *Annunciation*, c. 1445. Photo courtesy Fitzwilliam Museum, Cambridge / Art Resource, New York.

calling the convent's superiors "pimps, whores, and other such words."[64] It was the conjunction of Jew and monastic window that engendered unruly behavior and evaded spatial controls of propriety. Open windows, offering associations with the female body's private orifices, provided opportunity (if only symbolic) for miscegenation.[65] To protect chaste nuns from the sexuality of Jews, spatial barriers required reinforcement. Domenico Veneziano paints the Virgin's room, in Wolfthal's words, "shut tight, with small barred windows, enclosing walls, or bolted doors" to denote Marian purity; likewise, virginal nuns need their geographies defended from the Jews' visual potency (Figure 33).[66]

Through the senatorial directives to cover the exterior apertures of the ghetto complex, Venetian authorities sought to block the field of visibility, to blind the Jews' powers to opticality. Robert Bonfil writes, "The reception of Jews into Christian society was transformed by means of the ghetto from being exceptional and unnatural into being unexceptional and natural."[67] Bonfil insists that the formation of the ghetto paradoxically reintegrated Jews into Christian culture, thus allying segregation with integration. While the ghetto complex was indeed incorporated within the larger civic context of Venice, its urban involvements never naturalized the Jewish presence in Christian Venice. The Jews' religious difference and, of course, their so-called usurious practices, which themselves were based on the invisibility of Jewish production that made money merely from the passage of time, promoted the ghetto's distinction. The complex and its inhabitants always maintained a subordinated status, as the marginality conferred on the Jews created displacements physical and discursive. With the vertical expansion of the ghetto, the Jews' panoramic views polarized the community as such vistas remained intrinsically unnatural and juridically reprehensible. What remained at issue, and at stake, was the Jews' gaze. Although Christian guards were to patrol the ghetto twenty-four hours a day, it was the Jews from their windows and rooftop belvederes who possessed a room with a view – a view eventually obstructed to prohibit sight.

3

WINDOWS AS SITES OF VISUAL DISTURBANCE

IN WILLIAM SHAKESPEARE'S *THE MERCHANT OF VENICE*, SHYLOCK personifies the greed of the archetypal Jew whose usurious practices perhaps attract money-seeking Christians but also repel his own flesh and blood, his daughter Jessica. Shylock instructs his beloved daughter to "look to my house" (II.v.16) while he is away fleshing out, as it were, the terms of a future bond. Despite the Jew's command to look after his house in his absence, he warns Jessica not to look out from it. Indeed, Shylock urges Jessica not to take in the views from the windows:

> Hear you me, Jessica:
> Lock up my doors; and when you hear the drum
> And the vile squealing of the wry-necked fife,
> Clamber not you up to the casements then,
> Nor thrust your head into the public street
> To gaze on Christian fools with varnished faces;
> But stop my house's ears – I mean my casements (II.v.28–34)

Both Shylock's house and the restricted views from it are architectonic signifiers of property. Shylock seeks not only to protect his home and the wealth it houses through bolted doors, but also to safeguard his personal asset, the vulnerable Jessica, from the dangerous views of the Christian world from his casements. He insists on the closure of doors and windows, for such architectural apertures place his interior (Jewish) world of paternity and pledges in ongoing contact with the exterior (Christian) world. Doors may be shut to prohibit passage and to close off communication with the outside; however, windows maintain intimate engagement with the environment even perhaps when locked tight. As noted in this scene, Shylock's command to "clamber not you up to the casements" designates the window as a site for the senses. Anthropomorphized as the "house's ears," windows funnel the cacophony of the street to the interior. Windows also frame the gazes of spectacle. In fact, the public staging of Christian revelry is made conspicuous from Shylock's window. Seeing intersects with the act of masking off, as the concealing properties of the varnished Venetian mask further accentuate the transparency of the window. Indeed, the window reinforces vision.

Windows produced anxiety in early modern Europe precisely because they punctured the stability and opacity of the wall. The window perforated the architectural integrity of concealment, exposing the permeability of place. That Jessica would forsake her father is foreshadowed architecturally through the window. Immediately following Shylock's directive to seal his house, the outspoken servant Lancelot Gobbo whispers in Jessica's ear:

> Mistress, look out at window for all this:
> There will come a Christian by
> Will be worth a Jewès eye. (II.v.40–42)

Jessica's abandonment of her father and conversion to Christianity is marked at that window. The contested site of the casement in Shakespeare's verse engenders a new form of spatial relations that challenged the infrastructure of social acceptability. To situate a beautiful Jewess at a window was to transcend the threshold of respectable behavior, to give public accessibility to the socially marginal.

Jessica's invitation to enjoy the window vistas was particularly fraught given her gender and religious difference. Lisa Lampert, in her literary study of the hermeneutics of such difference, observes, "The bifurcated representations of woman and Jew … reflect the uneasy figurations of women and Jews as both insiders and outsiders to Christian society."[1] Jessica brings together these two constructed categories, woman and Jew, creating a dual layer of alienation. Her conversion to Christianity could not mitigate her marginalization, as she herself repeatedly questions her capability to "escape a Jewish essence."[2] Yet to call her to the window before that conversion was even complete was to challenge the essentialist claims of her Jewishness and her gender.[3] The window, a liminal space joining the interior of a building with its exterior, provided Jessica with an agency that neither women nor Jews, and certainly not its aggregate Jewess, historically possessed.

Jessica's casement may not have previously elicited scholarly attention, but Shakespeare's sensitivity to the window is celebrated on a Veronese veranda in *Romeo and Juliet*. Whereas Juliet encounters her fair Romeo at the balcony overlooking a private enclosed garden, Jessica's window view of Christian revellers is distinctly public and specifically prohibited.[4] In *The Merchant of*

Venice, it is the windowscape that proved precarious for both Christians and Jews. Windows produce spatial occasions for looking and being looked at that, I argue, reinforced social difference and created profound cultural fissures.[5] That is, windows pierce walls, thereby producing a privileged gaze onto the spaces of the street that transgressed the boundary between interior and exterior.

As John Ruskin writes in his mid-nineteenth-century *The Stones of Venice*, "It is the approachability of the window, that is to say, the annihilation of the thickness of the wall, which is the real point to be attended to."[6] In this chapter, I seek to attend to the early modern window and other building apertures both formally as applied to architecture and ideologically as associated with views and viewing. Though interested specifically in the fenestral designs and representations of Venice, this chapter takes an excursion, if only briefly, to early modern London. Like Venice, London possessed a prominent foreign presence that inspired the work of artists. British artists perhaps did not paint images of Turkish delegates or African gondoliers akin to the "eyewitness style" of Carpaccio and other Venetian painters, but they did present images of resident outsiders on the theatrical stage.[7] The preoccupation with the Other in *The Merchant of Venice*, dramatized by characters such as Shylock and Jessica, draws Shakespeare's London into a compelling comparative with Venice. Both cities attracted a growing foreign presence owing to their interests in commercial trade. Both cities categorized community based on the participatory involvement of its citizenry that distinguished the incorporated from the cities' disenfranchised aliens. Civic community in London and Venice was predicated on genealogy and residence that promoted spaces for differentiation and subordination. The spatial practices conjoining social marginality and geographic propinquity in these two urban centers orient us to the window, where gazes crossed. This chapter expands on the fenestral exchanges treated in the previous chapter to situate the window within the broader context of architectural apertures. The window played an integral role in the activities, processes, and relations constituting the city and its constituency, functioning both as mediator of and barrier to the animated scenes of urban life. To study the window is to study the demarcation between public good and private plurality, between the citizen and the subordinated Other.

Injurious London

Early modern architectural treatises grant the window a prime position in the anatomy of design. Italian Renaissance humanist Leon Battista Alberti writes in *De re aedificatoria* of c. 1452 that windows were required of any edifice for proper ventilation and illumination.[8] Alberti, whose architectural authority informed construction projects in early modern Europe and beyond, insists "every part of the house should have a window to allow the air within to breathe and be regularly renewed, otherwise it will decay and become stale."[9] The health of a building was shaped by its windows as well as governed by the placement, size, and number of them. Alberti turns to the lessons of classical antiquity and the writings of Ammianus Marcellinus to provide a cautionary tale for contemporary construction. During the time of Marc Anthony, Alberti recounts, soldiers plundered Seleucia and brought its spoils, including the temple statue, to Rome. Before their departure, Roman footmen discovered a narrow opening in the temple previously sealed off by Chaldean priests. They ordered the space opened, which released "an infectious vapor ... so offensive and detestable that from Persia to Gaul everything was infested with loathsome and fatal disease."[10] Early modern architects respected the functional requirements of the window. Puncturing the surface of the wall was the only way to ensure adequate aeration. The window, regardless of its formal arrangement or aesthetic embellishment, was structurally necessary to protect those living within the building and without from the dangers of complete enclosure.

Admitting light also presented practical and aesthetic requirements for all buildings and all chambers within those buildings. The ancient architect and writer Vitruvius notes in *De architectura* that the washbasin in Roman baths must be situated under a window "so that those standing around it will not obscure the light by casting shadows."[11] Renaissance theorists repeated Vitruvius's attention to interior illumination. For Alberti, doors, stairwells, and colonnades permitted objects to pass through a building; "windows serve for light."[12] The utility of a given room depended on the amount of lighting that room received. Reception chambers, for example, may require more light than a bedchamber; nevertheless, the location of the windows on the wall remained approximately equivalent. On window placement, Alberti specifies that "any opening intended to admit light should also allow a view out to the sky, and any windows constructed for this purpose ought never to be given a low position: light is seen by the face, not by the feet."[13] Consider the theoretically compelling pragmatics of this Albertian instruction. Alberti advises that windows must be situated at eye level to allow the room to maximize the benefits of the sun's rays. He warns that to position the openings too low is to throw the room into darkness. This method of locating windows permits sufficient illumination through the placement of wall apertures set to the "view out to the sky." Fenestration in early modern architectural treatises thus treats the lighting of the room with consideration to the views outside it. To "receive the direct sun," as Alberti prescribes, window apertures must engage the eyes of the building's inhabitants.[14] In other words, to allow the sun in, residents must be able to look out.

This theoretical position noted textually in treatises of the period is further complicated in coeval practice. In late medieval and early modern London, for instance, residents sought adjudication to defend the light and air of their homes from obstruction. When a building project encroached on neighboring windows, the London Assize of Nuisance, a juridical body consisting of municipal leaders and construction specialists, rendered judgment to protect the health and beauty of the city.[15] In a case involving Master Hales and his neighbor (identified as J. S.), local attorneys in 1636 maintained that impediments to the efficacy of the plaintiff's window created a civic nuisance that required immediate redress. As Master Christopher Wray, who was involved in the case, argued, "For when this light and air are taken from him [Master Hales], his house remaineth as a dungeon."[16] The case of Hales versus J. S. presents the window as essential to the private liberties of London's citizenry. Lawyers argued that blocking the window was "altogether unlawful and unreasonable" since it put the aggrieved resident in a condition of confinement.[17] Window obstruction was a form of internment that could not be tolerated as it jeopardized the well-being of citizens and brought dishonor to the city.

Such disrespect of the city also took the form of physical damage to London's windows with manifold meanings and motives. For example, Emma Bacchus's windows were broken as a mark of her lasciviousness. Bacchus was labeled "a bawd … and thow diddest breake thy glasse windowes because thow wouldest have thy house knowne to be a whore house."[18] Broken windows, a scandalous signifier of a bawdy home, were associated with all that was salacious and immoral. Protecting the home from this architectural language of insult required overseeing all impaired windows as well as the light and air passing through them. Londoners refused to allow their homes to become a conspicuous symbol of public scorn or private confinement.[19] The sight of London's liberties, according to case law, issued forth architecturally from its windows.

As window obstruction evoked fears of infirmity and incarceration linked to a larger culture of civic dishonor, so the shattering of windowpanes evolved as a ritualized form of violence that avenged assaults against the city and citizenry. Renzo Dubbini remarks, "In the opposition that it sets up between social space and the individual microcosm, between mobility and immobility, the window remained a dual and contradictory shape."[20]

The oppositional relationship of the interior and exterior worlds framed by the window lays claim to its civic complexities. The window in the urban context was especially vulnerable, exposed to the diverse elements of its constructed sociopolitical milieu. Such vulnerability distinguishes urban space from natural space in that the colliding relationships of the London metropolis do not correlate to life in the English country house. The casements of the English lodge, situated in the depths of the forest, produced verdant views of the gentry, as those of the villa, built in "the Subburbes of the Cittie, because ... the place is healthy, and through the distance from the bodye of the Towne, the noyse not much," offered the pleasant tranquility of the countryside.[21] The city window, on the contrary, surveyed the disparate and interactive networks of urbanity. It joined the quiet spaces of the interior with the bustling activities of the urban world. Its prominence of position at the threshold of social practice and civic exchange induced citizens and their governing agencies to act promptly to rectify inconveniences or improprieties at the window. Window obstruction or destruction was a socially coded form of civil disorder that repeatedly provoked the administrative concerns of local authorities.

Complaints filed with the London Assize of Nuisance confirm how emotions ran high when the integrity of the window was compromised. Offenses committed among neighbors led the Assize to pronounce verdicts related to the sensory encroachment of smells, sounds, and sights (or at times the lack thereof) afflicting citizens in their own homes. As Diane Shaw explains in her research on the Assize, the conception of the neighbor in densely populated London identified more than the next-door resident. The neighbor performed a vital role in the production of space by delineating boundaries and constituting borders. Shaw structures her definition of the English neighbor around the fault lines of urban planning, where the category "neighbor" demarcated the boundaries of personal property separating land. She emphasizes that "size and location [of such property] were presented not in terms of independent physical measurement, but in the social nomenclature of neighborly proxemics."[22] According to this definition, the physical outlines of an individual Londoner's real estate were measured socially through the identity of those who lived on its borders. Such borders delimiting the places of private life also represented the categorical exclusions essential to a cohesive community.[23] Arbitration on the emissions of light, air, sounds, or even privy odors through windows or other architectural openings was important to the city because it distinguished the contours of private space through the invasion of that space, as Shaw aptly notes. However, windows also crystallized the community at large by providing a totalizing image of the city. The window mediated the level of civilization from within a building and the exhibited decorousness seen from without. It filtered dialogues of reciprocity and exchange through its symbolically charged panes of glass to reveal fragmentary vignettes of the community's collective body. To barricade a window was to identify the outsiders living within city limits, to create the conditions of an internal urban exile that spatially marked the city's alterity.

This was no metaphorical division, as early modern London regulated alien subjects through architectural restrictions. Refugees, particularly Protestants from the Low Countries and elsewhere, received the city's protection from religious persecution but were denied the right to economic freedom. Their status as a "community of strangers" excluded them during Henry VIII's reign from owning, inheriting, or leasing property, and from opening and maintaining a shop. While in 1556 London's Chamberlain closed off the shop windows of aliens visible from the public street with concealing latticework, later attempts to prevent consumers from purchasing foreign-made goods required modifications to the architecture itself. The Crown under Elizabeth permitted aliens their shops in 1587, on condition that passersby could neither see nor purchase the strangers' wares from store windows or doors. Shop apertures were to be "made in such sort as people passing by may not see them [the aliens] at work, and so as their wares and merchandizes ... give no open show to any people passing by."[24] Such windows, nevertheless, must "leave convenient light for them to work."[25] To deny the transparency of the window was to curtail the economic potential of the foreign worker and to remove him as competition in the English marketplace. Elizabethan London permitted aliens their windows for the transmission of light but disallowed them direct access to English consumption and consumerism and, therefore, to profit.

Plural Venice

If London measured community by the appellation of its citizens, Venice then defined itself against the resident aliens in its midst. If London manifested self-interest by its property laws that economically disenfranchised foreign Protestants, Venice then blocked windows to protect the rights of Christian (i.e., Catholic) citizens from the unwanted views of the Other. The community in Venice was defined spatially by its common belief in Christianity, and not through the diversity of its parts. To symbolize the *polis* as Christian, Venetian authorities legislated fenestration constrictions for religious outsiders.[26] Among the urban spaces to exercise window closures was Venice's Jewish ghetto. In 1560, the Cinque Savi alla Mercanzia ordered the walling up of windows, balconies, and doors in the Ghetto Vecchio to prohibit Jews ocular contact with Christians. The 1516 legislation that ushered Jews, specifically Italian and German Jewish communities, into the overcrowded quarters of the Ghetto Nuovo expanded in 1541 with the establishment of the Ghetto Vecchio. The Collegio, comprising Venice's doge and the city's highest-ranking councilors, ruled in July 1541 that the Ghetto Nuovo could not adequately lodge the influx of migrating Levantine Jews owing to the complex's restricted space.[27] Levantines, exiles from the Iberian Peninsula who settled in Ottoman territories, therefore took up residence within the ghetto's growing perimeters. The charters authorizing the Jewish presence in the city permitted Levantine Jews to reside in the newly portioned Ghetto Vecchio but prohibited them from opening shops (*far botteghe*), including the banks and stores selling secondhand goods (*arte della strazzaria*) that characterized commerce in the original Ghetto Nuovo. Levantine Jewish merchants were to serve the city in a way that the Italian and German Jews in the Ghetto Nuovo did not. Whereas the Jews in the Ghetto Nuovo traded in money and used merchandise, Sephardic Jews in the Ghetto Vecchio redirected eastern trade in luxury items across the Mediterranean.[28] Venice literally made room in the city for Levantine merchants because of their economic potential and trade relations with the East. At its inception in the sixteenth century, the ghetto under Christian stewardship distinguished where Jews lived through calculations as to how they contributed to Venice's mercantilism and maritime trade.

Venetian zoning practices institutionalized the Jewish presence in distinct areas of the ghetto. These residential regulations also determined what Jews could and could not see from their ghetto homes. On August 3, 1560, the Cinque Savi demanded that the Levantine Jews in the Ghetto Vecchio seal up all windows, balconies, and doors (*tutte le fenestre over balconi, et porte siano murate*) along the Cannaregio because they feared the views from the ghetto's apertures could potentially "inconvenience" neighboring Christians and disturb their "serenity."[29] The documented binary of Jew and Christian in this legislation is striking given that Venice was a city in which geographic divisions were continually crossed in demonstration of the unity of the Venetian polity.[30] In Venice, rich and poor cohabitated around a single courtyard and ritual ceremonies traversed the city's *sestieri* (districts). Jacopo de' Barbari's bird's-eye view of Venice, executed in 1500, provides visual expression to the unity of the urban geography (Figure 12). The synoptic structure of de' Barbari's map presents the harmonious totality of the city and, as Bronwen Wilson states, "conveys the Venetian rejection of magnificence, the subordination of the individual to the collective."[31] The urban practices that bound Venice's topography also partitioned it. The city's claim to the collective at times clashed with its aggressive commercialism, which permitted outsiders in Venice but monitored their actions and interactions. Representing the urban spaces of Venice required delineation and constant observation. As a result, the government posted four guards and two boat patrolmen to keep close watch on the ghettoized Jews throughout the day and night.[32] The social geography of Venice may well have acquired republican meaning from its corporate identity, but challenges to the contiguous contours of the property arose when its margins were populated by the socially marginal.

The walling up of architectural apertures in Venice, the contested site of the enclosed window in London – the differences among these urban practices are central to the conception of community. Citizens of late medieval and early modern London denounced window obstruction as a wrongful act that opposed responsible property management and challenged the customs of the city. As resident aliens in London possessed no legal claims to property, civil authorities closed shop windows to protect the city's consumption networks. Domestic windowscapes remained a matter of London's citizenry. Damaging a Londoner's window advanced a social discourse of domestic impropriety, yet damaging the views of a Londoner's window was analogous to subjecting the resident to the noxious stench of a nearby latrine or eavesdropping on a private conversation from the next-door garden. All these disparate offenses were associated with the neglectful act of the public nuisance.[33] The offensive practices performed at London's windows, such as limiting range of sight, introducing fetid odors, or listening in on a neighbor's private conversation, violated the well-being of citizens and their claims to moral rectitude and civic honor. As these examples suggest, neighborly negligence in London drew from abuses affecting all the senses. Intrusions of sights, sounds, and smells were equally injurious, as indicated by the arbitration of the London Assize of Nuisance.

The documentary language in contemporary Venice instead gives sensory primacy to sight, although sight's sister senses, particularly hearing (or touch, as noted in Chapter 4) also induced anxieties around the ghetto's architectural openings.[34] Architectural apertures framed Venice's surveillance system. Seeing in or looking out evolved as an exercise in power in early modern Venice that motivated the government to station watchmen in restricted areas of the city and to prohibit visual access to Venice to certain members of the city's constituency. The Venetian window provided the site with an exchange of gazes that proved problematic in buildings housing foreigners. Gazing on the city's urban form was not necessarily wrongful, but in the Venetian context it ignited civic concern that went beyond the boundaries of the neighborhood and exceeded the localized encroachments of a nuisance. Given the diverse social forces inhabiting Venice, access to the window transformed from a neighborly pleasure to a state-sanctioned privilege.

The archival voice of Venetian authorities, governmental and ecclesiastical, records the attention afforded windows and their vistas. The window in Venice presented more than a social or economic anxiety as in London; rather, the public regarded the Jews' windowscapes as blasphemous. In the ghetto, window access incited government attention when allegations circulated accusing Jews of committing irreverent acts against Christ and Christians from their casements. Ghetto architecture, founded on the notion of surveillance, was difficult to patrol thoroughly due to the height of its apartments. Veiling vision in the ghetto was an arduous task given the dizzying elevation of the buildings atop Venice's scarce lagoon ground. The height of the ghetto buildings, soaring with acute perpendicularity up to nine stories, yielded extraordinary city sights (Figure 2). If Venice, seen from its streets, offers a localized picture of the city, ascending the wooden staircases to the top of the attenuated ghetto tenements promised sweeping city views. Christian guards kept a watchful eye on the Jews during their twenty-four-hour patrol, but it was the Jews from their tall towers who possessed a panoramic view of Venice and the Venetians.

In 1560, the Cinque Savi required Jews to obstruct their canal-side view outside the Ghetto Vecchio in order to submit both the Jews and their ghetto vistas to regulatory discipline. The renegotiation of the Jews' visual access to Christians in the vicinity conveys the Venetian authorities' attempt to define the edges of urban space, to overcome the visual reciprocity, through the occluded views of the ghetto. The optical interference of the ghetto proved so vexing to its urban surroundings that state officials, in an attempt to define better the limits of the neighborhood, built window restrictions into the sequestered quarters of other Others, including Turks. As discussed in Chapter 2, the confinement of Muslim Turks in the Fondaco dei Turchi in the early seventeenth century followed the model of Jewish ghettoization from the previous century.[35] Situated along the Grand Canal in the parish of San Giacomo dell'Orio, the Fondaco dei Turchi formerly belonged to the dukes of Ferrara until Venetians repossessed the grand palace (Figure 30).[36] On December 11, 1620, the Collegio charged the Cinque Savi to oversee the alterations necessary to transform the building from a luxurious private palazzo befitting a Renaissance prince to a warehouse and living quarters for itinerant Turkish merchants traveling between the Ottoman Empire and their trading post in Venice. The regulations conceived by the Cinque Savi in May 1621 specified that no Turk could move into the fondaco until all doors on the landward side of the building were walled up, the balconies along the Grand Canal were sealed, and the wall along the Grand Canal where the Turks unload their merchandise was raised another four feet. Additionally, the magistracy indicated that "it shall be made impossible to see into the courtyard of the house [fondaco] from the landward side: either a wall shall be erected to block the view, or else all the windows and openings shall be stopped up, so that the Turks cannot be seen by their neighbors."[37] In this example, the fondaco's rules of operation demonstrate how sightlessness was bilateral. Blocked windows, balconies, and doors blinded Turkish merchants from the scenes of Venice, whereas the elevated wall fronting the fondaco equally precluded Christian observation of local Turks. Only the Christian guard posted at the fondaco with "twenty-five lamps burning throughout the night" had a cycloptic view of both worlds that endured throughout the day and night.[38]

To barricade the Turks in the fondaco was to define the limits of the neighborhood. Despite their designated presence in the city, Muslim merchants architecturally represented their outsider status within the Venetian urban topography through an enumerated list of house rules. The magistracy of the Cinque Savi curtailed access to the fondaco, both physical and visual, through the enclosure of the building's apertures and erection of a high wall, thereby making the Turks invisible in the eyes of the Christian community. Authorities appointed Venetian guardians to protect the integrity of this out-of-sight policy with penalties ranging from pecuniary to corporal for all transgressors. Venetian urban planning struck such an unneighborly offensive since authorities feared the presence of Turks both for their religious difference and for the imperial strength of the sultan. As a consequence, Turks remained outsiders within city limits, as their residency in the city became a condition of an internal exile. Dennis Romano observes in the context of Venetian urbanism that exile was in fact proscriptive: "it tells the victim what he cannot do, but it leaves open a wide range of options."[39] Certainly Turks had the freedom to leave their bounded strictures during the day to conduct commerce beyond the perimeters of the fondaco. Nevertheless, the everyday space of their confinement ensured that most fondaco business was performed out of sight of their Venetian neighbors.

While civic magistrates permitted difference to dwell within the city, they simultaneously required protection from the foreign observers' gaze. At the time of the fondaco's foundation, Venetians covered windows and built concealing walls and other optical obstructions so as to protect the privacy of Christians. This privacy had been breached in the ghetto, where Jews directed their ocular attention to the world outside its guarded walls. From their ghettoized interior, the Jews entangled their domestic space with public spectacle to trespass on the exterior world belonging exclusively to Christians. The ghetto window disturbed the strict segregation of Venetian urbanism. As a result, the ghetto required ongoing legislation even a century after its establishment to ensure its urban isolation, both within and without.

Controlling the Jews' cityscape began at the level of the lagoon and ascended as high as the clouds. *Rive*, the private embankments used to transfer merchandise from the canals to the city's buildings, were closed off to Jews to protect the integrity of their confinement. On January 15, 1619, legislation passed in the Senate that reiterated the sixteenth-century ban on "opening the ghetto *rive*, in the houses or businesses of particular Jews."[40] To uphold the "pristine authority" of the offices charged with overseeing the Jewish communities and to avert civic "scandal," magistrates inscribed *riva* closure in the Jews' charters of residence.[41] Authorities occasionally furnished exceptions to the Ghetto Nuovo bankers, whose small loans against pledges of modest value to the Christian impecunious benefited private credit markets and public finance. Simon di Calimani Banchier profited from this exemption when the magistracy of the Cattaveri authorized, on April 27, 1588, the opening of the *riva* supplying his two banks, with the appended caveat of a fifty-ducat fine if the embankment remained open after sundown.[42] Similarly, Nassimben de Calimani received licensed access to his *riva* from the Council of Ten on December 16, 1614.[43] Officials the previous month had commanded Nassimben to wall up his Ghetto Nuovo *riva* or submit to significant penalty. The Jew's service to the state, however, inspired the injunction's annulment. Nassimben de Calimani owned a secondhand goods business that provided the government with fine tapestries and other luxury items used in civic ceremonies. Authorities therefore permitted Nassimben his *riva* but obliged him to lock the quay at night and return its keys to patrolling ghetto guards. Entrepreneurial Jews from the Ghetto Vecchio also retained occasional access to *rive* when moving merchandise. Benjamin Ravid explains that *riva* contact was conditional, based on records left with ghetto guards that listed the Jewish merchant's name and destination as well as a report drafted by the Jew and submitted to civic magistrates the following morning to verify his whereabouts.[44] Access to architectural apertures engendered a series of legislative checks and balance, reports for *rive* or licenses paid for rooftop belvederes called *altane*, to ensure Christians their controlled surveillance.[45] These scrutinized openings in the ghetto's design provided Jews a means of doing business and admitting light in their sequestered spaces. Through regulatory restrictions, such apertures afforded Venetians a means of control that guided the sun's rays into the ghetto even as they refracted the city's persistently surveilled image.

Balconies too came under scrutiny. On March 28, 1587, the Cinque Savi reinstated legislation requiring bars on all balconies facing Christians in the vicinity.[46] In 1604, officials prompted Camilla and Zuane Minotto, the Christian proprietors renting space to Jews in the Ghetto Vecchio, to hasten the installation of iron grilles on all "low balconies."[47] The Cattaveri issued a warning about such balconies again in 1616, demanding that the Jews in both ghettos summarily comply with the legislative mandates to cover up their exposure to adjacent Christians. The Jews responded with resistance. Jewish community leaders who made up the self-governing body of the Small Assembly (Congrega Piccola) recorded their opposition in a translated text now known as the *Libro grande*. Suspicious of the Jews' loyalty to the Venetian state, the office of theological jurisconsult charged Sebastian Venier to translate from Hebrew to Italian the Jewish community's records dating from the early seventeenth century.[48] The *Libro grande* illuminates facets of the Jews' daily lives, including statutes on sumptuary laws, dietary restrictions, and the ordination of rabbis. David Malkiel's examination of the volume reveals how singular the Small Assembly's opposition to the architectural modifications was, given the Jews' general alacrity in executing all state orders.[49] The Small Assembly decisively lobbied against barring balconies, insisting "this is impossible, on account of the health of the inhabitants of these places."[50] The *Libro grande* does not treat the nature of the health concerns, but as Alberti theorized in his mid-fifteenth-century treatise, proper ventilation and illumination were necessary to the structural integrity of a building and to the health of a community. Enclosing the ghetto apertures therefore posed a severe health hazard, a risk Venetians understood during outbreaks of the plague when releasing Jews from their ghetto confines.[51] The Jewish communities' staunch nonconformity on issues related to balcony obstruction presents the politics behind anxieties over hygienics. Following the Cattaveri's decision, the Small Assembly raised funds and elected groups of lobbyists to fight the Venetian state for open access to their balconies and visual contact between their isolated interiors and the world outside.

As a space of transmission and exchange, the window most tenaciously mediated the crossed glances of ghetto life. According to Hubert Damisch, "Windows are always only one of the many gazes that the city opens onto itself. But a privileged gaze insofar as it is singular, individual, *private*, and one through which not only the street but also the labyrinth of the city can erupt into the space in which the subject resides."[52] It was the Jew from his well-framed window who solicited the spectacle of the city. The window formed a physical marker between inside and outside that was not merely a threshold to be traversed but a space to be transgressed.[53] That transgression took the form of accusations of Jewish sacrilege at ghetto windows. Cardinal Lorenzo Priuli, Patriarch of Venice, expressed concern to civil authorities prior to the renewal of the Jews' charter about the ghetto's structural frailties. In a memorandum dated 1596, Priuli accused Jews of committing several offenses that required immediate state response. One of the nine Jewish abuses he enumerates maintains that Jews would stand at their windows during processions of the holy sacrament and scream insults at the Eucharist, "il vero Dio."[54] In this instance, sound combines with sight to desecrate the Host. Similar charges of eucharistic defilement reemerged in 1625, indicting Levantine Jews of blaspheming the holy sacrament as it passed daily along the *fondamenta* (embankment) of Cannaregio to serve infirm parishioners unable to attend mass.[55] The charges blame Jews of deriding the *Santissimo Sacramento* three times during the day from their unrestricted and open windows. As Priuli's memorandum to Venetian civil authorities suggests, the protection of Christ (and Christians) from bodily impurities required controlling access to ghetto windows. The ongoing conflicts related to ghetto apertures corresponded to the boundaries (physical, social, symbolic) marked out by religious difference that limited Jewish participation in civic life and denied Jews contact with rites of Christian sacrality.

The establishment of the ghetto, in part, served to defend the holy and its Christian celebrants, as the Venetian historian Marin Sanudo chronicles in his diaries. On Good Friday of 1515, the year preceding the formation of the Venice ghetto, Sanudo writes: "I do not wish to ignore a depraved custom that has developed from the continuous commerce that people have with these Jews, who inhabit this city in great numbers at San Cassan, Santo Agustin, San Polo, Santa Maria Mater Domini. It used to be that from before Palm Sunday to after Easter they were not to be seen. This year they were out and about until yesterday [Holy Thursday], and this is a very bad thing."[56] In the Christian consciousness, Jewish proximity to the Eucharist, particularly during Holy Week celebrations, threatened the sanctity and unity of the city. For a Jew to deprecate the body of Christ concomitantly dishonored, denounced, and disrupted the body politic of Venice, the "corporate body having its own honor to protect and redress."[57] Spatial controls defended the sacred barriers of eucharistic practice to distinguish the boundaries between Christian purity and Jewish perfidy, a division eventually contributing to the social and symbolic geographies of ghetto-ization. Yet the sacramental separations noted by Sanudo had been well established long before the erection of the high walls of Venice's ghetto in 1516. As early as 538, the Third Council of Orleans specified: "As we are governed, with God's grace, by Catholic kings, the Jews shall not presume to go out among Christians nor mix with the Catholic populace, in any place or for any reason, from the Cena Domini day until the second day after Pascha Saturday, that is, that four-day period."[58] Separation between Jews and Christians during Holy Week continued throughout the Middle Ages, gaining doctrinal support in the thirteenth century. After the Fourth Lateran Council's establishment of the doctrine of transubstantiation in 1215, Christians throughout Europe feared for the safety of the sacred Host in the presence of Jews.[59] As a consequence, the Council of Vienna in 1267 prohibited Jews from occupying the streets during eucharistic processions and ordered them to stay behind closed doors and windows when the consecrated Host passed in the vicinity of their homes. Anxieties over Jewish contact with the Eucharist were not limited to sacred processions. The Fourth Lateran Council forced Jews to withdraw to their homes throughout the duration of Holy Week to prevent them from mocking Christ's Passion.

Although church officials promulgated this edict in the late Middle Ages, secular rulers throughout the early modern period also supported the seasonal confinement of Jews. Late fifteenth-century court documents indicate that the Gonzaga princes of Mantua, for instance, repeatedly mandated that the Jews of their northern Italian dominion remain inside their homes during *Septimana Sancta*.[60] In sixteenth-century Venice, the convergence of sacred ritual and identity politics likewise relocated Jews indoors during Holy Week. Venetian magistrates inscribed detention in the Jews' charters of sojourn from Holy Thursday to Holy Saturday.[61] City officials obliged Jews to keep their doors and windows shut (*tener sempre serrate le porte et fenestre*) during this period to ensure complete enclosure.[62] While accusations of desecration generally took the form of physical injury to the Host in which Jews were charged with attacking the consecrated wafer with knives, fire, and boiling water until it bled to show the presence of Christ, the allegations of eucharistic defilement in Venice reveal that the Jews complicit in the sacrilege did not lay a hand on the Host.[63] Optical interference, coupled with the clamor of alleged verbal taunts, could also provoke charges of profanation. As Kenneth Stow observes in a case involving the Jews of Frankfurt am Main, the annual celebrations of the Eucharist required protection from "wrongful contact with Jews, even eye contact."[64] In 1462, Pope Pius II complained to city officials that the Jews and their synagogue were housed too close to Frankfurt's principal church of Saint Bartholomew, the sights and sounds of Christian ceremony giving Jews sensory access to the consecrated Host. To alleviate scandal, Pius recommended that Emperor Frederick III oblige "the Jews to move their synagogue to an unobtrusive place in the city, hidden from view."[65] As Jews looked out from their windows onto the performances of Christian ritual, they ignited controversy by their physical proximity to the Eucharist. Windows permit the transmission of sounds and sights that, in the words of Pius II, proves "opprobrious and brings infamy to the Christian religion and the divine cult."[66] It may be for this reason that in early modern Umbria, among other regions, the *sassaiola* (stoning) of Jews' homes accompanied the annual Holy Week enclosures. This (often) bloodless ritual, following the Easter procession, targeted roofs, walls, and windows. Ariel Toaff explains, "The volley of stones against the windows avenged the Messiah, punished the Jewish loan-shark, satisfied those who threw them, and silenced the rantings of the Observant friars, at least temporarily."[67] Authorities monitored the violence to prevent significant damage, but such architectural assaults denote the anxiety the Jews' homes, particularly their windows, provoked in the Christian consciousness. These examples demonstrate how the geographic propinquity of Jew and Christian remained detrimental to the achievement of eucharistic purity and communal propriety. Civil authorities thus removed the Jews from sight.

In the age of the ghetto, defense of the Corpus Christi prohibited the physical and visual proximities of Jews and Christians through two distinctive yet not incompatible projects of confinement. Both the enclosed spaces of sacred ceremony and the ghettoized dwellings of civic life closed the Jews' windows as an architectural metaphor for their rejection of Christ. The reprobate practices of Jews treated in the *Adversus Judaeos* tradition of the Church Fathers required Jewish blindness to define Christian identity and to mark Jewish beliefs and rituals as obsolete.[68] The window, shut tight to elude sight, thus acts metonymically for the Jews' obstinacy, allying ghetto architecture with the bodies housed within. The two types of domestic internment veiling Jewish vision, however similar they may be in their protection of the Christian corpus, nonetheless offer conceptual nuances of confinement. Holy Week enclosures in Venice and beyond performed a cyclical and seasonal role in the construction of difference. The ephemeral in-house incarceration created a momentary detention in which recurrence was controlled and inevitable.[69] The transitory appearance of this ritualized quarantine reasserted a well-established social discourse of civic piety based on variable representations in time and space.

By contrast, the walling up of ghetto windows symbolized a permanent mark of domestic exile, an architectonic march toward civic isolation, that built subjugation into the urban form. Ghettoïzation institutionalized a city of alienating environments that inscribed religious difference into the urban fabric and in it prescribed a larger social order. The Venetian call for the closure of ghetto windows strove not only to safeguard the body of Christ as it passed in the streets but also to ensure that the surveillance of the social body was defined from the inside out. The workings of the city depended on the distribution of individual outsiders and close scrutiny of the location of those bodies in space. To equate the ghetto's fenestral enclosures solely with Holy Week detentions is to dismiss the centralized role surveillance played in the everyday life of early modern Venice. The unremitting division between Jews and Christians that came with bricking up ghetto windows imposed a vision of an idealized urban geography that inhibited the Jews' status as fully sighted onlookers. The conflicts over ghetto vistas in Venice reveal the ongoing contestation between Christian and Jew, between social order and disorder. Only the Jews' complete fenestral blindness could assure social order. Windows shaped politics that crystallized community and redefined neighborliness. Their closures in Venice advanced public policies of social control that impeded the Jews' gaze, quieted the ghetto interiors, and protected all that was holy.

4

WALLS AS BOUNDARIES OF THE NIGHT

IN HIS 1936 ESSAY "THE WORK OF ART IN THE AGE OF MECHANICAL Reproduction," Walter Benjamin describes the shifts in human sense perception associated with the advent of new media such as film and photography. Though he seeks specifically to apprehend the modern through an examination of the reproducible image, Benjamin observes that his reception theories have a longer history. He posits that architecture "since primeval times" has participated in a complex network of sensory information, arguing:

> Buildings are appropriated in a twofold manner: by use and by perception – or rather, by touch and sight. . . . On the tactile side there is no counterpart to contemplation on the optical side. Tactile appropriation is accomplished not so much by attention as by habit. As regards architecture, habit determines to a large extent even optical reception. . . . For the tasks which face the human apparatus of perception at the turning points of history cannot be solved by optical means, that is, by contemplation, alone. They are mastered gradually by habit, under the guidance of tactile appropriation.[1]

Benjamin contends that long before the art of photography or the landscape of modern urbanism, inhabitants of the built environment received architecture in a state of distraction. It is not attentiveness that makes humans order their architectural occupancy. It is habit. Habit catalyzes the aesthetic encounter as the spaces of everyday life stimulate the senses. Habit guides the body through architectural space, the quotidian qualities of the encounter evoking a bodily response. Habit naturalizes urban onlookers to wander within that which they do not quite see.

Benjamin reminds us that architecture cannot be captured exclusively with the eyes. As three-dimensional objects on a habitable scale, buildings preclude full visualization. Katherine Fischer Taylor notes that "the impossibility of ever *seeing* a building in a single synthetic view" makes optical appropriation unachievable.[2] The architectural experience requires the contemplative capacities of opticality and the materialist impulses of tactility to render building intelligible on a spatial scale. Vision and touch become interconnected sensoria in the act of perception. Constituents in a reciprocal spatial relationship, sight and touch nevertheless obey distinct laws of perception. Their differences are measured in distance. While sight permits viewers direct access to an object without proximal contact, touch requires closeness and connection. Viewers are able to keep the object of their gaze in sight without the need for physical engagement; touch alternatively demands bodily proximity. Boundaries mark such distinctions. Elizabeth Harvey states that sight, like hearing and smell, "extend[s] the body beyond its own boundaries," whereas touch breaks down those physical barriers to insist on the corporeal and the contiguous.[3] Architecture creates the conditions for visual detachment and tactile closeness no matter on which side of its walls you stand. The physical embodiment of the wall defines the space within and its exclusivity from without. Through its irreducible separation and touchable materiality, the wall emblemizes the city and the senses that sustain it.

This chapter explores the architectural wall as it implicates the seeing and touching bodies it houses from within and protects from without. The wall is not, as sociologist Georg Simmel claimed, a mute architectural element.[4] It speaks. It tells spatial stories of the processes, movements, and relationships of urban life. It makes manifest the interconnected networks of urbanity. The wall can never be a neutral structure, for it constructs a place where intersecting social relations congregate. In this chapter, I explore the social relations that cluster and adhere around walls, specifically Venice's ghetto walls. I am interested in the paradoxical qualities of the wall that simultaneously obstruct our views and provoke our desire for passage. To this end, I examine the senatorial directives that erected ghetto walls to contain the Jews at night and to conceal them from sight. I then shift my analysis to moments when Jews crossed their enclosures, when the vulnerabilities of the ghetto wall gave Jews tactile engagement with the city. Walls, while characterized by the physical and social divisions they construct, overcome that division to challenge the very order they sought to create. It is the opacity of the wall that challenges sight's supremacy and motivates the impulse "to pass through, visually and bodily."[5] Walls necessitate tactile contact to test their rigidity and shape the textured edges of the urban fabric. Here I study sight and touch to query the boundaries erected around the senses, to interrogate sensing as a mediator of urban experience. I examine the ghetto's sensory involvements from both sides of its walls to suggest that architectural reception conjoins both the visual and the tactile, inevitably acknowledging their sensory interdependence.

Whereas Benjamin mined human sense perception for its cognitive and haptic possibilities, I seek instead to understand the representations of sight and touch erected around walls and the protean qualities of their construction. I study buildings and bodies to identify how the spatial experience of the wall structures vision and affects the shape of touch. If architecture, as Benjamin suggests, stimulates the visual and the tactile conditions of perception, then the Jewish ghetto of early modern Venice offers a unique venue to pursue the limits of the senses of space. In 1516, the Venetian Senate founded the ghetto as a state-controlled institution with specific spatial and temporal dimensions. Jews were free to traverse Venice's streets, squares, and canals during the daytime hours but were compelled to return to their segregated space at sunset. Ghettoization evolved as a nocturnal pursuit grounded in fears surrounding the senses. Venetians locked Jews up at dusk and guarded ghetto gates at the moment when vision was occluded and suspicion of cutaneous contact between Christians and Jews was at its highest. Threats to the body and the soul were thought to multiply as the sky turned black as pitch, when nighttime transgressions were invisible to the naked eye. "Because the darkness of the night offers everyone the possibility of doing evil," declared Venice's Council of Ten, the city had to defend the boundaries of night from potential unruliness.[6] The Venetian ghetto was at the center of this sensorial politic because the fear of the Jew, as I will argue, was most concentrated at night.

Boundary Marking

Venice was singular in its nocturnal sociability. The city, set against the watery backdrop of the northern Adriatic, shimmered with the illuminations of the night sky off the lagoon waters. Such an improbable natural environment created a unique setting for evening encounter, both pious and political. Crepuscular processions filled the city streets and canals during major civic celebrations, most notably during Christmastide and Carnival season.[7] Night provided the solemn atmosphere to observe the feasts and festivals of the liturgical calendar and to commemorate momentous events in Venetian history. After a Saturday sunset in July 1592, a cross-section of the city assembled around the classically inspired votive church sited on the Giudecca in celebration of the Feast of the Redeemer. Venice's doge and senators initiated the evening proceedings by walking across a specially fabricated pontoon bridge from the Zattere to Giudecca en route to the mass held at the Church of the Most Holy Redeemer (Il Redentore, Figure 34). This church, famously executed by Andrea Palladio, and the

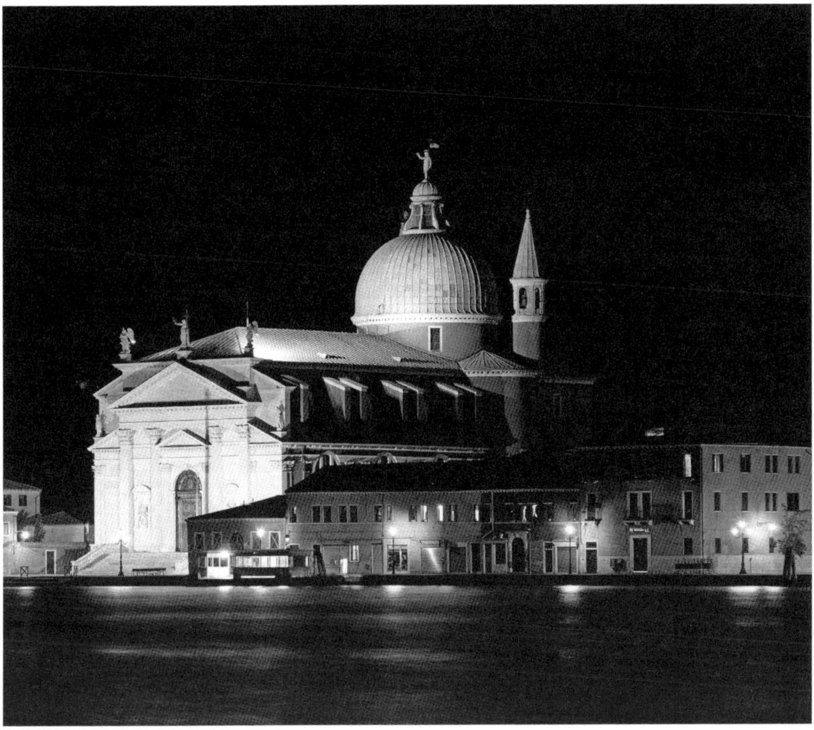

34. Andrea Palladio, Il Redentore, Isola della Giudecca, Venice, completed 1592. Photo: author.

annual celebrations surrounding its construction acknowledged Venice's gratitude for deliverance from the devastating plague that struck the city beginning in 1575, killing over 50,000 inhabitants.[8] The departed pestilence inspired the erection of ecclesiastical architecture as well as numerous history paintings that further documented the feast's civic significance. Joseph Heintz the Younger, in a painting dated 1648, depicts the doge attended by prominent ecclesiastics and patricians on the steps of the church (Figure 35). Heintz the Younger, a German artist who painted in an Italianate style, enjoyed considerable success in Venice portraying the city's vibrant religious and civic celebrations. In this image, the northern artist incorporates anecdotal details of the feast, including Venetian nobles gliding in gondolas, a boy wrestling a dog, beggars asking for alms along the embankment, and a young girl losing her high platform shoc (known as a chopine) to the waters. In the eighteenth century, Gabriel Bella located the feast later into the night with a full moon rising above the bridge-bound procession (Figure 36). His bodies in motion emblemize the city and animate

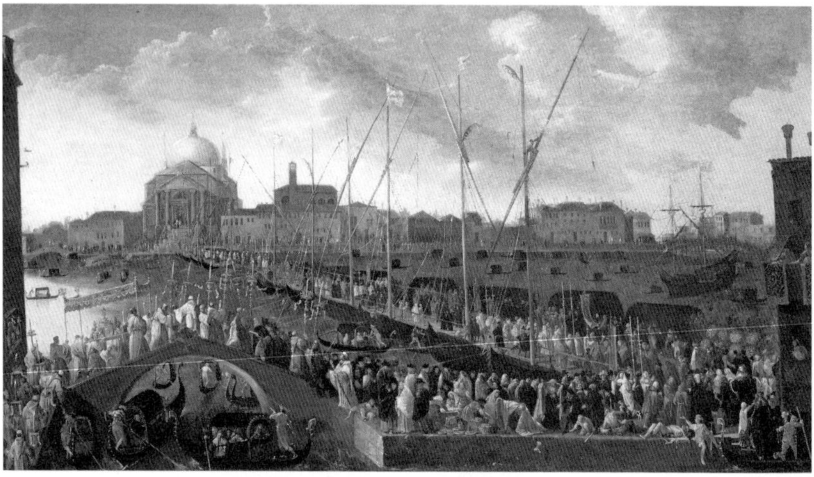

35. Joseph Heintz the Younger, *Procession of the Redentore*, c. 1648. Venice, Museo Correr. Photo courtesy Alinari / Art Resource, New York.

its nocturnal rites and rituals. Bella saturates the canvas with the colors of night and spectacle. These early modern works orient reception in space and time. Concentrating the city's constituency around the watery surroundings of Palladian architecture, the Feast of the Redeemer promoted new understanding of the nocturnalization of urban space, whose specific parameters derived from the Venetians embodied in it.

Religious ritual in Venice enjoyed the tenebrous ambience of the night, but the pragmatics of the city's maritime commerce and statecraft also required access to the night. Small oil lamps, known as *cesendele*, permitted wayfarers to travel throughout the canals on moonless nights by distinguishing city from sea.[9] In the Doge's Palace, torches blazed after curfew bells sounded to set the scene for political performance. If crucial legislation lingered after nightfall, the Senate forged ahead in the dark, lighting candles to shed light on matters foreign and domestic. The Sala del Maggior Consiglio shone with "an infinite number of torches" when politics intermingled with the revelry of social gathering.[10] During a visit to Venice in 1493, Duchess of Milan Beatrice d'Este celebrated the beauty of the night under lighted torches that hung from the ceiling of the Great Hall. Beatrice writes in a letter to her husband, Ludovico Sforza, that the late night event included theatrical allegories with performers who "danced round Justice, and after dancing for a while, their balls exploded, and out of the flames, an ox, a lion, an adder, and a Moor's head suddenly appeared."[11] In honor of the duchess's visit, an evening of lights exploded into pyrotechnics. Night begot flames and fireworks.

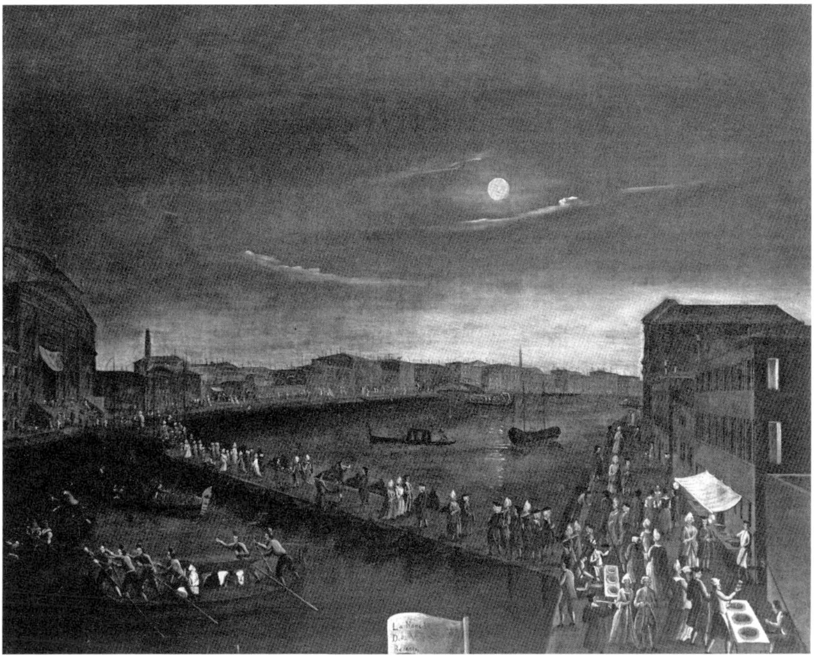

36. Gabriel Bella, *Night of the Redeemer*, late eighteenth century. Venice, Museo della Fondazione Querini Stampalia. Photo courtesy Fondazione Querini Stampalia Onlus.

However spectacularly Venice reflected the lights of the night, accessibility to that nocturnal city was limited. Obstruction was manifold, based in part on the conceptual distance class, gender, and ethnicity wrought on constructions of urbanity. Jews were particularly vulnerable to night-wrapped Venice. On March 29, 1516, the Senate instructed Jews to move to the Ghetto Nuovo, the edict specifying that Jews posed a potential danger to the city after dark:

> To prevent the Jews from going about all night, provoking the greatest discontent and the deepest displeasure on the part of Jesus Christ, be it determined that, on the side towards the old Geto, where there is a little bridge, and likewise on the other side of the bridge, two doors shall be made, one for each of these two places. These doors must be opened in the morning at the sound of the *marangona* [the bell rung at sunrise], and in the evening they shall be shut at the twenty-fourth hour [sunset] by four Christian guards. . . . If by chance any Jew is found by officials or public servants outside the Geto after the hours specified above, they shall be bound to arrest him at once for his disobedience.[12]

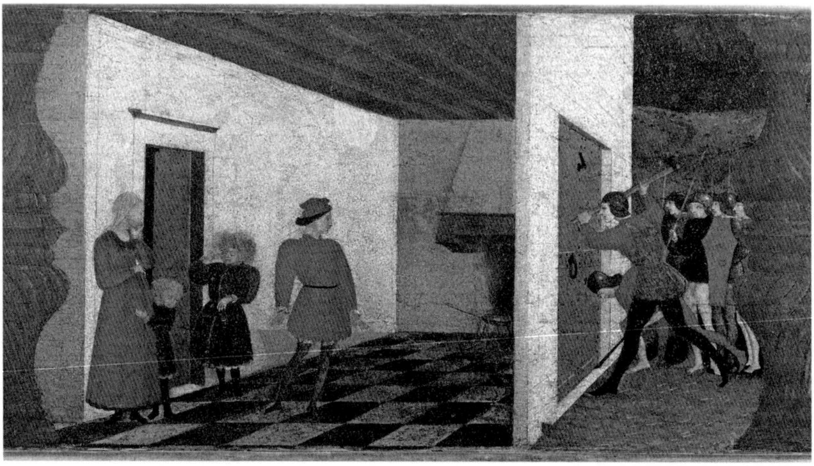

37. Paolo Uccello, *Miracle of the Profaned Host*, predella from the Corpus Domini Altarpiece, 1468, detail of scene 2. Urbino, Galleria Nazionale delle Marche. Photo courtesy Erich Lessing / Art Resource, New York.

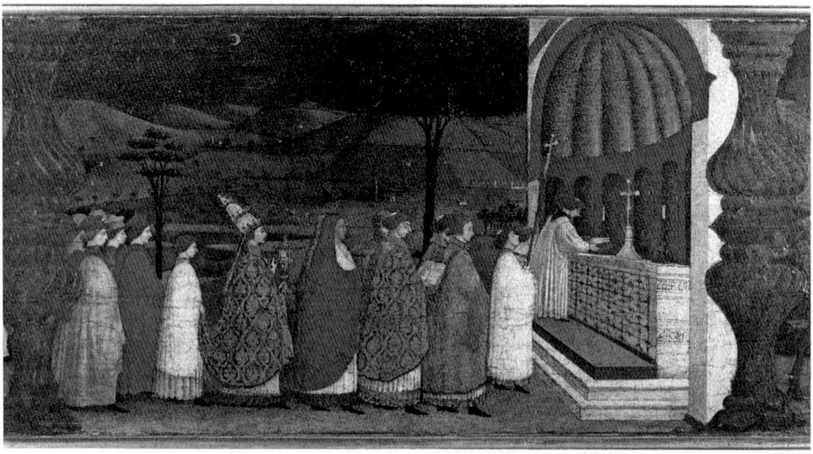

38. Paolo Uccello, *Miracle of the Profaned Host*, predella from the Corpus Domini Altarpiece, 1468, detail of scene 3. Urbino, Galleria Nazionale delle Marche. Photo courtesy Erich Lessing / Art Resource, New York.

The mandate further stipulated that the Jews would be locked into the ghetto at night and watched by Christian guards twenty-four hours a day. Strategically situated on both sides of the ghetto walls, guards kept close watch on the Jews by day and by night. No time of the day provoked greater insecurity and instability than the evening hours. The chiaroscuro of late night Venice proved vexing to Venetian state officials because, as A. Roger Ekirch writes, "night brutally robbed men and women of their vision, the most treasured of human senses. None of sight's sister senses, not even hearing or touch, permitted individuals such mastery over their environs."[13] Control of the city required sight. The efficacy of Venetian surveillance was dulled by the night, as ill-lit streets obstructed the gaze of power. Night obscured the identity of friend and foe, leaving the city vulnerable to potential acts of malfeasance. The formation of the ghetto sought to mitigate the vulnerabilities of the night. The ghetto created a restrictive place for early modern Jews to live within the boundaries of the lagoon city while separating them from Christians from sundown to sunrise.

The construction of the ghetto was a strategy of control to reorganize and redefine the spatial boundaries of the night. The ghetto offered Venetians a visible place where Jews could submit to the regulatory discipline of uninterrupted surveillance and enforced curfews, a sequestered space that prevented Jews from infiltrating society after the evening bells tolled.[14] Night in early modern Europe possessed an element of the horrific and the sublime; that is, the darkness of the night induced both demonic acts of violence and spiritual visions.[15] The nocturnal vignettes of Paolo Uccello's Corpus Domini predella of 1468, representing the desecration of the Eucharist, incorporate both aspects of night. The artist situates the Jew's bloody attempt to destroy the Host and the Christians' recovery of it within a vast nightscape, replete with a crescent moon above (Figures 37–38). Here darkness is made to reaffirm eucharistic truth and fortify Christian faith while perpetuating the notion of the Jew as demonic.[16] Christian allegations of Jewish nighttime violence were not unusual in the Renaissance. According to a ritual murder case in Trent in 1475, a guard testified that he heard the Christian child Simon Unferdorben screaming from Samuel Ebreo's house at night (Figure 39).[17] The myth of ritual murder placed suspicion on the Jews' nocturnal activities to allege "bloodthirsty" abuses of Christian children.

For the ghettoized Jews, a ghettoized nighttime affected the practice of their religion, which already situated the night as a temporal focus for faithful activity. Bereshit, the Hebrew title for the book of Genesis, begins with darkness over the void. God created light and "called the light Day, and the darkness He called Night. And there was evening and there was morning,

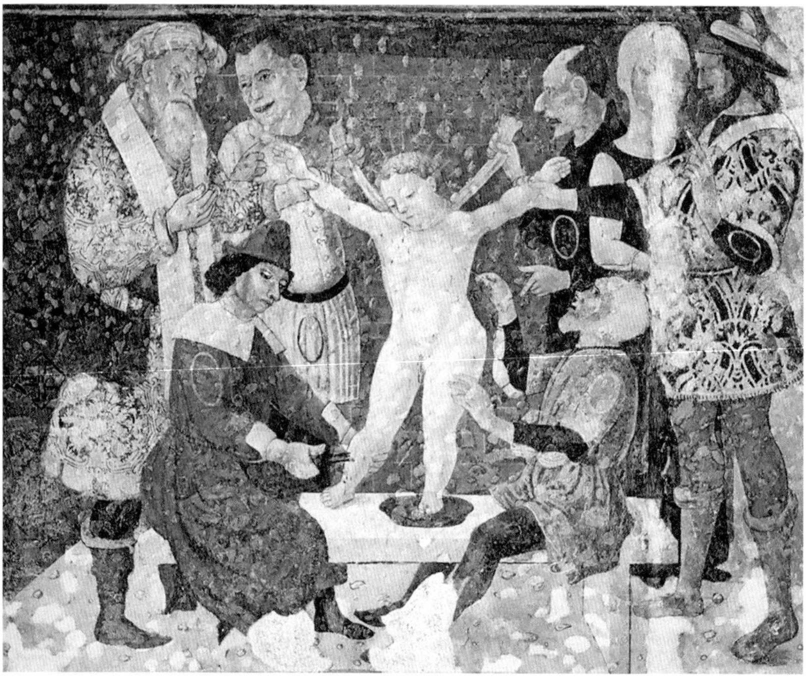

39. *Ritual Murder of Simon of Trent*, late fifteenth century. Cerveno, Parrocchia San Martino. Photo: author, with the consent of the Ufficio Beni Culturali Ecclesiastici della Diocesi di Brescia.

a first day."[18] The day, following the words of Torah, opens with the onset of night. Night serves as the temporal protagonist in Jewish ritual to map the movement from darkness to light. In early modernity, Jews often filled the night with devotion. In Venice and cities including Ancona and Mantua, the establishment of the ghetto coffeehouse in the seventeenth century initiated a new form of piety inspired by the silence and isolation of the twilight hours.[19] Following Maimonides's *Hilchot Talmud Torah* (3.13) in which he states "it is only at night that a person acquires most of his wisdom," the study of Torah became a nocturnal endeavor.[20] Maimonides emphasizes that "a person who desires to merit the crown of Torah should be careful with all his nights, not giving up even one to sleep."[21] Coffee and its capacity to instill wakefulness in those who imbibe it created an innovative form of nighttime study and male sociability outside the home. The energizing effects of coffee coupled with the words of Torah enlivened the early modern night to perpetuate Christian fears of Jewish nocturnal violence. Inherent to the night were manifestations of the sinister as well as the spiritual. For example, the veil of darkness incited Jews in sixteenth-century northern Italy to engage in carnivalesque behavior on the eve of a young Jewish boy's circumcision. As a physical mark placed on the male member, circumcision emerged as a sign of Jewish genealogy that distinguished Jew from non-Jew. Beginning in the Middle Ages, the ritual practice of circumcision also evolved as a rite of passage that marked the transition from night to day, profane to sacred. On the seventh night following the birth of a boy, the Jewish communities of central and southern Europe celebrated the event with all-night amusements of drinking, dancing, gambling, and singing obscene verse. Civic statutes in Cremona indicate that in 1575 the Jewish community attempted to purify the *veglia* of the circumcision by banning games of chance.[22] In 1697, a Venetian regulation further sought to minimize the profane aspects of the pre-circumcision vigil by limiting access to the night's events to blood relatives, thus barring entry to neighbors and friends. Elliott Horowitz observes that beginning in Venice "a policy emerged in the Italian communities of transforming the pre-circumcision vigil from an open observance into a relatively closed one. This, of course, went hand in hand with the weeding out of its more profane elements, for controlling who goes in has much to do with controlling what goes on."[23] As noted in Venice as well as other northern Italian cities, control of the night required communal authorities to restrict the Jews' movement on the city's darkened streets so as to prevent alleged nighttime misconduct.

Subjecting Jews to a strict ghetto curfew similarly sought to avert Jewish nocturnal abuses. Although the sounding of the evening bell warned all of Venice's inhabitants to repair to their homes, Venice bustled with activity late into the night with curfew remaining unenforced and unenforceable. Jews, however, were generally exempt from active participation in the night. The Venetian ghetto instituted a regulatory system that reorganized the spatial and temporal qualities of the urban nightscape to assuage Christian fears. Night was not a neutral category but an expression of power whose measured limits were imprecise and policed. Maintaining law and order required authorities to patrol Venice's shadowy streets to ensure that from sundown to sunrise the labyrinth of the city was protected from darkness. An economy of vision developed around the night. In Venice, as in other medieval and early modern Italian cities, the magistracy of the Signori di Notte (Officers of the Night) maintained jurisdiction over the dimly lit cityscape, their presence symbolizing governmental control over the night. Prosecution of civil disturbances and violent crimes came under the Signori di Notte's punitive precincts, which beginning in the fourteenth century included rooting out the activities of counterfeiters and sodomites.[24] The archival records in Venice related to the civil and criminal branches of the Signori di Notte, though only partially extant, indicate no significant Jewish nocturnal activity during the early modern period.[25] Some of the documented cases involve admonitions against Jews engaged in the *arte della strazzaria* (the selling of secondhand goods) from trading in new items, warnings against breaking and entering, and allegations of petty theft.[26] Although the Signori di Notte did not frequently hold Jews on suspicion of nocturnal malfeasance, the gatekeeping mentality of the Senate evidence concern in the Christian consciousness of Jewish nighttime abuses. The absence of light induced fears of the illicit: economic, sexual, and even architectonic. As Bryan Palmer remarks, "Night can be understood as lowering curtains on … domains of dominance, introducing theaters of ambiguity and transgression that can lead toward enactments of liberation. But night has also been a locale where estrangement and marginality found themselves a home."[27] Early modern conceptions of darkness redefined architecture's relationship to alterity. Architecture evolved as a circumscription of space that demarcated difference to house nocturnal estrangements. Architectural confinement redefined the role of marginality in discourses of space and the role of space in discourses of night. To understand the allegations of nefarious nocturnal acts is to interrogate the ambiguities and ambivalences in night's spatial rhetoric. To distinguish the subtleties of social marginality in Venice and its role in the formation of a cohesive community is to stimulate the senses and to offer marginality a home.

Ghetto architecture came to separate within from without with varying degrees of permeability. How Jews and Christians experienced ghetto enclosure differed markedly throughout the day. In the autobiography *The Life of Judah*, the seventeenth-century Venetian rabbi Leon Modena describes the porousness of the ghetto walls during the daytime hours when the ghetto doors remained open: Jews ventured out to work, shop, gamble, visit Christian friends, and teach Christian children, while Christians entered the ghetto compound in search of loans and trade.[28] After nightfall, however, the Venetian government restricted contact between Jews and their Christian counterparts. The safe conducts conferred on Jews repeatedly specified that they could not leave the ghetto after hours without pecuniary penalty and imprisonment. The establishment of the Venetian ghetto promoted commercial interactions during the day when the ghetto remained opened and prohibited social interrelations at night when guards closed the ghetto gates.

The spatial practices of isolation that came with the night disenfranchised the Jews of Venice. When Jews crossed nocturnal boundaries to trespass on the spatial homogeneity of the night, they repudiated the prescribed divisions of society and its bounds of civility. Night required limitations to regulate difference and protect the categorical exclusions dividing the community. Enforcement of the nocturnal streets was a constituent part of that process, as exemplified in a quattrocento chase scene in nocturnal Mantua. On September 17, 1491, Alexio Beccaguto charged Hercule Turco, the chief law enforcement officer of Mantua, with falsely accusing a group of Jews of going out at night without lighting a torch.[29] Beccaguto explains that the Jews were coming home one Thursday evening after attending a party celebrating the birth of a Jewish boy (most likely, the nighttime event that took place on the eve of the circumcision ceremony). Turco's foot soldiers confronted the Jews and would not permit them to enter their homes. The Jews began screaming and fled, during which time their torches blew out. The soldiers finally caught and arrested them, injuring one of them. The night travels of Mantua's Jews attracted police attention because Jews were thought to threaten nocturnal security. Although nighttime activities typically kept Jews indoors and off the streets after curfew, the formation of the ghetto in Mantua in 1612 would later require their nocturnal confinement.[30] As this archival anecdote suggests, the flourishing of the Renaissance did not end the social tensions between Christians and Jews, even in the so-called tolerant regions of the Italian Renaissance courts.[31] Turco's nighttime pursuit, moreover, sheds light on the important role the torch played in the early modern night sky. Following the advent of public street lighting in the seventeenth century, authorities in Europe's leading cities intended the new system of illumination to secure civic order against nighttime intrusion and to encourage respectable traffic on the nocturnal streets.[32] Prior to the seventeenth century, residents walking the streets at night had to carry torches or candle lanterns to bathe their path with light, not to aid the passerby ambling around in the dark but rather the police standing guard nearby. Lighting remained an ordinance of the night watch. "Failure to illuminate oneself was considered evidence of shadowy intentions," writes Craig Koslofsky.[33] The nightwalking Jews of Renaissance Mantua, whose religious difference associated them with the terrors of the night, transgressed the prescriptions of the evening hours when allegedly venturing out without torches lit.

Authorities tightly supervised the night, yet anonymities of darkness often breached that system of surveillance. One Sunday night in Rome in 1551, a group of young Jewish men converged in the local tavern, amusing themselves with game and wine until "the fifth or sixth hour [of the night]."[34] This form of nighttime sociability would not have been possible four years later when Paul IV issued the papal bull *Cum nimis absurdum* that ghettoized the Jews of the Papal States. Not yet confined behind the ghetto gates of the Rione Sant'Angelo, this band of Roman Jewry was still tipsy from drink and the freedoms of the night air. They made their way to the Piazza Giudea, where they encountered a Christian man, a visitor from Naples, carrying a cord of rope over his shoulder. The Neapolitan identified himself as a torch-maker who had just purchased the rope to use its fibers in plying his trade. In this nocturnal scene, the torch of the torch-maker failed to illuminate the shadowy intentions of the Jewish pack. As Thomas V. Cohen recounts, the Jews convinced the torch-maker that they were the (Christian) police arresting him for stealing the coil of rope. The night's rowdy adventures unfolded in a series of pranks that transformed tomfoolery into theft when the Jews stole money from the torch-maker's purse. The Jewish assailants ultimately ended up in the Campidoglio dungeon after Roman authorities cleared the air on this evening of mischief. A night that changed a group of Jews into Christian cops changed them back to Jews in the light of day.

As exemplified in the Mantuan and Roman nightscapes, night generated anxieties in the early modern imagination that afforded Jews the darkened streets to harm their Christian neighbors. Night obstructed sight, thereby fomenting fears of Christian vulnerability and violability. To allow Christians to sleep more soundly, Venetian authorities passed legislation that prohibited the Jews' passage into the night. The magistracy of the Cattaveri punished those Jews found outside the ghetto walls after hours. The penalty obliged the Jews to pay 100 lire for the first offense, 200 lire for the second, and 500 lire and two months in prison for the third. Ghetto architecture played a significant role in the construction of night by designating the Jews' placement within the city. Jews experienced an instability of space when Jewish Venice transformed from day to night. Venetians barricaded Jews behind ghetto walls after dusk to identify the outsiders living within city limits, to create the conditions of an internal urban exile that spatially designated the city's alterity. To abscond from the ghetto at night and to defy that difference came at a cost.

Ghetto walls thus played an integral role in the spatial production of nocturnal Venice. When senators passed legislation in 1516 that mandated the Jews' segregated housing in the Ghetto Nuovo, they emphasized the spatial integrity of the walls enclosing the complex: "Furthermore, two high walls shall be built to close off the other two sides [of the ghetto], which rise above the canals, and all the quays attached to the said houses shall be walled in."[35] When authorities expanded the ghetto compound with the establishment of the Ghetto Vecchio in 1541, the Collegio required the Cinque Savi alla Mercanzia to "connect with walls along the right and left side [of the ghetto along the Cannaregio]; in this wall a door shall be made to enter and exit; this wall shall continue along the boundaries of the said ghetto … in order that there is no exit along the Cannaregio other than the door."[36] On August 3, 1560, Jewish residents in the overcrowded Ghetto Nuovo submitted an appeal to the Cinque Savi to move to the Ghetto Vecchio. The magistrates approved the request with the condition that the windows, balconies, and doors of the Jews' homes abutting Christian houses be walled in and a wall be erected "of equal height and length" so as to block the Jews' view.[37] In March 1633, the Cinque Savi established the Ghetto Nuovissimo when authorizing the construction of twenty new apartments adjacent to the Ghetto Nuovo for wealthy Levantine and Ponentine Jews.[38] Although the Ghetto Nuovissimo residences were more comfortable and ornate than the tenement apartments of their Jewish neighbors, enclosing walls remained an essential element in their construction (Figure 10). The Cinque Savi required that the Ghetto Nuovissimo homes maintain the strictures of *clausura* before any Jew was permitted to move into the new space. The history of ghetto construction in Venice reveals how the spatial arrangement of enclosure was maintained by the walling up of available surface that gave Jews access to the night. The high walls of ghetto homes completed this enclosure. In June 1758, for example, the Cattaveri charged Domenico Gregorin Murer to renovate the collapsing façade of Simon and Salamon Germani Todeschi's Ghetto Nuovo apartments located near the wooden bridge on the Rio di San Girolamo, the documents specifying that the "new walls [of the façades] were necessary in carrying out the enclosure of the aforementioned ghetto."[39]

The walls of the ghetto denoted sharp separation. In general, walls imply isolation. They inhibit passage. Richard Sennett writes that the wall "is an urban construction which literally closes in a city."[40] Indeed, Venice's ghetto walls configured enclosure on an urban scale. When the sky went dark, Jews were locked into the ghetto and encased within the high walls of their tenements. The construction of ghetto walls constituted an idea of the city based on the spatial restrictions of communal incongruity. In his seventh-century *Etymologiae*, Isidore of Seville distinguished the physical boundaries of community from their symbolic representation: "a city is so-called on account of its inhabitants rather than its walls."[41] Here the idea of the city takes on a human dimension, as the physiognomies of community are set apart from architectural considerations. The emphasis on the communal collective in Isidore's definition stands in marked contrast to the material places of the city mapped in early modern Venice, which present space as a physical location. Community in Venice evolved not only as a result of lineal and affinal relations but also as a mark of spatial incorporation.[42]

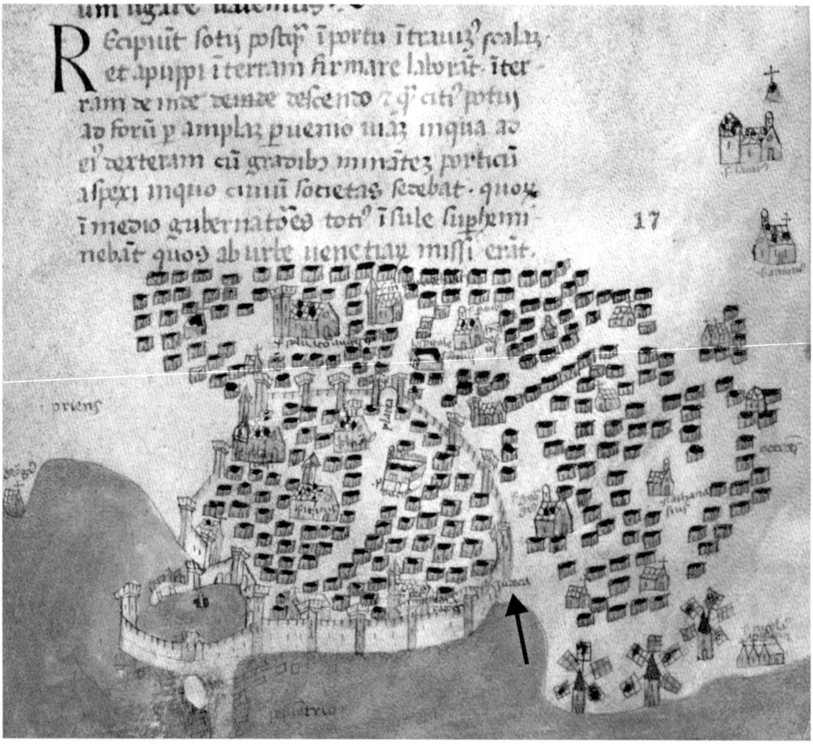

40. Cristoforo Buondelmonti, *Candia*, in *Descriptio insulae Candiae*, c. 1419, arrow indicating the location of the *Judeca* (Judaica) added to original by author. Florence, Biblioteca Medicea Laurenziana, Ms. Plut. 29.42, c. 17r. Photo courtesy Ministero dei Beni e delle Attività Culturali e del Turismo. È vietata ogni ulteriore riproduzione con qualsiasi mezzo.

The idea of community was built on boundaries that distinguished the incorporated Christians from the city's intimate outsiders. Social fissure and urban fragmentation gave rise to the concept of community in Venice to situate and temporalize the city's geographical constraints.

Walls were a prominent feature of the early modern city. Yet how Jews traversed (or transgressed) those boundaries presented particularities symbolic of enclosure. Walls, for instance, surrounded the Jewish quarter of mid-fifteenth-century Candia, the capital of the Venetian colony of Crete, which Venice ruled from 1211 to 1669. The Judaica was situated inside city walls in an area of the island that had little appeal to Venetians or Greeks because the neighborhood was vulnerable to outside invasion and adjacent to a tannery that emitted foul odors and waste (Figure 40). Although Venice's Maggior Consiglio had compelled Jews to reside within the perimeters of the

Judaica in 1334, walls did not delineate the contours of that quarter until the fifteenth century.[43] As Maria Georgopoulou notes, "In the early fourteenth century, no walls enclosed the Judaica of Candia, nor was there a guarded gate controlling the movement of Jews in and out of their quarter."[44] In the fifteenth century, Venetian officials increased the number of walls demarcating the urban spaces of the Jewish quarter of Candia when accusations circulated that Jews had sensory access to ecclesiastical ceremony. According to archival documents, Dominicans living in the monastery of St. Peter the Martyr alleged that Jews from their windows and balconies could see "all the way into the space of the church and over the altar ... and through the entire monastery ... and this could also bring about a risk for the souls of the monks of this monastery."[45] To alleviate this concern, Venetian authorities obliged the Jews of Candia to erect, at their expense, "a wall from stone and limestone ... high enough that they are able to fill in the space and to block their view."[46] This wall visualized social marginality by dividing inside from outside, pious from perfidious. Whereas the coastal wall defined the outside perimeter of the Jewish quarter and circumscribed the older section of the city, this high wall was erected inside the Judaica to obstruct the Jews' view and leave them out of sight of their Dominican neighbors. It protected the privilege and privacy of the friars, but it never prohibited passage. Instead, the walls of the Judaica were porous, unaccompanied by guarded gates. They defined the separation of the Jews' surroundings, but they neither limited access nor restricted movement.

"It is thus obvious," writes David Jacoby, "that the principle of compulsory residential segregation physically implemented in the colonies preceded by about two centuries its application in Venice and may have served as a precedent for the creation of the Venetian Ghetto in 1516."[47] Jewish populations in the Venetian colonies were often differentiated residentially from Christian neighborhoods. As the Cretan city of Rethymno delineated the perimeters of their Jewish quarter with crosses, colonial Candia erected walls to mark the constricted space of Jewish segregated housing. However Candia delimited the spaces of Jewish occupancy, the walls of that enclosure remained perforated. In fact, Venetian officials in 1464 required the Candiote Jews to pay for the enlargement of the Judaica gate in order to facilitate the free passage of merchants, Jews and others, in and out of the Jewish quarter. The Judaica walls denoted division, but their social construction never intended isolation. The walls in Candia's Jewish quarter represented an urban district of compulsory residence that continually heralded relations outside its segregated space.

The Venice ghetto, on the contrary, defined egress and entry through a system of surveillance regulated by bolted gates and watchful guards. "Boundaries," explains Mark Wigley, "are only established by the intersection between a walled space and a system of surveillance which monitors all openings in the walls."[48] In Venice, an economy of vision developed around ghetto walls to insist on an isolation that was closely bound up with the night. The wall initiated a partitioning process "related to the isolation between two opposites."[49] It constructed the space where identity drew its limits. In his architectural treatise *De re aedificatoria* (c. 1452), Leon Battista Alberti stresses that a city plan must incorporate walls to frame the urban landscape: "The best means of dividing a city is to build a wall through it. This wall, I believe, should not run diametrically across the city but should form a kind of circle within a circle."[50] Venetians did not follow Alberti's urban plan of walled concentric circles. Venice was unusual in that it was an open city that did not rely on defensive fortifications.[51] The city wall, which Henri Pirenne describes as a "*privilege* which [no medieval city] lacked," for it symbolized civic status and independence, was not essential to Venice's urban image.[52] The waters of the lagoon gave Venice the impression of a self-contained world impregnable to outside invasion.[53] Venetians may not have used the wall defensively to demarcate city limits, but officials did employ walls internally to striate spaces of difference. Ghetto walls were a principal feature of that difference. The walls partitioned space as they structured the lives of those folded within their geometries. What mattered was not necessarily that Jews were out of sight after dark, but rather that their compulsory and segregated confinement was made conspicuous throughout the day and night.[54] Ghetto walls colonized the eye. The elevations of the ghetto visualized, physically and symbolically, the Jews' marginalized presence in the city. The demographic pressures of the community caused Jews to build upward, constructing multistory and multifamily structures anomalous within the Venetian skyline.[55] Ghetto walls stood implacably high to divide the constituent members of the city and to signify protection from the night. Such walls, soaring and surveilled, became the key tool in stimulating vision against night's miasma to defend the senses of space.

Boundary Crossing

The prominence of ghetto walls functioned to realign urban disparities. Walls articulate the oppositional relationship of the interior and exterior worlds to enforce a sense of distance and separation. Erected to construct detachment, walls nonetheless lay claim to their vulnerabilities and expose the conflicting elements of their social construction. As Henri Lefebvre writes, "Visible boundaries, such as walls or enclosures in general, give rise for their part to an appearance of separation between spaces where in fact what exists is an ambiguous continuity."[56] Walls provoke paradox in that the points of differentiation between the walls' two faces are also their common points. In their liminal position between inside and outside, they open themselves through direct contact to what lies beyond their perimeters. It is the approachability of the walls, the urge to scale them or to find their perforated points, that distinguishes their architectonic allure. It is the stories narrated at the threshold of enclosure "between a (legitimate) space and its (alien) exteriority" that determines the walls' contradictions.[57] Spaces that delimit can also appropriate. Walls that separate can also be crossed. The act of drawing boundaries challenges the very nature of the operation and underscores the spatial stories that polarize and cohere community in the same discursive moment.[58]

The walls of the Venice ghetto may well have defined the nocturnal limits of community, but they also told stories of their own permeability. Such walls created an architectural skin around Venice's Jewish corpus to enforce separation from Christians after nightfall. Frenchman Nicolas Audeber remarked on this spatial separation during his visit to Venice in the mid-seventeenth century: "[The Jews] all resid[e] together in a single place enclosed by high walls that, on the outside, are removed from contact with the houses of the city, and there they are crammed as if in a cloister to keep them separated from the Christians. . . . In Venice it is called 'the ghetto.'"[59] Audeber observes how the architectural wall operated to carve the ghetto out from its urban environs and to denote the Jews' symbolic segregation. Yet these ghetto walls also remained distinctly porous. As Marin Sanudo points out in his contemporary chronicle, the establishment of ghetto enclosures came with manifold exemptions. Sanudo specifies that on July 29, 1516, only four months after the Senate founded the Ghetto Nuovo, legislation passed that permitted Jewish doctors to leave the confines of the ghetto in order to visit patients and attend medical gatherings late into the night.[60] Levantine and Ponentine Jewish merchants upon settlement in Venice's ghetto complex also received special dispensation from the Cinque Savi alla Mercanzia to have nighttime access to the seas for their commercial needs. Because the Cinque Savi had concerns that resident émigré merchants, Jews and others, traded in stolen objects and smuggled goods at night to avoid customs, Venetian officials legislated a system of checks and balances to secure reliability in market practices.

In response to the nocturnal activity of German merchants, Venetian administrators known as the Visdomini decreed as early as 1366 that the warehouse windows of the Fondaco dei Tedeschi be barred with iron grilles in order to prevent grave harm to the community.[61] The closure of the fondaco served to protect the mercantile economy by architecturally preventing Germans from smuggling wares at night. Sennett remarks that "nighttime proved the busiest part of the day for the Germans," whose attempts to avoid paying legislated duties led them to illegal nocturnal acts when absconding to and from their windows with merchandise.[62] Windows and doors were a building's most vulnerable points. Their closure offered protection from wind and rain as well as from unwanted entry or exit.[63] While Venetians shut windows, doors, and *rive* (quays) tight to lock out nighttime intruders, they also locked in German merchants with iron bars to guard against the hazards that came with the night. In effect, Venetians reinforced the German warehouse in an attempt to provide its apertures with a sense of impermeability.

The Jewish ghetto was similar to the Fondaco dei Tedeschi in that communal authorities required its nocturnal confinement. With the ghetto's spatial restrictions came the constant surveillance of guards, who left detailed records of all licensed Jews leaving their residence after dusk for extra-ghetto business.[64] The conditions of this privilege stipulated that Jews had to verify their whereabouts the following morning to city magistrates, or undergo further investigation and punishment. When the government granted Jews privileges to stay outside the ghetto after curfew, stipulations specified that they were to avoid "forbidden" spaces, presumably referring to brothels and the houses of respectable Christian women. The ghetto gates, which swung open at night to allow in wealth from maritime trade and to allow out succor for the infirm, shut tight to guard against sexual contact between Jews and Christians. Illegal business practices may have instituted a bureaucratic paper trail with infractions punished by secular authorities; however, illicit sexual activity in a community defined by rigid endogamy ignited communal fears that destabilized categories secular and sacred. Giorgione and Titian may have painted images of allegorical nudes on the exterior walls of the Fondaco dei Tedeschi (now in ruinous condition and preserved in Venice's Ca' d'Oro), but decoration of the ghetto wall with pictorial flourishes, particularly nude imagery, was inapposite to the Jews' constricted space. City officials sought not to conceal ghetto walls with illusory imagery but to accentuate their opacity. Ghetto walls were debordering structures that represented physical separation with Christian and Jewish bodies occupying diverse living environments. Such separation served to protect not only

Venice's commercial interests but also the city's sexual honor. The guarded walls of the Venice ghetto connected architecture with ongoing prohibitions against interfaith touching to control private life and to reinforce discourses of exclusivity and alterity.

Touching, specifically interfaith touching, was a form of sexual transgression that collapsed religious boundaries and spatialized social controls. "To touch," writes Cary Howie, "is to experience a limit and open a connection. Whether this touch is figured visually, hermeneutically, or sexually, it traces the outlines of a community ... given over to bodies, texts, and buildings."[65] The materiality of the physical world (bodies, books, buildings) inherently arouses a desire to touch, yet these impulses in the early modern period also came with spatial consequences when sites of difference became proximate. To guard against the interfaith impulse to touch, authorities, both ecclesiastical and lay, advocated prophylactic campaigns of segregation to divide that difference. In 1423, Fra Bernardino da Siena sermonized in neighboring Padua a series of prohibitions, reiterating directly the terms of canon law, that proscribed immediate physical contact between Christians and Jews: "It is a mortal sin to eat or drink with Jews"; "It is a mortal sin to seek the help of a Jewish doctor"; "Christians are not allowed to bathe in the company of Jews"; "It is a mortal sin for Christians to socialize with Jews in their homes"; "It is a mortal sin for Christians to act as wet nurses or otherwise help to raise the children of the Jews or serve as midwives for them, even to wash the newborn child."[66] Bernardino's canonical codes of conduct provided moralizing instruction that insisted on the physical separation of Christians and Jews during the day's routines and rituals. Civil authorities in Venice did not always enforce these injunctions, which prompted Patriarch of Venice Cardinal Lorenzo Priuli in 1596 to advocate analogous interdictions. In a memorandum issued to the Venetian government prior to the renewal of the Jews' *condotta* (charter of sojourn), Priuli urged officials to prohibit Jews from eating with Christians; hiring Christians to work in Jewish homes as servants; soliciting Christian wet nurses to suckle Jewish children; and inviting Christians "of either sex" into the ghetto at night.[67] Such charters, which Priuli found too lenient and in practice readily abused, had from their inception specified that Jews could not hire Christians to work in their homes under penalty of a pecuniary fine and imprisonment for the Jews involved as well as temporary banishment for the implicated Christian.[68]

Regulations over conditions of contact correlated not only with canon law but also with the dictums of *ius commune*. For example, the *De Iudaeis et aliis infidelibus* of Marquardus de Susannis, first published in Venice in 1558, treats the dangers of illicit sexual behavior between Christians and Jews in a judicial handbook that combined common law and canon.[69] De Susannis understood the carnal communion of Jew and Christian legally as an insult against Christianity. Jews, in de Susannis's opinion as jurisconsult and ambassador for the Republic of Venice, maintained the status of "enemies of the cross and blasphemers of the name of Christ"; therefore, he deemed the sexual union of a Jew and a Christian as a violation of the holy, a pollution of the Christian corpus.[70] Kenneth Stow explains in his study of the *De Iudaeis*, "when Christian men have sexual relations with Jewish women, they commit the same crime that is committed by having relations with a nun, namely, that of insulting both baptism and Christianity."[71] To prevent such abuses of faith, de Susannis underscores the important function dress served in distinguishing Jews from Christians. Lawyers, as well as ecclesiastics, thought if Jews were visibly recognizable through, for example, the use of badges, veils, or head coverings, then Christians would avoid overly familiar contact with them.[72] That is, the sight of a Jew marked as "Jew" could help counteract the touch of miscegenation. De Susannis's judgment on dress was not innovative for the period, the precedent originating from Canon 68 of the Fourth Lateran Council (1215): "it sometimes happens that by mistake Christians mingle with Jewish or Saracen women, and Jews or Saracens with Christian women. Therefore, lest they, under the cover of error, find an excuse for the grave sin of such mingling, we decree that these people [Jews and Saracens] of either sex and in all Christian lands and at all times be readily distinguishable from others by the quality of their clothing."[73] As a symbolic marker of Jewish difference, distinguishing garb endured as a legal imperative in early modern common law in part because it helped resolve questions of intent. If there was no doubt that a Jew and a Christian were ignorant of their crime, de Susannis concludes that they could not be indicted for "sexual relations with an infidel."[74] Judges commuted their penalty to the crime of fornication. The sartorial marking of the Jew, however, made it difficult to plead ignorance. The distinctively dressed Jew found guilty of carnal misconduct with a Christian could instead be charged with "the intent of causing opprobrium to the faith," which carried a penalty of death and loss of property.[75]

The *De Iudaeis* addresses variations in penalty, the punishment contingent on the intent and identity of the accused. Sexual intercourse among members of the opposite faith was an ecclesiastical crime; nevertheless, canon law did not set a punishment for such a crime. Judges most often sentenced the defendants following the guidelines of local statutes, turning to common law if the community in which the crime occurred did not treat interfaith intercourse in their registries. In Venice, local statutes explicitly addressed the consequences of this sex crime nearly a century before Jews had settled permanently in the archipelago. Maintaining sexual boundaries became a legislative imperative in Venice, where the touching of the opposite-sexed outsider prompted swift justice. As early as July 19, 1424, the Venetian government unanimously passed legislation that forbade sexual relations between Jewish men and Christian women. The penalty for such an act depended on the Christian woman's station. Authorities fined Jews 500 lire and sentenced them to six months in jail when found with a prostitute from the Rialto. The pecuniary fine remained the same when a Jew had carnal relations with a Christian woman of higher social stature, additionally subjecting him to one year in prison.[76] In 1443, the Senate revisited this punishment. Benjamin Ravid explains, "To prevent relations with Christian women, the fine was increased from five hundred lire to five hundred ducats, an increase of 620%, and the jail sentence extended from one year to two."[77] The Avogadori di Comun also penalized Christian men severely (*ad maiorem penam*) when found having sexual relations with Jewish women. Venetian statutes could not tolerate the carnal communion of Jew and Christian, which polluted the civic body as well as the Corpus Christi.[78]

Sennett associates the alienations implicit in the Jew's touch with claims of contagion; Jews were thought to spread syphilis, leprosy, plague, and other diseases.[79] Despite chimerical allegations circulating Europe that indicted Jews as agents of pollution, the *noli me tangere* policy in Venice may have had less to do with anxieties over the touch of infectious contagion than with suspicions over miscegenation. Venetians, in fact, placed Jews in contiguous contact with Christians and contagion when permitting Jewish doctors to leave the confines of their ghettoized enclosure, day or night, to care for the health of the civic body.[80] The Cattaveri even temporarily released Jews from the ghetto during times of plague, thereby sanctioning a Jewish presence throughout the city's *sestieri* when infection was at its most concentrated.[81] Jacopo Abenini and his family, for instance, moved to a storeroom they rented from Lunardo de Pesaro outside ghetto walls in the parish of Santa Lucia for six months during the plague that struck the city in 1630; however, authorities warned the Abenini not to wander the city scandalizing (Christian) neighbors.[82] Concerns over bodily proximity involved not solely the risks of infection but also, more specifically, threats to the sexual health of the Christian corpus. The cohesion of the Corpus Christi in Venice required spatial reinforcement to protect the sexual boundaries of the city and the bodies, Jew and Christian, that set those boundaries in motion.

The barriers established around the ghetto consigned sex to a patrolled status contained behind brick walls. Those walls, nonetheless, did not abate fears of the Jews' sexuality in Venice or in early modern Europe more generally.[83] The Jews' sexualized bodies aroused constant scrutiny. For instance, Jewish women were thought to be sexually suspicious with enhanced libidos that triggered an uncontrollable attraction to Christian men. Long before Shakespeare's alluring Jewess Jessica threatened Christian bloodlines with her desirable beauty, medieval theologians rendered Synagoga, the collective image of the Jewish community, as a personified woman seducing Christianity.[84] The carnality of Synagoga displayed in medieval thought and art cogently suggests feminine wantonness. As Sara Lipton argues, Synagoga, the archetypal Jewess, is "perversely and destructively fertile, [and] has brought forth progeny only to doom them to Hell by her unwifely and immodest behavior."[85] The seductive qualities of Synagoga render her a shameful temptress difficult to repress in the sexual imagination of Christian society. Contemporary Jewish women provoked similar fascinations that enticed the minds of Christian men. Thomas Coryat, the Englishman who wrote of his Venetian travels in 1611, describes the Jewish women he encountered in the ghetto:

> In the roome wherin they [Jews] celebrate their divine service, no women sit, but have a loft or gallery proper to themselves only, where I saw many Jewish women, whereof some were as beautiful as ever I saw, and so gorgeous in their apparel, jewels, chaines of gold, and rings adorned with precious stones, that some of our English Countesses do scarce exceede them, having marvailous long traines like Princesses that are borne up by waiting women serving for the same purpose.[86]

Shakespeare perhaps never set eyes on the Venetian Jewess that served as his play's muse, but his contemporary Coryat lingers over her body with rich description to acknowledge the temptation of her physical appearance. Coryat scrutinizes this bedecked and bejeweled beauty from head to toe to reveal a Jewess socially inscribed with the carnality of Synagoga. English diarist John Evelyn likewise references the physicality of the Jewish women he observed at a wedding in the Venetian ghetto on March 24, 1646. His brief description centers on "The Bride clad in White, sitting in a lofty chaire, & coverd also with a white vaile," but his eye wanders to the "divers very beautifull *Portuguez*-Jewesses, with whom we had some conversation."[87] The exotic beauty of the Jewess seduced Christian senses.[88] It was the temptation of the irredeemable body beneath her beauty that Venetian authorities attempted to thwart through collective punishment and urban enclosure. The nighttime lockdown of Jews within ghetto walls acted to avert sexual forays *entre* Jew and Christian. Preventing carnal contact between Christians and Jews was hardly original to cinquecento Venice. What was new was the use of architecture to prohibit it. The fortified and surveyed ghetto walls prevented midnight trysts turned transgressions, infidelities turned blasphemies. Authorities instituted architectural enclosure that obstructed access to interfaith attraction. Ghettoization sought to control carnal lust under the cover of darkness, thereby precluding the possibility of miscegenation. Domestic detachment impeded the temptation to touch.

City officials thus sought to bind the sexed corporeality inhabiting Venice through the strategic segregation of space.[89] The ghetto provided the order and organization to polarize the sundry bodies of Venice by limiting the mobility of the Jews' bodies on the nocturnal streets. If night provided the fertile ground for sexual encounter, the ghetto controlled the bodily world of Venice against intimate contact. The city that restricted the nighttime movement of Jews through high walls and guarded gates also gave urban expression to the Jews' corporeal presence. The ordering of social space in Venice situated Jews within an architecture of embodiment that in fact reinscribed their bodies (physically, socially, discursively) in the larger urban form. The ghetto contained the Jews' contested bodies as those bodies then projected themselves onto the sociocultural cityscape of Venice. A reciprocal relationship materialized between the body and the city. Elizabeth Grosz maintains, "The city is made and made over into the simulacrum of the body, and the body, in its turn, is transformed, 'citified,' urbanized as a distinctively metropolitan body."[90] Bodies and cities are inextricably linked to reveal the social construction inscribed in their material makeup. Architectural treatises from antiquity onward acknowledge the reciprocity of the body with building. Vitruvius, for example, anthropomorphizes architecture in Book Three of *De architectura* to reveal the proportions of the human body beneath the harmony of the temple structure, while modern architectural theory, such as that espoused by Finnish architect Juhani Pallasmaa, embed the body in its environment: "I experience myself in the city, and the city exists through my embodied experience. The city and my body supplement and define each other. I dwell in the city and the city dwells in me."[91] The city engenders an indivisible relation to the body, even when that body is marginal. Venice, for example, cultivated, as it controlled, the corporeality of the Jew. The ghetto's walled boundaries that subordinated the Jews' bodies could not contain those bodies continually or completely. Walls can never fully sequester bodily mobility. Instead, they beckon us to move through their material space. Boundaries, though established as observed limits, are actualized only through the act of passage, and Jews articulated the transience of their bounded strictures when accessing Venice's urban life after dark.[92]

Entry to the evening outside ghetto walls often ended with carnal consequences. The Cattaveri permitted Jews only a brief encounter with nocturnal Venice, requiring them to return to the ghetto at a specific hour of the night. At times Jews transgressed the stipulations of their license. In September 1609, Rachel Hebrea Cantarina, accompanied by her brother Marco and father Jacob, was granted permission to leave the ghetto after curfew to sing in the homes of respectable members of society (*in casa di gentilhuomeni, cittadini, et altre persone honorate*). Instead of entertaining Venetian patricians and citizens with song, Rachel and her family were found eating, drinking, and behaving dishonestly (*mangiando, bevendo et praticando dimesticamente*) with Christian commoners.[93] The magistrates viewed the incident as an affront to God and a bad example to all, and amended Rachel's nighttime privilege to include a proviso that all three members of the Cattaveri must unanimously approve any future request for leave submitted by the female performer. Modification to this proviso transpired over time; nevertheless, the details of that license never impressed Rachel, who in June 1613 was found singing around Venice *in gondola* at night without proper permission.[94] The nocturnal anxiety Rachel provoked motivated civic and moral censure when she gained unregulated contact to darkened Venice. It was the allure of her sonorous voice in the context of a metropolitan center that delighted in leisure that gained her access to the night and made magistrates tolerant of her transgressions. She personified the seductive powers of Synagoga with a recognizable carnality that threatened proscriptions to touch. Cavorting with Christians after dark raised concerns of illicit sexuality, which Rachel initially attempted to conceal behind the thin veneer of sanctioned domestic socializing.

Women in the urban spaces of early modern Europe often experienced a nightlife set within the domestic interior. In seventeenth-century London, aristocratic men enjoyed nighttime leisure in the city's public houses and cafés, whereas their wives strengthened social networks with visits to the homes of other gentlewomen. In this nocturnal scenario, class and gender played a principal role in designating entrance to the city at night. From Paris to London, Vienna to Leipzig, non-noble women out after dusk, for work or for play, raised suspicions of unrestrained female sexuality and awakened a nighttime temptation difficult to constrain in men.[95] "Whoever holds the piazza always is master of the city," writes the Florentine chronicler Giovanni

Cavalcanti in his early fifteenth-century *Istorie fiorentine*.[96] The master of the city was no neutered subject. Cavalcanti's remarks underscore the explicit gendering of early modern urban geographies. Whereas men occupied the piazza and its public architecture, women were ensconced within the folds of the private interior. To be sure, exemptions existed that allowed women the diurnal crossing of certain topographies. The Italian humanist Francesco Sansovino records in his 1581 guide to Venice that patrician brides traveled *in gondola* when visiting family members sequestered in convents throughout the city.[97] In Corneto, outside Rome, women entered the town hall to testify before the tribunal, notwithstanding communal statutes that firmly barred their access to the public space of the communal palace.[98] In Florence, lower-class women worked within and outside their homes in textile markets, food production, and local inns, while in Venice women of the laboring *popolani* class sewed canvas sails for the Arsenale, the compound of shipyards and armories in the Castello district that manufactured the city's naval power.[99] The gendered geographies of women at times permitted access beyond the domestic interior, despite women's restricted autonomy and limited freedom of movement.[100] Nevertheless, circumambulation at night remained a privileged pursuit. A woman could not stray from her home at night for fear that the ensuing intrigue would tarnish the reputations of the honorable men joined to her by blood or marriage. Inhabited by a patriarchal world, night lacked the infrastructure to support women's public presence without incrimination. Local ritual permitted patrician women their occasional escorted excursion, either fête or feast, but unaccompanied women provoked associations with nightwalking prostitutes. Maintaining morality within the city was dialectically linked with keeping the peace, both processes requiring a surveilled space to safeguard women's vulnerability, secure civil order, and mediate boundaries of social difference. While the night offered opportunity for barriers between inside and outside, public and private, fascination and fear, to be traversed, decorum prohibited such barriers from being transgressed.

Certainly Venice's Jewish minstrel Rachel did not possess the social standing to legitimate her moonlit forays. As a working-class Jewess, with the traditional trappings of Synagoga's feminine profligacy, Rachel unequivocally destabilized the boundaries city officials so carefully spelled out in statutory definition and in architectural applications to the urban form. Despite legislative exclusions prohibiting Jews physical contact with the world outside the ghetto, in the darkness Rachel rediscovered her siren powers of voice and her delicacy of touch when encroaching perilously on

Venice's sexualized borders. As exemplified in this case, the law could not prohibit the very mingling it sought to restrict.

The porousness of ghetto walls that provided Rachel a path to Venice's orderly night disquieted city officials. Pier Cesare Ioly Zorattini documents a case in which a Jew *secretamente* returned to his family in the ghetto at two in the morning after escaping the lazzaretto, the mandatory quarantine for Venice's plague-stricken on a small lagoonal island.[101] Here the ailing Jew traverses the Venetian night to journey from one form of confinement to another. This story provides the context and coordinates that animate the permeability of Venice's compulsory enclosures. Once again the walls of the ghetto are breached, this time to allow a Jew to come back through its shadowy perimeters. In his 1596 memorandum to city officials, Cardinal Lorenzo Priuli addressed the ghetto's structural frailties when accusing Jews of exiting ghetto enclosures by night through unfortified windows and unguarded quays. Specifically, he alleged that such architectural apertures allowed Jews nocturnal access to Venice during which time they would impregnate defenseless Christian women and later steal the newborn children to raise them (as Jews) in the ghetto.[102] Trial records also reveal the permeability of the ghetto night, as Jewish men left the confines of *clausura* to engage in *commercio carnale*. In 1715, authorities accused (but later acquitted) Zacaria da Pesaro Ebreo of engaging in sexual relations with a Christian woman named Matia Cantona in a dark courtyard near the Ponte dal Aseo, while in 1717 Abram Treves Ebreo dal Zante and Vita Almeda Ebreo were found living day and night outside the ghetto in the home of a Christian woman (*ad abitare di giorno, e di notte fuori del Ghetto, in casa d'una donna Cristiana*), who allegedly received payment for her sexual services.[103] The ghetto, which sought to control the Jews' sexed corporeality through a system of surveillance that protected the innocence of Christians by night, also heightened anxieties about the Jews' sexualized mobility. As Priuli's claims suggest, the ghetto's tall tenements never mitigated the sexual politics embodying the Jews. Instead, it catalyzed fantasies about their furtive touch. Beatriz Colomina observes, "The politics of space are always sexual, even if space is central to the mechanisms of the erasure of sexuality."[104] In Venice, the ghetto evolved as an institution of exclusion that regulated Jewish sexuality, but such an exclusion of sexuality itself became a sexual act in that it aroused in the Christian imagination an explicit world of Jewish carnality.

* * *

Machiavelli writes in *The Prince*, "In general, men judge more by sight than by touch. Everyone sees what is happening, but not everyone feels the consequences. Everyone sees what you seem to be; few have direct experience of who you really are."[105] For Machiavelli, sight and touch occupy a sensory hierarchy that did not necessarily align with the ocularcentric traditions of Greek philosophy.[106] Hellenic models provided sight higher sensorial status due in large part to the corporeal associations of tactility. Touch relies not on localized receptors for perception but on the sensitivities of the skin enwrapping the entire body. Tactile stimulation accentuates the material impulses of the flesh, heightening the bodily desire for physical contact with the outside world. In Machiavellian terms, the power to touch shaped human subjectivity. Sight might provide the discerning eye a view to the intention and integrity of a man, but, as he observes, it is only through the physically proximate connection to touch that one might truly know a man. Seeing and touching, perhaps inherently antithetical, become entwined experiences of the bodily sensorium. Perception emerges from the desire to see and to feel. As Walter Benjamin reflects on the sensorial implications of architecture, he likewise concludes that building exploits the visual and the tactile to insist on a reception based on distraction. Architectural appropriation comes to light only out of focus with an emphasis on the hand-eye mechanisms of haptics. With its appeals to the tactile imagination, architecture enlivens our kinesthetic impulses and our need to experience the proximities and intimacies of space. Certainly navigating the Venetian nightscape, armed with candles and oil lanterns, required an acute sense of sight. Investments in looking, however, became shortsighted when vision was occluded at day's close and impetuousness pervaded the early modern night sky. There in the darkness the contours of buildings blurred and rested bodies turned restless. And as those bodies moved through space they provoked associations both sensual and contentious, as fantasies of interfaith touching broke down nocturnal boundaries and carnal desires filled the night air.

CONCLUSION

"We went after dinner one Saturday to see the Jews Synagogue. Among other things I heard here a Rabbin make a Homily to his flock. He looked like a French Minister, or Puritanical Lecturer, in a short cloak and hat. The snafling through the nose made all the edification that I saw in it: It was in Italian, but the coldest discourse that I ever heard in any language," writes Richard Lassels in *The Voyage of Italy* (1670).[1] If Grand Tour travel to the continent completed the education of the English gentleman, Lassels designates himself in his book as the model teacher.[2] Formerly a Catholic priest educated at the English College in Douai, Lassels includes the Jewish ghetto within his treatise-cum-guidebook as a site that offers the inquisitive tourist potential enlightenment. Visuality conjoins with aurality to present the ghetto as a pedagogic space for social critique. For Lassels, "travelling makes us acquainted with a world of our kindred we never saw before. For, seeing we are all, come from one man at first, and consequently all a kin to one another; its but a reasonable thing, that a man should once at least in his life time, make a journey into forrein Cou[n]tries, to see his Relations, and visit this kindred."[3] Through travel, Grand Tourists acquired knowledge of the past and present, of economics and politics, of art and architecture, which they believed would transform them into cultural connoisseurs.

Lassels's *Voyage* was not novel in directing visitors to Venice's Jewish quarter. In fact, Grand Tour travelers for decades had standardized their itineraries of Venice to include visits to the ghetto.[4] Their travelogues offer firsthand impressions of the city's daily activities and annual ceremonies, such as early morning transactions of fruits and flowers along the Rialto, tackle making at the Arsenale, and Corpus Christi processions through the Piazza San Marco.[5] Yet sightings of ghetto tenements were also a prominent feature of the *giro d'Italia* after 1630. John Evelyn, John Raymond, Edmund

Warcupp, and Philip Skippon, among others, provide insights into the urban life of Jewish Venice with their reported conversations with rabbis and architectural accounts of synagogues.[6] Venice's ghetto thus became a conventional site of Grand Tour sightseeing through the eighteenth century.

Nineteenth-century writers rarely allude to the ghetto, however.[7] Henry James's *Italian Hours* – informed by John Ruskin's *The Stones of Venice* – makes reference to Jews working as peddlers along the Grand Canal but does not take note of their ghetto tenancy.[8] It seems the Jews' enclosure no longer inspired penned response toward the end of the eighteenth century, particularly with the end of ghettoization in 1797. With the fall of the Venetian Republic to Napoleon Bonaparte's army in that year came the demolition of Venice's ghetto gates. French soldiers took the gates off their hinges and burned them in the public square amid celebratory music and dance.[9] Under the French, Jews enjoyed Venetian citizenship and new civil rights. Months later, the French ceded the city to the Austrians with the signing of the Treaty of Campo Formio, and the Austrians summarily restricted the Jews' civil liberties, including prohibiting their participation in municipal government.[10] Nevertheless, Venice's ghetto gates were never again reinstalled. Under Austrian occupation, Jews could purchase real estate in any part of the city.[11] Enclosure of Jews no longer had a place in Venice. In this post-enclosure context, the architectural attraction of the Jewish quarter waned among travelers. No longer did the ghetto occupy a space in the usual patterns of continental pilgrimage. As a result, observations of the ghetto rarely accompany records of Venetian sightseeing in the nineteenth century.

One notable exception was Ohio author William Dean Howells, who began a four-year sojourn in Venice in December 1861 as American consul. Melancholy, a basic tenet of his literary realism, mixes with fascination in his descriptions of the city's decayed magnificence.[12] Among the sites recorded in his *Venetian Life*, published in 1866, is the Jewish ghetto.[13] For Howells, the mid-nineteenth-century Venetian ghetto is a "noisome and dirty" place, but it remains worthy of exploration precisely because it no longer houses "an oppressed people."[14] The architecture of the ghetto may have changed very little since its erection in the Renaissance, but the complex's social function had changed by the nineteenth century. Indeed, Howells concludes that social relations between Christians and Jews in Venice had improved through the centuries to alleviate anti-Jewish anxieties. The stereotyped Shylock is now dead.[15]

In *Venetian Life*, Howells describes the residential mobility of the Jews that resulted from the removal of the gates: "[The Jews] dwelt peacefully in their Ghetto till the lofty gates of their prison caught the sunlight of modern civilization, and crumbled beneath it. Then many of the Jews came out and fixed their habitations in different parts of the city."[16] He explains how affluent Jews moved from the overcrowded quarters of the ghetto to occupy opulent spaces of Venetian living, including "the famous and beautiful Ca' Doro" and "the *appartamento signorile* in the palace of Cardinal Bembo."[17] Yet Venice's Jews did not empty the ghetto complex. Impecunious Jews, writes Howells, "clung to the spot where their temples still remain, and which was hallowed by long suffering. . . . So, although you find Jews everywhere in Venice, you never find a Christian in the Ghetto, which is held to this day by a large Hebrew population."[18]

Howells's ghetto gazing long postdates the dismantling of the ghetto gates. He looks at and beyond the time of the Jews' enclosure to leave his readers looking forward. *Venetian Life* chronicles the spatial complexity of the ghetto through the bodily movement of Venice's Jews over time. Napoleon may have opened Venice's ghetto spaces, but the Venetian urban form preserved the area of the former enclosure as a Jewish space. Temporalities converge in this demographic account to mark the ghetto with the collective memory of Venice's Jews.[19] The ghetto thus becomes a familiar place of corporeal experience of the Jews' lived bodies that literally situates memory on site. "I do not understand," Howells remarks, "why any class of Jews should still remain in the Ghetto, but it is certain, as I said, that they do remain there in great numbers. It may be that the impurity of the place and the atmosphere is conducive to purity of race."[20] According to Howells, the dirt and fetid odors of the ghetto cleanse the Jews to purify them collectively and petrify them in place. Individual Jews may be *unplaced* from the ghetto when moving beyond its boundaries; however, the space itself remains a home for Venice's Jews. For Howells, the memory of the Jews of Venice takes place in the place of the ghetto. Time and space saturate the ghetto with the delimiting perimeters of memory, such that there can be no memory of the ghetto without the Jew.

To this day Venice's ghetto remains a locus of Jewish identity, despite the scattering of Jews throughout the city, country, and beyond. Memory of the ghetto's past is vicarious; it derives not from those living within its tall brick buildings but from the mind's eye that houses ghetto histories.[21] Contiguous associations of place fix a Jewish presence onto Venice's ghetto spaces. Venetians and visitors alike reconstitute the topography of memory linking the extant site to its former Jewish inhabitants through acts of historical recollection. The irrepressible will to remember prevents the site from breeding amnesia. March 29, 2016 marked the quincentennial of the Jewish ghetto of Venice, and the city commemorated the ghetto's 500th anniversary with events that highlighted the Jewish character of that historical Jewish quarter. The late eighteenth century perhaps saw the end of ghetto enclosures, but this area of Venice – with its Jewish Museum, Murano glass menorahs, and kosher restaurants – still maintains its Jewishness. From Venice we learn that the ghetto neither naturalized nor neutralized Jewish difference. On the contrary, it established the indelibility of a Jewish identity that endures today.

NOTES

Introduction

1. Rainer Maria Rilke, "A Scene from the Venice Ghetto," in *Stories of God*, trans. Michael H. Kohn (Boston: Shambhala, 2003), 57; and Rainer Maria Rilke, "Eine Szene aus dem Ghetto von Venedig," *Geschichten vom lieben Gott* (Wiesbaden: Insel, 1955), 94.
2. Rilke, "A Scene from the Venice Ghetto," 58–60; and Rilke, "Eine Szene aus dem Ghetto von Venedig," 95–97.
3. Since its erection, the ghetto complex in Venice has undergone continuous restoration programs. The interior spaces no longer resemble those of the sixteenth century, but the buildings' exterior with its irregular fenestration patterns and soaring heights is a distinguishing formal element dating to the early modern period.
4. On the relationship between Jews, Christians, and civic vision in medieval Europe, see Sara Lipton, *Dark Mirror: The Medieval Origins of Anti-Jewish Iconography* (New York: Metropolitan Books, 2014).
5. On the subjectivity of the gaze, see Jacques Lacan, "Of the Gaze as *Objet petit a*," in *The Four Fundamental Concepts of Psycho-Analysis*, ed. Jacques-Alain Miller, trans. Alan Sheridan (New York: W. W. Norton, 1978), 67–119. The Lacanian gaze is not the look we direct onto the world around us. Instead, it acknowledges the presence of an exterior eye looking back at us. Slavoj Žižek's study of pornography and perversion in popular culture informed this analysis in that he problematizes the antinomic relation of gaze and eye articulated by Lacan: "This antinomy of gaze and view is lost in pornography – why? . . . Contrary to the commonplace according to which, in pornography, the other (the person shown on the screen) is degraded to an object of our voyeuristic pleasure, we must stress that it is the spectator himself who effectively occupies the position of the object. The real subjects are the actors on the screen trying to rouse us sexually, while we, the spectators, are reduced to a paralyzed object-gaze." Slavoj Žižek, *Looking Awry: An Introduction to Jacques Lacan through Popular Culture* (Cambridge, MA: MIT Press, 1991), 110.
6. On theories of spatial and social practice informing this book, see Michel Foucault, *Discipline and Punish: The Birth of the Prison*, trans. Alan Sheridan (New York: Vintage Books, 1979); Michel de Certeau, *The Practice of Everyday Life*, trans. Steven Rendall (Berkeley: University of California Press, 1984); and Henri Lefebvre, *The Production of Space*, trans. Donald Nicholson-Smith (Oxford: Blackwell, 1991). See also how the spaces of the modern city and their relationship to social control frame studies of preindustrial urbanism in Marvin Trachtenberg, *Dominion of the Eye: Urbanism, Art,*

and Power in Early Modern Florence (Cambridge: Cambridge University Press, 1997); and Renzo Dubbini, *Geography of the Gaze: Urban and Rural Vision in Early Modern Europe*, trans. Lydia G. Cochrane (Chicago: University of Chicago Press, 2002); as well as "Maps of Authority: Conflict in the Medieval & Early Modern Urban Landscape," ed. Annabel Wharton, special issue, *Journal of Medieval and Early Modern Studies* 26, no. 3 (Fall 1996).

7. On the history of the Venetian ghetto, see Ennio Concina, Ugo Camerino, and Donatella Calabi, *La città degli ebrei: Il ghetto di Venezia, architettura e urbanistica* (Venice: Albrizzi, 1991). See also David Cassuto, "The Scuola Grande Tedesca in the Venice Ghetto," *Journal of Jewish Art* 3–4 (1977): 40–57; Umberto Fortis, *The Ghetto on the Lagoon: A Guide to the History and Art of the Venetian Ghetto (1516–1797)*, trans. Roberto Matteoda (Venice: Storti, 1988); Vivian B. Mann, ed., *Gardens and Ghettos: The Art of Jewish Life in Italy* (Berkeley: University of California Press, 1989); Roberta Curiel and Bernard Dov Cooperman, *The Venetian Ghetto* (New York: Rizzoli, 1990); Richard Sennett, *Flesh and Stone: The Body and the City in Western Civilization* (New York: W. W. Norton, 1994), 212–51; Riccardo Calimani, *The Ghetto of Venice*, trans. Katherine Silberblatt Wolfthal (Milan: Arnoldo Mondadori, 1995); Richard Goy, *Venice: The City and Its Architecture* (London: Phaidon, 1997), esp. 86–93; Francesca Brandes, ed., *Venice and Environs: Jewish Itineraries, Places, History, and Art* (Venice: Marsilio, 1997); Donatella Calabi, "The 'City of the Jews,'" in *The Jews of Early Modern Venice*, ed. Robert C. Davis and Benjamin Ravid (Baltimore: Johns Hopkins University Press, 2001), 31–49; and Annie Sacerdoti, *The Guide to Jewish Italy*, trans. David Kerr (New York: Rizzoli, 2004).

8. The Senate decree of 1516 specifies that the rent on ghetto property would increase with the arrival of the Jews: "the Jews must pay a rent which will be higher by one third than that received at present by the landlords of the aforesaid houses." Archivio di Stato di Venezia (hereafter ASVe), Senato, Terra, registro 19, fols. 78r-79r, March 29, 1516. See David Chambers and Brian Pullan, eds., *Venice: A Documentary History, 1450–1630* (Toronto: University of Toronto Press, 2001), 338. Despite the fact that Jews by law could not own real estate, the ghettoized Jews of Venice were able to secure a *jus gazaka*, a right of possession that was akin to a permanent lease. The *jus gazaka* was a socially and ecclesiastically sanctioned contract that could be sold as well as passed by inheritance to younger generations of Jews. See, for example, Cecil Roth, *History of the Jews in Venice* (New York: Schocken, 1958), 109. The nineteenth-century historian Ferdinand Gregorovius describes the *jus gazaka* in the Roman ghetto: "Imprisoned in the ghetto, Jews became subject to outside owners. For the houses of the quarter belonged to Romans. . . . When they removed they remained landlords, and the Jews tenants. But because they were to be limited to the quarter forever they had to establish a permanent rental arrangement. . . . So a law was instituted which ordained that the Romans should retain the title to the dwellings rented to Jews, but that the leasehold of the Jews should be hereditary. The owner might never force the Jewish tenant to vacate, as long as he paid his rental properly, and the rental might never be raised; furthermore the Jew might alter or enlarge his house at will. This law was . . . called *jus gazaga*." Ferdinand Gregorovius, *The Ghetto and the Jews of Rome*, trans. Moses Hadas (New York: Schocken, 1966), 70–71. Although ghetto rental property could be passed down to future generations, alterations to ghetto architecture required state permissions.

On the complexities of property and possession related to ghetto real estate in Venice, see Ennio Concina, "Owners, Houses, Functions: New Research on the Origins of the Venetian Ghetto," *Mediterranean Historical Review* 6, no. 2 (December 1991): 180–89; and Benjamin Ravid, "The Minotto Family and an Unapproved Construction Project in the Ghetto Vecchio of Venice, 1608–1609," in *Daniel Carpi Jubilee Volume*, ed. Minna Rozen, Anita Shapira, and Dina Porat (Tel Aviv: Tel Aviv University, 1996), 91–108.

9. ASVe, Senato, Terra, registro 19, fols. 78r-79r, March 29, 1516. See Chambers and Pullan, eds., *Venice: A Documentary History*, 338.
10. See Maristella Botticini, "A Tale of 'Benevolent' Governments: Private Credit Markets, Public Finance, and the Role of Jewish Lenders in Medieval and Renaissance Italy," *Journal of Economic History* 60, no. 1 (March 2000): 164–89.
11. William Thomas, *The History of Italy (1549)*, ed. George B. Parks (Ithaca, NY: Cornell University Press, 1963), 69.
12. During an era of ceaseless warring and bad harvests, Renaissance rulers sought Jewish capital and expertise in the credit market. For this reason, Italian authorities permitted Jewish subjects to lend money to the poor at a rate of interest at times greater than that offered by Christian lenders but would reclaim that money in the form of exorbitant taxes. In this way, the Jews were made to serve as tax collectors for these states; the money they amassed would be transferred to the state, while the Jews would suffer the Christian community's condemnation for their excessive charges. See Botticini, "A Tale of 'Benevolent' Governments," 164–89.
13. Jacques Le Goff, *Your Money or Your Life: Economy and Religion in the Middle Ages* (New York: Zone Books, 1988), 93. Regarding usury, see Benjamin Nelson, *The Idea of Usury: From Tribal Brotherhood to Universal Otherhood* (Princeton, NJ: Princeton University Press, 1949); John Noonan, *The Scholastic Analysis of Usury* (Cambridge, MA: Harvard University Press, 1957); Robert Bonfil, *Jewish Life in Renaissance Italy*, trans. Anthony Oldcorn (Berkeley: University of California Press, 1994), 79–98; R. Po-chia Hsia, "The Usurious Jew: Economic Structure and Religious Representations in an Anti-Semitic Discourse," in *In and Out of the Ghetto: Jewish-Gentile Relations in Late Medieval and Early Modern Germany*, ed. R. Po-chia Hsia and Hartmut Lehmann (Cambridge: Cambridge University Press, 1995), 161–76; and Joel Kaye, *Economy and Nature in the Fourteenth Century: Money, Market Exchange, and the Emergence of Scientific Thought* (Cambridge: Cambridge University Press, 1998), especially 79–115.
14. On April 6, 1515, Marin Sanudo wrote, "Non voglio restar di scriver una prava consuetudine venuta per il continuo comercio si ha con questi zudei, quali stanno in questa terra gran numero, San Cassan, Santo Agustin, San Polo, Santa Maria *Mater Domini*, che prima de la Domenica di l'Olivo non si vedevano più fin passà Pasqua. Hora fino eri sono andati atorno, et è malissimo facto, e niun li dice nulla, perchè mediante le guerre, hanno bisogno di loro; e cussì fanno quello voleno." Marino Sanuto, *I diarii di Marino Sanuto: Dall'autografo Marciano ital. cl. VII codd. CDXIX-CDLXXVII*, ed. Federico Stefani, Nicolò Barozzi, and Guglielmo Berchet, vol. 20 (Venice: Fratelli Visentini, 1887), 98. See also Marin Sanudo, *Venice, Città Excelentissima: Selections from the Renaissance Diaries of Marin Sanudo*, ed. Patricia H. Labalme and Laura Sanguineti White, trans. Linda L. Carroll (Baltimore: Johns

Hopkins University Press, 2008), 337–38. I use the Venetian spelling of Sanudo's name; however, his name was Tuscanized as Marino Sanuto.

15. ASVe, Senato, Terra, registro 19, fols. 78r–79r, March 29, 1516. See Chambers and Pullan, eds., *Venice: A Documentary History*, 338.

16. The Venetian government ultimately eliminated the boat patrol; nevertheless, Christian surveillance remained a permanent feature of ghetto life. Authorities posted four Christian guards in the ghetto complex twenty-four hours a day and required them to live within its walls without their families. See Benjamin Ravid, "The Venetian Government and the Jews," in *The Jews of Early Modern Venice*, ed. Robert C. Davis and Benjamin Ravid (Baltimore: Johns Hopkins University Press, 2001), 10.

17. On the Jewish ghettos in early modern Italy, see Kenneth Stow, "Hatred of the Jews or Love of the Church: Papal Policy Toward the Jews in the Middle Ages," in *Antisemitism Through the Ages*, ed. Shmuel Almog, trans. Nathan H. Reisner (Oxford: Pergamon Press, 1988); Kenneth Stow, "The Consciousness of Closure: Roman Jewry and Its *Ghet*," in *Essential Papers on Jewish Culture in Renaissance and Baroque Italy*, ed. David B. Ruderman (New York: New York University Press, 1992); Kenneth Stow, "Sanctity and the Construction of Space: The Roman Ghetto as Sacred Space," in *Jewish Assimilation, Acculturation, and Accommodation: Past Traditions, Current Issues, and Future Prospects*, ed. Menachem Mor (Lanham, MD: University Press of America, 1992); Kenneth Stow, "Ethnic Rivalry or Melting Pot: The *Edot* in the Roman Ghetto," *Judaism* 41, no. 3 (Summer 1992): 286–96; Kenneth Stow, "A Tale of Uncertainties: Converts in the Roman Ghetto," in *Shlomo Simonsohn Jubilee Volume: Studies on the History of the Jews in the Middle Ages and Renaissance Period*, ed. Daniel Carpi et al. (Tel Aviv: Tel Aviv University, 1993); Kenneth Stow, "Marriages Are Made in Heaven: Marriage and the Individual in the Roman Jewish Ghetto," *Renaissance Quarterly* 48, no. 3 (Autumn 1995): 445–91; Kenneth R. Stow, *Theater of Acculturation: The Roman Ghetto in the Sixteenth Century* (Seattle: University of Washington Press, 2001); Howard Tzvi Adelman, "Jewish Women and Family Life, Inside and Outside the Ghetto," in *The Jews of Early Modern Venice*, ed. Robert C. Davis and Benjamin Ravid (Baltimore: Johns Hopkins University Press, 2001), 143–65; Diane Wolfthal, *Picturing Yiddish: Gender, Identity, and Memory in the Illustrated Yiddish Books of Renaissance Italy* (Leiden: Brill, 2004); and Stefanie B. Siegmund, *The Medici State and the Ghetto of Florence: The Construction of an Early Modern Jewish Community* (Stanford, CA: Stanford University Press, 2006). See also Maria Georgopoulou, "Mapping Religious and Ethnic Identities in the Venetian Colonial Empire," *Journal of Medieval and Early Modern Studies* 26, no. 3 (Fall 1996): 467–96.

18. Goy, *Venice: The City and Its Architecture*, 46. For a history of architecture in Renaissance Venice, see such studies as John McAndrew, *Venetian Architecture of the Early Renaissance* (Cambridge, MA: MIT Press, 1980); Ralph Lieberman, *Renaissance Architecture in Venice, 1450–1540* (New York: Abbeville, 1982); Richard J. Goy, *Venetian Vernacular Architecture: Traditional Housing in the Venetian Lagoon* (Cambridge: Cambridge University Press, 1989); Ennio Concina, *Storia dell'architettura di Venezia: Dal VII al XX secolo* (Milan: Electa, 1995); trans. Judith Landry as *A History of Venetian Architecture* (Cambridge: Cambridge University Press, 1998); Deborah Howard, *Venice & the East: The Impact of the Islamic World on Venetian Architecture, 1100–1500* (New Haven, CT: Yale University Press, 2000); and

Deborah Howard, *The Architectural History of Venice* (New Haven, CT: Yale University Press, 2002).

19. Calimani, *The Ghetto of Venice*, 133. The most common types of wood used for the construction of Venetian buildings were larch, fir, and oak. At times, elm was also used. See Goy, *Venice: The City and Its Architecture*, 48.
20. Curiel and Cooperman, *The Venetian Ghetto*, 36.
21. Rilke, "A Scene from the Venice Ghetto," 58; and Rilke, "Eine Szene aus dem Ghetto von Venedig," 95.
22. ASVe, Senato, Mar, registro 26, cc. 45v–46r, June 2, 1541. See also Benjamin Ravid, "The Religious, Economic, and Social Background and Context of the Establishment of the Ghetti of Venice," in *Gli ebrei e Venezia: Secoli XIV-XVIII*, ed. Gaetano Cozzi (Milan: Edizioni Comunità, 1987), 250–251; Benjamin Arbel, *Trading Nations: Jews and Venetians in the Early Modern Eastern Mediterranean* (Leiden: Brill, 1995), 197–200; and Chambers and Pullan, eds., *Venice: A Documentary History*, 344. For a genealogy of the term Levantini, see E. Natalie Rothman, *Brokering Empire: Trans-Imperial Subjects between Venice and Istanbul* (Ithaca, NY: Cornell University Press, 2012), 211–47.
23. See James S. Ackerman and Myra Nan Rosenfeld, "Social Stratification in Renaissance Urban Planning," in *Urban Life in the Renaissance*, ed. Susan Zimmerman and Ronald F. E. Weissman (Newark: University of Delaware Press, 1989), 21–49.
24. ASVe, Inquisitorato alle Arti, busta 102, fascicolo "Casi tra li Cattaveri con li Cinque Savii sopra le case delli Hebrei," August 3, 1560.
25. With the fall of the Venetian Republic to Napoleon Bonaparte's army came the demolition of Venice's ghetto gates in 1797. The French were determined to "remove that mark of separation between the Jewish Citizens and the other Citizens, where no such mark should exist." With the Treaty of Campo Formio (signed October 18, 1797), Austria annexed Venice and proceeded to reinstate restrictions on the city's Jews. Robert C. Davis, "Introduction," in *The Jews of Early Modern Venice*, ed. Robert C. Davis and Benjamin Ravid (Baltimore: Johns Hopkins University Press, 2001), vii–viii.
26. In 1364, the humanist Francesco Petrarca celebrated Venice as the ideal city: "The august city of Venice rejoices, the one home today of liberty, peace and justice, the one refuge of honorable men, the one port to which can repair the storm-tossed, tyrant-hounded craft of men who seek the good life. Venice – rich in gold but richer in fame, mighty in her resources but mightier in virtue, solidly built on marble but standing more solid on a foundation of civil concord, ringed with salt waters but more secure with the salt of good counsel!" Francesco Petrarca, *Letters from Petrarch*, trans. Morris Bishop (Bloomington: Indiana University Press, 1966), 234. On the myth of Venice and a rich bibliography related to Venetian mythmaking, see Edward Muir, "Images of Power: Art and Pageantry in Renaissance Venice," *American Historical Review* 84, no. 1 (February 1979): 16–52; Edward Muir, *Civic Ritual in Renaissance Venice* (Princeton, NJ: Princeton University Press, 1981), 13–61; Benjamin Ravid, "Between the Myth of Venice and the Lachrymose Conception of Jewish History: The Case of the Jews of Venice," in *The Jews of Italy: Memory and Identity*, ed. Bernard Dov Cooperman and Barbara Garvin (Potomac: University Press of Maryland, 2000), 151–92; reprinted in *Studies on the Jews of Venice, 1382–1797* (Aldershot: Ashgate,

2003); David Rosand, *Myths of Venice: The Figuration of a State* (Chapel Hill: University of North Carolina Press, 2001); and Iain Fenlon, *The Ceremonial City: History, Memory and Myth in Renaissance Venice* (New Haven, CT: Yale University Press, 2007).

27. "Questi per il negotio, sono opulentissimi & ricchi, & dimorano più volentieri in Venetia che in altra parte d'Italia. Percioche non si usano loro violenze ne tirannidi come altrove, & sono sicuri in ogni occorrenza delle facultà loro, & conseguiscono giustitia contra qualunque si sia percioche riposandosi in singolarissima pace, godono questa patria quasi come vera terra di promissione." Francesco Sansovino, *Venetia, citta nobilissima et singolare, descritta in XIIII. libri* (Venice: Iacomo Sansovino, 1581), fol. 136v.
28. Dora Liscia Bemporad argues that the Jewish ceremonial art donated to Italian synagogues after the establishment of the ghetto signified a new sense of security for Jews. She writes, "It is highly probable that the certainty of being able to remain in one place indefinitely, albeit under conditions of humiliating segregation, favored the growth, if not the birth, of ceremonial art that enriched and embellished places of worship to a degree that went beyond ritual needs." Dora Liscia Bemporad, "Jewish Ceremonial Art in the Era of the City States and the Ghettos," in *Gardens and Ghettos: The Art of Jewish Life in Italy*, ed. Vivian B. Mann (Berkeley: University of California Press, 1989), 111. On the role the Jews' *haggadot* played on the senses, see Adam S. Cohen, "La Haggadah multi-sensorielle," *Cahiers de civilisation médiévale* 55 (2012): 521–39.
29. Leon Modena, *The Autobiography of a Seventeenth-Century Venetian Rabbi: Leon Modena's "Life of Judah,"* ed. Mark R. Cohen (Princeton, NJ: Princeton University Press, 1988), 103.
30. Leon Modena complained of the cost of living in Venice, where he earned 175 ducats annually and where the price of food was much higher than in Ferrara. See Howard E. Adelman, "Leon Modena: The Autobiography and the Man," in *The Autobiography of a Seventeenth-Century Venetian Rabbi: Leon Modena's "Life of Judah,"* 25, n. 50.
31. Muir, *Civic Ritual in Renaissance Venice*, 15.
32. Alberti writes, "The presence of an elegant portico, under which the elders may [stroll] or sit, take a nap or negotiate business, will be an undoubted ornament to both crossroad and forum. Furthermore, the presence of the elders will restrain the youth, as they play and sport in the open, and curb any misbehavior or buffoonery resulting from the immaturity of their years." Leon Battista Alberti, *On the Art of Building in Ten Books*, trans. Joseph Rykwert, Neil Leach, and Robert Tavernor (Cambridge, MA: MIT Press, 1988), 263; and Leon Battista Alberti, *De re aedificatoria libri decem*, ed. Eberhard Tappe (Argentorati: M. Iacobus Cammerlander Moguntinus, 1541), lib. 8, cap. 6: fol. 121r. See also Gene A. Brucker, *Renaissance Florence* (Berkeley: University of California Press, 1983), 43; and Sharon T. Strocchia, "Theaters of Everyday Life," in *Renaissance Florence: A Social History*, ed. Roger J. Crum and John T. Paoletti (New York: Cambridge University Press, 2006), 67.
33. Alberti, *On the Art of Building in Ten Books*, 263; and Alberti, *De re aedificatoria*, lib. 8, cap. 6: fol. 121r.
34. Andrea Palladio, *The Four Books on Architecture*, trans. Robert Tavernor and Richard Schofield (Cambridge, MA: MIT Press, 1997), 213; and Andrea Palladio, *I quattro libri dell'architettura* (Venice: Domenico de' Franceschi, 1570), libro IV: Proemio à i Lettori, 3.

35. Palladio, *The Four Books on Architecture*, 213; and Palladio, *I quattro libri dell'architettura*, libro IV: Proemio à i Lettori, 4.
36. Alina A. Payne, *The Architectural Treatise in the Italian Renaissance: Architectural Invention, Ornament, and Literary Culture* (Cambridge, MA: Cambridge University Press, 1999), 51.
37. Muir, *Civic Ritual in Renaissance Venice*, 15.
38. On the authority of visuality, see Nicholas Mirzoeff, *The Right to Look: A Counterhistory of Visuality* (Durham, NC: Duke University Press, 2011), 1–10.
39. Nicholas Mirzoeff, ed., *The Visual Culture Reader* (London: Routledge, 2013), xxx.
40. Svetlana Alpers, Emily Apter, Carol Armstrong, et al., "Visual Culture Questionnaire," *October* 77 (Summer 1996): 25–70. Visual culture is an expanding field of inquiry; see, for example, Chris Jenks, ed., *Visual Culture* (London: Routledge, 1995); Marita Sturken and Lisa Cartwright, *Practices of Looking: An Introduction to Visual Culture* (Oxford: Oxford University Press, 2001); W. J. T. Mitchell, "Showing Seeing: A Critique of Visual Culture," *Journal of Visual Culture* 1, no. 2 (August 2002): 165–81; James Elkins, *Visual Studies: A Skeptical Introduction* (New York: Routledge, 2003); and Mirzoeff, ed., *The Visual Culture Reader.*
41. Sylvia Lavin, "Visual Culture Questionnaire," *October* 77 (Summer 1996), 50.
42. Lavin, "Visual Culture Questionnaire," 51.
43. See Katherine Fischer Taylor, "Architecture's Place in Art History: Art or Adjunct?," *Art Bulletin* 83, no. 2 (June 2001): 342–46.
44. Lefebvre, *The Production of Space*, 98.
45. W. J. T. Mitchell, "There are No Visual Media," in *The Visual Culture Reader*, ed. Nicholas Mirzoeff (London: Routledge, 2013), 12.
46. Michael Baxandall, *Painting and Experience in Fifteenth-Century Italy: A Primer in the Social History of Pictorial Style* (Oxford: Clarendon Press, 1972). For other examples of the art historical engagement with sight, see Norman Bryson, *Vision and Painting: The Logic of the Gaze* (New Haven, CT: Yale University Press, 1983); Hal Foster, ed., *Vision and Visuality* (Seattle, WA: Bay Press, 1988); Jonathan Crary, *Techniques of the Observer: On Vision and Modernity in the Nineteenth Century* (Cambridge, MA: MIT Press, 1990); Norman Bryson, Michael Ann Holly, and Keith Moxey, eds., *Visual Theory: Painting and Interpretation* (Cambridge: Polity Press, 1991); Robert Nelson, ed., *Visuality Before and Beyond the Renaissance: Seeing as Others Saw* (Cambridge: Cambridge University Press, 2000); and Jaś Elsner, *Roman Eyes: Visuality and Subjectivity in Art & Text* (Princeton, NJ: Princeton University Press, 2007).
47. Dianne Harris and D. Fairchild Ruggles, eds., *Sites Unseen: Landscape and Vision* (Pittsburgh, PA: University of Pittsburgh Press, 2007), 28. See also Denis Cosgrove, *Geography & Vision: Seeing, Imagining and Representing the World* (London: I. B. Tauris, 2008); and Trachtenberg, *Dominion of the Eye.*
48. Harris and Ruggles, eds., *Sites Unseen*, 11.
49. Hubert Damisch, *Skyline: The Narcissistic City* (Stanford, CA: Stanford University Press, 2001), 16.
50. Walter Benjamin, *Illuminations*, ed. Hannah Arendt (New York: Schocken, 1968), 240.
51. Mitchell, "Showing Seeing," 166.
52. Stuart Clark, *Vanities of the Eye: Vision in Early Modern European Culture* (Oxford: Oxford University Press, 2007).

Margins as Laboratories of Urban Planning

1. On Giovanni Merlo, see Juergen Schulz, "The Printed Plans and Panoramic Views of Venice (1486–1797)," *Saggi e memorie di storia dell'arte* 7 (Florence: Leo S. Olschki, 1970), esp. 28–29, 73–75, 101–02, 142–47, 162–65. See also Marco Folin, *Rappresentare la città: Topografie urbane nell'Italia di antico regime* (Reggio Emilia: Diabasis, 2010).
2. Louis Marin distinguishes the ideal city from the uninhabited and uninhabitable imaginary city. See Louis Marin, "The City's Portrait in Its Utopics," in *Utopics: Spatial Play*, trans. Robert A. Vollrath (Atlantic Highlands, NJ: Humanities Press, 1984), 208.
3. On the early modern cartographic tradition, see, for example, Lucia Nuti, "The Perspective Plan in the Sixteenth Century: The Invention of a Representational Language," *Art Bulletin* 76, no. 1 (March 1994): 105–28; Lucia Nuti, "Mapping Places: Chorography and Vision in the Renaissance," in *Mappings*, ed. Denis Cosgrove (London: Reaktion, 1999), 90–108; Renzo Dubbini, *Geography of the Gaze: Urban and Rural Vision in Early Modern Europe*, trans. Lydia G. Cochrane (Chicago: University of Chicago Press, 2002); Naomi Miller, *Mapping the City: The Language and Culture of Cartography in the Renaissance* (London: Continuum, 2003); and Francesca Fiorani, *The Marvel of Maps: Art, Cartography and Politics in Renaissance Italy* (New Haven, CT: Yale University Press, 2005).
4. Jacopo de' Barbari's view of Venice informed the compositional design of Merlo's map. In her discussion of de' Barbari's *Venetie*, Bronwen Wilson similarly observes that the Rialto Bridge functioned as "the pictorial and topographical centre of the woodcut." Bronwen Wilson, *The World in Venice: Print, the City, and Early Modern Identity* (Toronto: University of Toronto Press, 2005), 28. On Jacopo de' Barbari's map, see also Juergen Schulz, "Jacopo de' Barbari's View of Venice: Map Making, City Views, and Moralized Geography before the Year 1500," *Art Bulletin* 60, no. 3 (September 1978): 425–74.
5. Wilson, *The World in Venice*, 34.
6. The Senate in Venice first ghettoized Italian and Ashkenazi Jews, Jews of German descent, followed by Levantine Jews (Levantini), exiles from Spain and Portugal who settled in the Ottoman Empire. As Ottoman subjects, Levantini received commercial privileges in Venice, including the right to "sail the seas freely both to windward and to leeward, as Venetian citizens do; and . . . [to] pay duties at the same rate as Venetian citizens." David Chambers and Brian Pullan, eds., *Venice: A Documentary History, 1450–1630* (Toronto: University of Toronto Press, 2001), 346–47. Ponentine ("Western") Jews, many *marrani* or converts of Iberian origin, also benefited from commercial networks established with Iberia and the Ottoman Empire. Ponentine Jews were the third and wealthiest group to settle in the Venice ghetto. On the changing tenor of these terms in early modern Venice, see E. Natalie Rothman, *Brokering Empire: Trans-Imperial Subjects between Venice and Istanbul* (Ithaca, NY: Cornell University Press, 2012).
7. Bryan D. Palmer, *Cultures of Darkness: Night Travels in the Histories of Transgression* (New York: Monthly Review Press, 2000), 5. On city margins in medieval art, see Michael Camille, *Image on the Edge: The Margins of Medieval Art* (London: Reaktion, 1992), esp. 129–52.

8. Edward Muir and Ronald F. E. Weissman, "Social and Symbolic Places in Renaissance Venice and Florence," in *The Power of Place: Bringing Together Geographical and Sociological Imaginations*, ed. John A. Agnew and James S. Duncan (Boston: Unwin Hyman, 1989), 87.
9. On theories of outside architecture, see Elizabeth Grosz, *Architecture from the Outside: Essays on Virtual and Real Space* (Cambridge, MA: MIT Press, 2001).
10. Elena Fasano Guarini, "Center and Periphery," *Journal of Modern History* 67, supplement: "The Origins of the State in Italy, 1300–1600" (December 1995): S74–S96.
11. Benjamin Arbel, "Venice's Maritime Empire in the Early Modern Period," in *A Companion to Venetian History, 1400–1797*, ed. Eric R. Dursteler (Leiden: Brill, 2013), 125–253. See also Reinhold C. Mueller, "Aspects of Venetian Sovereignty in Medieval and Renaissance Dalmatia," in *Quattrocento Adriatico: Fifteenth-Century Art of the Adriatic Rim*, ed. Charles Dempsey (Bologna: Nuova Alfa, 1996), 29–56; and Monique O'Connell, *Men of Empire: Power and Negotiation in Venice's Maritime State* (Baltimore: Johns Hopkins University Press, 2009).
12. Rothman, *Brokering Empire*, 18–20, 219.
13. Wilson, *The World in Venice*, 69.
14. Wilson, *The World in Venice*, 25.
15. Philippe de Commynes, *The Memoirs of Philippe de Commynes*, ed. Samuel Kinser (Columbia: University of South Carolina Press, 1973), 2:489–90.
16. On Philippe de Commynes's *Mémoires* as an instruction of princes, see William J. Bouwsma, "The Politics of Commynes," *Journal of Modern History* 23, no. 4 (December 1951): 315–28. On the "mirror-for-princes" genre, see the classical commentaries in Allan H. Gilbert, *Machiavelli's "Prince" and Its Forerunners: "The Prince" as a Typical Book "De regimine principum"* (Durham, NC: Duke University Press, 1938); Felix Gilbert, "The Humanist Concept of the Prince and *The Prince* of Machiavelli," *Journal of Modern History* 11, no. 4 (December 1939): 449–83; and Quentin Skinner, *The Foundations of Modern Political Thought*, vol. 1 (Cambridge: Cambridge University Press, 1978), esp. 118–38. See also Peter Stacey, *Roman Monarchy and the Renaissance Prince* (Cambridge: Cambridge University Press, 2007).
17. Skinner, *The Foundations of Modern Political Thought*, 125.
18. Commynes, *The Memoirs of Philippe de Commynes*, 2:493.
19. In his 1611 *Coryat's Crudities*, English traveler Thomas Coryat remarks on the diversity of Venice's inhabitants: "There you may see many Polonians, Slavonians, Persians, Grecians, Turks, Jewes, Christians of all the famousest regions of Christendome, and each nation distinguished from another by their proper and peculiar habits." Thomas Coryat, *Coryat's Crudities* (Glasgow: James MacLehose and Sons, 1905), 1:318. See also Rothman, *Brokering Empire*, 2–3.
20. "Si les venoient acheter droitement en Venise Alemans et Baivers, Franceis et Lonbars, Toscans et Ongrés, et totes gens qui vivent de merchandies, et les condusoient en lors pays." Martino da Canale, *Les Estoires de Venise: Cronaca veneziana in lingua francese dalle origini al 1275*, ed. Alberto Limentani (Florence: Leo S. Olschki, 1972), 38.
21. On Venice and its minorities, see Giorgio Fedalto, "Le minoranze straniere a Venezia tra politica e legislazione," in *Venezia: Centro di mediazione tra oriente e occidente, secoli XV-XVI: Aspetti e problemi*, ed. Hans-Georg Beck, Manoussos Manoussacas, and

Agostino Pertusi (Florence: L. S. Olschki, 1977), 1:143–63; Giorgio Fedalto, "Stranieri a Venezia e a Padova," *Storia della cultura veneta*, ed. Girolamo Arnaldi and Manlio Pastore Stocchi (Vicenza: Neri Pozza, 1976–1986), vol. 3/I: *Dal primo Quattrocento al Concilio di Trento* (1980), 499–535; Giorgio Fedalto, "Stranieri a Venezia e a Padova, 1550–1700," *Storia della cultura veneta*, ed. Girolamo Arnaldi and Manlio Pastore Stocchi (Vicenza: Neri Pozza, 1976–1986), vol. 4/II: *Dalla Controriforma alla fine della Repubblica. Il Seicento* (1984), 251–79; Donatella Calabi, "Gli stranieri e la città," in *Storia di Venezia. Dalle origini alla caduta della Serenissima*, ed. Gino Benzoni and Antonio Menniti Ippolito, 14 vols. (Rome: Istituto della Enciclopedia Italiana, 1991–2002), vol. 5: *Il Rinascimento. Società ed economia*, ed. Alberto Tenenti and Ugo Tucci (1996), 913–46; Reinhold C. Mueller, *Immigrazione e cittadinanza nella Venezia medievale* (Rome: Viella, 2010); and Benjamin Ravid, "Venice and Its Minorities," in *A Companion to Venetian History, 1400–1797*, ed. Eric R. Dursteler (Leiden: Brill, 2013), 449–85.

22. In a letter to the Doge of Venice, Bessarion explains his gift: "As all peoples of almost the entire world gather in your city, so especially do the Greeks. Arriving by sea from their homelands they debark first at Venice, being forced by necessity to come to your city and live among you, and there they seem to enter another Byzantium (*quasi alterum Byzantium*). In view of this, how could I more appropriately confer this bequest than upon the Venetians to whom I myself am indebted and committed by obligation because of their well known favors to me, and upon their city, which I chose for my country after the subjugation of Greece and in which I have been very honorably received and recognized." Deno John Geanakoplos, *Greek Scholars in Venice: Studies in the Dissemination of Greek Learning from Byzantium to Western Europe* (Cambridge, MA: Harvard University Press, 1962), 35–37.
23. See Jonathan Harris, *Greek Emigres in the West, 1400–1520* (Camberley: Porphyrogenitus, 1995), 25.
24. Dominique Kirchner Reill, *Nationalists Who Feared the Nation: Adriatic Multi-Nationalism in Habsburg Dalmatia, Trieste, and Venice* (Stanford, CA: Stanford University Press, 2012), 24. On Venetian Dalmatia, see Larry Wolff, "Venice and the Slavs of Dalmatia: The Drama of the Adriatic Empire in the Venetian Enlightenment," *Slavic Review* 56, no. 3 (Autumn 1997): 428–55; Larry Wolff, "The Enlightened Anthropology of Friendship in Venetian Dalmatia: Primitive Ferocity and Ritual Fraternity among the Morlacchi," *Eighteenth-Century Studies* 32, no. 2 (Winter 1998/99): 157–78; and Larry Wolff, *Venice and the Slavs: The Discovery of Dalmatia in the Age of Enlightenment* (Stanford, CA: Stanford University Press, 2001).
25. Chambers and Pullan, eds., *Venice: A Documentary History*, 328.
26. Chambers and Pullan, eds., *Venice: A Documentary History*, 328.
27. Blake de Maria, "The Patron for Pordenone's Frescos on Palazzo Talenti d'Anna, Venice," *The Burlington Magazine* 146, no. 1217 (August 2004): 548–49; and Blake de Maria, *Becoming Venetian: Immigrants and the Arts in Early Modern Venice* (New Haven, CT: Yale University Press, 2010), 99–106.
28. De Maria, "The Patron for Pordenone's Frescos on Palazzo Talenti d'Anna," 549.
29. Richard Goy, *Venice: The City and Its Architecture* (London: Phaidon, 1997), 60–85, 94–107.
30. Chambers and Pullan, eds., *Venice: A Documentary History*, 333.

31. Goy, *Venice: The City and Its Architecture*, 86–93.
32. On the Jews' charters of sojourn, see Benjamin Ravid, "An Introduction to the Charters of the Jewish Merchants of Venice," in *The Mediterranean and the Jews: Society, Culture and Economy in Early Modern Times*, ed. Elliott Horowitz and Moises Orfali (Ramat-Gan: Bar-Ilan University Press, 2002), 2:203–46; reprinted in *Studies on the Jews of Venice, 1382–1797* (Aldershot: Ashgate, 2003). See also Benjamin Ravid, "The Third Charter of the Jewish Merchants of Venice, 1611: A Case Study in Complex Multifaceted Negotiations," *Jewish Political Studies Review* 6, no. 1/2 (Spring 1994): 83–134.
33. Galit Hasan-Rokem and Alan Dundes, eds., *The Wandering Jew: Essays in the Interpretation of a Christian Legend* (Bloomington: Indiana University Press, 1986).
34. Jean-François Lyotard, *Heidegger and "the jews,"* trans. Andreas Michel and Mark S. Roberts (Minneapolis: University of Minnesota Press, 1990), 22.
35. As Brian Pullan notes, "Ghettoes, in the strict sense of the word, were always imposed by legislation, and were generally established on remote and inconvenient sites." Brian Pullan, *The Jews of Europe and the Inquisition of Venice, 1550–1670* (London: I. B. Tauris, 1997), 156.
36. Piero Camporesi, *The Incorruptible Flesh: Bodily Mutation and Mortification in Religion and Folklore*, trans. Tania Croft-Murray (Cambridge: Cambridge University Press, 1988), 79.
37. Residency increased in Frankfurt's *Judengasse* from 110 registered inhabitants in 1463, 250 in 1520, 900 in 1569, to nearly 3,000 in 1610. *Encyclopaedia Judaica*, "Frankfurt on the Main," ed. Michael Berenbaum and Fred Skolnik, vol. 7, second edition (Detroit, MI: Macmillan, 2007), 207–12.
38. Rosemarie Schuder and Rudolf Hirsch, *Der gelbe Fleck: Wurzeln und Wirkungen des Judenhasses in der deutschen Geschichte: Essays* (Cologne: Röderberg im Pahl-Rugenstein, 1988); Fritz Backhaus, "The Jewish Ghetto in Frankfurt," in *The Life and Times of N. M. Rothschild, 1777–1836*, ed. Victor Gray and Melanie Aspey (London: N. M. Rothschild & Sons, 1998), 23–33; Eoin Bourke, "The Frankfurt Judengasse in Eyewitness Accounts from the Seventeenth to the Nineteenth Century," in *Ghetto Writing: Traditional and Eastern Jewry in German-Jewish Literature from Heine to Hilsenrath*, ed. Anne Fuchs and Florian Krobb (Columbia, SC: Camden House, 1999), 11–24; Egon Wamers and Markus Grossbach, *Die Judengasse in Frankfurt am Main: Ergebnisse der archäologischen Untersuchungen am Börneplatz* (Stuttgart: Jan Thorbecke, 2000); and Fritz Backhaus, Gisela Engel, et al., eds., *The Frankfurt "Judengasse": Jewish Life in an Early Modern German City* (London: Vallentine Mitchell, 2010). See also Alfred Haverkamp, "The Jewish Quarters in German Towns during the Late Middle Ages," in *In and Out of the Ghetto: Jewish-Gentile Relations in Late Medieval and Early Modern Germany*, ed. R. Po-chia Hsia and Hartmut Lehmann (Cambridge: Cambridge University Press, 1995), 13–28; and Maria Boes, "Jews in the Criminal-Justice System of Early Modern Germany," *Journal of Interdisciplinary History* 30, no. 3 (Winter 1999): 407–35.
39. The Altstadt (old town) is the historic center of Frankfurt am Main that houses the Cathedral of Saint Bartholomew and the Römer city hall. City officials segregated the Jews outside the city center to an area that remained scarcely populated until the eighteenth century.

40. Ania Loomba, *Shakespeare, Race, and Colonialism* (Oxford: Oxford University Press, 2002), 9.
41. Gilles Deleuze, *Foucault*, trans. Seán Hand (Minneapolis: University of Minnesota Press, 1988), 96–97.
42. Donatella Calabi, "The 'City of the Jews,'" in *The Jews of Early Modern Venice*, ed. Robert C. Davis and Benjamin Ravid (Baltimore: Johns Hopkins University Press, 2001), 31.
43. Regarding the Jews of Padua and Modena, see Antonio Ciscato, *Gli ebrei in Padova (1300–1800): Monografia storica documentata* (Bologna: Forni, 1967); and Katherine Aron-Beller, *Jews on Trial: The Papal Inquisition in Modena, 1598–1638* (New York: Manchester University Press, 2011). See also Federica Francesconi, "From Ghetto to Emancipation: The Role of Moisè Formiggini," *Jewish History* 24, no. 3/4 (2010): 331–54; and Federica Francesconi, "Dangerous Readings in Early Modern Modena: Negotiating Jewish Culture in an Italian Key," in *The Hebrew Book in Early Modern Italy*, ed. Joseph Hacker and Adam Shear (Philadelphia: University of Pennsylvania Press, 2011), 133–55.
44. See Kenneth Stow, *Catholic Thought and Papal Jewry Policy, 1555–1593* (New York: Jewish Theological Seminary of America, 1977); and Kenneth Stow, *Theater of Acculturation: The Roman Ghetto in the 16th Century* (Seattle: University of Washington Press, 2001). On Jewish Rome, see also Ettore Natali, *Il ghetto di Roma*, vol. 1 (Rome: Stabilimento Tipografico della Tribuna, 1887); Attilio Milano, *Il ghetto di Roma: Illustrazioni storiche* (Roma: Staderini, 1964); David B. Ruderman, "The Cultural Significance of the Ghetto in Jewish History," in *From Ghetto to Emancipation: Historical and Contemporary Reconsiderations of the Jewish Community*, ed. David N. Myers and William V. Rowe (Scranton, PA: University of Scranton Press, 1997), esp. 2–3; and Bernard D. Cooperman, "Ethnicity and Institution Building among Jews in Early Modern Rome," *AJS Review* 30, no. 1 (April 2006): 119–45. On debates surrounding the meaning of *Cum nimis absurdum*, see David Berger, "'Cum Nimis Absurdum' and the Conversion of the Jews," *Jewish Quarterly Review* 70, no. 1 (July 1979): 41–49; and Kenneth R. Stow, "The Proper Meaning of 'Cum Nimis Absurdum,'" *Jewish Quarterly Review* 71, no. 4 (April 1981): 251–52.
45. See Stow, *Theater of Acculturation*.
46. Ferdinand Gregorovius, *The Ghetto and the Jews of Rome*, trans. Moses Hadas (New York: Schocken, 1966), 86. For a similar description of Rome's ghetto, see Massimo d'Azeglio, *Dell'emancipazione civile degl'Israeliti* (Florence: F. Le Monnier, 1848), 24–25; and L. Scott Lerner, "Narrating over the Ghetto of Rome," *Jewish Social Studies*, New Series, 8, no. 2/3 (Winter-Spring 2002): 1–38.
47. Lerner, "Narrating over the Ghetto of Rome," 3. On the demolition of the Roman ghetto, see Alberto M. Racheli, "La demolitzione e ricostruzione del quartiere del Ghetto (1885–1911)," in *Roma capitale, 1870–1911. Architettura e urbanistica: Uso e trasformazione della città storica*, ed. Giorgio Ciucci and Vanna Fraticelli (Venice: Marsilio, 1984), 436–41.
48. Lerner, "Narrating over the Ghetto of Rome," 7. On the Roman synagogue, see also Bice Migliau, "Le vicende dell'edificio delle Cinque Scole," in *Roma capitale, 1870–1911. Architettura e urbanistica: Uso e trasformazione della città storica*, ed. Giorgio Ciucci and Vanna Fraticelli (Venice: Marsilio, 1984), 442–47; Carol Herselle Krinsky, *Synagogues of Europe: Architecture, History, Meaning* (Cambridge,

MA: MIT Press, 1985), 362–69; and Giovanni Ascarelli, Daniela Di Castro, et al., eds., *Il Tempio Maggiore di Roma: Nel centenario dell'inaugurazione della Sinagoga, 1904–2004* (Turin: Allemandi, 2004). On the Renaissance synagogue, see Barry Stiefel, *Jews and the Renaissance of Synagogue Architecture, 1450–1730* (London: Pickering & Chatto, 2014).

49. Stefanie Siegmund, *The Medici State and the Ghetto of Florence: The Construction of an Early Modern Jewish Community* (Stanford, CA: Stanford University Press, 2006). See also Umberto Cassuto, "I più antichi capitoli del ghetto di Firenze," *Rivista israelitica* 9 (1912): 203–11; Umberto Cassuto, *Gli ebrei a Firenze nell'età del Rinascimento* (Florence: Galetti e Cocci, 1918); and Umberto Cassuto, "La famille des Médicis et les Juifs," *Revue des études juives* 76 (1923): 132–45.

50. Contemporary diarist Agostino Lapini writes, "Di gennaio 1570 il signor principe di Firenze Francesco de' Medici cominciò a far murare il luogo dove abitano gli giudei, avendo prima compero case, magazzini e postribuli e botteghe et altre abitazioni dove erono state le pubbliche meretricie e meccaniche, grandissimo tempo. E vi fe' fare tutte l'abitazioni e botteghe che al presente si veggono in piazza giudea: che in su detta piazza di qua e di là erono le botteguzze, e stanzuzze delle meccanichissime meretrice, e si levorno e si murorno le stanze che vi sono; che spese detto signor Principe parecchi migliaja di scudi." Agostino Lapini, *Diario fiorentino di Agostino Lapini dal 252 al 1596*, ed. Giuseppe Odoardo Corazzini (Florence: G. C. Sansoni, 1900), 171.

51. Nicholas Terpstra, *Lost Girls: Sex and Death in Renaissance Florence* (Baltimore: Johns Hopkins University Press, 2010), 18. See also Gene Brucker, *The Society of Renaissance Florence: A Documentary Study* (New York: Harper & Row, 1971), 190–201; Richard C. Trexler, "La prostitution florentine au XVe siècle: Patronages et clientèles," *Annales. Économies, sociétés, civilisations* 36, no. 6 (November–December 1981): 983–1015; and John K. Brackett, "The Florentine Onestà and the Control of Prostitution, 1403–1680," *Sixteenth Century Journal* 24, no. 2 (Summer 1993): 273–300.

52. See Siegmund, *The Medici State and the Ghetto of Florence*, 201–206. In addition to residential restrictions, authorities forced Jews and prostitutes to wear sartorial markers to distinguish themselves from respectable Christians.

53. "che li zudei, quali sono in questa terra molti in diverse caxe et contrade et danno mal exempio a li christiani tutti, siano mandati ad habitar a la Zueca etc." Marino Sanuto, *I diarii di Marino Sanuto: Dall'autografo Marciano ital. cl. VII codd. CDXIX-CDLXXVII*, ed. Federico Stefani, Nicolò Barozzi, and Guglielmo Berchet, vol. 20 (Venice: Fratelli Visentini, 1887), 138. See also Marin Sanudo, *Venice, Città Excelentissima: Selections from the Renaissance Diaries of Marin Sanudo*, ed. Patricia H. Labalme and Laura Sanguineti White, trans. Linda L. Carroll (Baltimore: Johns Hopkins University Press, 2008), 338; as well as Robert Finlay, "The Foundation of the Ghetto: Venice, the Jews, and the War of the League of Cambrai," *Proceedings of the American Philosophical Society* 126, no. 2 (April 8, 1982), 146. Although Jewish quarters in the southern part of the Italian peninsula have been given the name Giudecca (from the Latin *Judaica* or "the Jewry"), in the Venetian example no extant evidence indicates that Jews ever lived in the Giudecca. According to Benjamin Ravid, the etymology of "Giudecca" most likely does not derive from *Judaica* but rather *Zudega*, from *giudicato* or "the judged." See Benjamin Ravid, "The Jewish Mercantile Settlement of Twelfth and Thirteenth Century Venice: Reality or Conjecture?," *AJS Review* 2 (1977): 201–25.

54. Pullan, *The Jews of Europe and the Inquisition of Venice*, 156; and Calimani, *The Ghetto of Venice*, 34.
55. Rose Marie San Juan, *Rome: A City Out of Print* (Minneapolis: University of Minnesota Press, 2001), 34.
56. Jews paid rent to Christians, such as the Minotto and da Brolo families, for the houses and shops they occupied on the lower floors of the ghetto complex. However, Jewish owners held the majority of rented property through possession of the *jus gazaka*. Ennio Concina compiled data on ghetto rental property in which Jews in the Ghetto Nuovo, Ghetto Vecchio, and Ghetto Nuovissimo paid 14,661 ducats in rent in 1661. From that sum, Christian proprietors received only 1,269 ducats while Jewish owners of the *jus gazaka* collected 13,392 ducats from rental property on the ghettos' upper floors. Ennio Concina, "Owners, Houses, Functions: New Research on the Origins of the Venetian Ghetto," *Mediterranean Historical Review* 6, no. 2 (December 1991): 188. See also Ennio Concina, "Parva Jerusalem," in *La città degli ebrei: Il ghetto di Venezia, architettura e urbanistica*, ed. Ennio Concina, Ugo Camerino, and Donatella Calabi (Venice: Albrizzi, 1991), 9–155; and Benjamin Ravid, "The Minotto Family and an Unapproved Construction Project in the Ghetto Vecchio of Venice, 1608–1609," in *Daniel Carpi Jubilee Volume*, ed. Minna Rozen, Anita Shapira, and Dina Porat (Tel Aviv: Tel Aviv University, 1996), 91–108.
57. On the etymology of the word "ghetto," see Benjamin Ravid, "From Geographical Realia to Historiographical Symbol: The Odyssey of the Word Ghetto," in *Essential Papers on Jewish Culture in Renaissance and Baroque Italy*, ed. David B. Ruderman (New York: New York University Press, 1992), 373–85. See also Kenneth Stow, "The Consciousness of Closure: Roman Jewry and Its *Ghet*," in *Essential Papers on Jewish Culture in Renaissance and Baroque Italy*, ed. David Ruderman (New York: New York University Press, 1992), 386–400; reprinted in *Jewish Life in Early Modern Rome: Challenge, Conversion, and Private Life* (Aldershot: Ashgate, 2007); and Sandra Debenedetti-Stow, "The Etymology of 'Ghetto': New Evidence from Rome," *Jewish History* 6, no. 1–2, The Frank Talmage Memorial Volume (1992): 79–85.
58. Katharine G. Bristol, "The Pruitt-Igoe Myth," *Journal of Architectural Education* 44, no. 3 (May 1991): 168. See also Charles A. Jencks, *The Language of Post-Modern Architecture* (New York: Rizzoli, 1984), 9–10; and Sudhir Alladi Venkatesh, *American Project: The Rise and Fall of a Modern Ghetto* (Cambridge, MA: Harvard University Press, 2000), 15–21.
59. Bristol, "The Pruitt-Igoe Myth," 166, 168. In her study of the Pruitt-Igoe myth, Bristol argues that socioeconomic factors, which impacted the buildings' architectural design, played the most significant role in the project's failure.
60. The Senate decree states, "Tuti li Zudei che de presenti se attrovano habitar in diverse contrade de questa cita nostra . . . siano tenuti & debino andar immediate ad habitar unidi in la corte de case che sono in Geto apresso San Hieronymo, loco capacissimo per sua habitacione." ASVe, Senato, Terra, registro 19, fol. 78r, March 29, 1516. See also Chambers and Pullan, eds., *Venice: A Documentary History*, 338.
61. Concerning the Venetian garden, see, for example, John Dixon Hunt, "The Garden in the City of Venice: Epitome of State and Site," *Studies in the History of Gardens and Designed Landscapes* 19, no. 1 (March 1999): 46–61; and John Dixon Hunt, *The Venetian City Garden: Place, Typology, and Perception* (Basel: Birkhäuser, 2009).

62. Giorgio Gianighian, "Building a Renaissance Double House in Venice," *Architectural Research Quarterly* 8, nos. 3–4 (December 2004): 301. For a history of architecture in Renaissance Venice, see such studies as John McAndrew, *Venetian Architecture of the Early Renaissance* (Cambridge, MA: MIT Press, 1980); Ralph Lieberman, *Renaissance Architecture in Venice, 1450–1540* (New York: Abbeville, 1982); Ennio Concina, *Storia dell'architettura di Venezia: Dal VII al XX secolo* (Milan: Electa, 1992); trans. Judith Landry as *A History of Venetian Architecture* (Cambridge: Cambridge University Press, 1998); Deborah Howard, *Venice & the East: The Impact of the Islamic World on Venetian Architecture, 1100–1500* (New Haven, CT: Yale University Press, 2000); Deborah Howard, *The Architectural History of Venice* (New Haven, CT: Yale University Press, 2002); and Patricia Fortini Brown, *Private Lives in Renaissance Venice: Art, Architecture, and the Family* (New Haven, CT: Yale University Press, 2004). On vernacular architecture in early modern Venice, see Egle R. Trincanato, *Venezia minore* (Milan: Edizioni del Milione, 1948); Paola Pavanini, "Abitazioni popolari e borghesi nella Venezia cinquecentesca," *Studi veneziani* 5 (1981): 63–126; Giorgio Gianighian and Paola Pavanini, *Dietro i palazzi: Tre secoli di architettura minore a Venezia, 1492–1803* (Venice: Arsenale, 1984); Richard Goy, *Venetian Vernacular Architecture: Traditional Housing in the Venetian Lagoon* (Cambridge: Cambridge University Press, 1988); and Giorgio Gianighian, "Building Castelforte," *Architectural Research Quarterly* 9, no. 1 (March 2005): 51–68. See also Juergen Schulz, *The New Palaces of Medieval Venice* (University Park, PA: Penn State University Press, 2004).
63. The drawing reproduced in Figure 26 originates from an eighteenth-century trial in which the Jewish tailor Israel Tedesco was sued for building a house beyond the confines of the Ghetto Nuovissimo. This document suggests that by the late eighteenth century the boundaries around the Venetian ghettos were blurred, as Christians and Jews cohabitated along the periphery of the ghetto complex. Despite such cohabitation, Jews and Christians maintained distinct spaces that segregated Jews vertically above the homes of their Christian neighbors. For information on the trial, see Donatella Calabi, "Il ghetto e la città," in *La città degli ebrei: Il ghetto di Venezia, architettura e urbanistica*, ed. Ennio Concina, Ugo Camerino, and Donatella Calabi (Venice: Albrizzi, 1991), 281–83.
64. "li Zudei, che habiteno in questa sua cita, et tutto el dominio, siano distincti et diversificati da li Christiani cossi in habito come sono in la fede." Archivio di Stato di Mantova, Archivio Gonzaga, busta 2038–39, fascicolo 9, fol. 2v. Canon 68 of the Fourth Lateran Council (1215) records the first church law obliging Jews to wear distinguishing garb: "In certain provinces of the church, divergence in clothing distinguishes Jews from Christians and Saracens from Christians; however in certain [provinces], there has arisen such confusion that no differences are discernible. Thus, it sometimes happens that by mistake Christians mingle with Jewish or Saracen women, and Jews and Saracens with Christian women. Therefore, lest they, under the cover of error, find an excuse for the grave sin of such mingling, we decree that these people [Jews and Saracens] of either sex and in all Christian lands and at all times be readily distinguishable from others by the quality of their clothing. Indeed, this very legislation is decreed for them [the Jews] also by Moses." Robert Chazan, *Medieval Stereotypes and Modern Antisemitism* (Berkeley: University of California Press, 1997), 100.

65. On the sartorial restrictions placed on the Jews of Venice, see Benjamin Ravid, "From Yellow to Red: On the Distinguishing Head-Covering of the Jews of Venice," *Jewish History* 6, nos. 1–2, The Frank Talmage Memorial Volume (1992): 179–210; reprinted in *Studies on the Jews of Venice, 1382–1797* (Aldershot: Ashgate, 2003). On dress and social marginalization, see also Diane Owen Hughes, "Distinguishing Signs: Ear-Rings, Jews and Franciscan Rhetoric in the Italian Renaissance City," *Past & Present* 112 (August 1986): 3–59; and Sara Lipton, *Images of Intolerance: The Representation of Jews and Judaism in the "Bible moralisée"* (Berkeley: University of California Press, 1999), esp. 15–19.
66. Thomas Coryat, *Coryat's Crudities* (Glasgow: James MacLehose, 1905), 1:370.
67. Coryat, *Coryat's Crudities*, 1:371.
68. On the ghetto and the foreign gaze, see Benjamin Ravid, "Christian Travelers in the Ghetto of Venice: Some Preliminary Observations," in *Studies on the Jews of Venice, 1382–1797* (Aldershot: Ashgate, 2003), 111–50; and Calabi, "The 'City of the Jews,'" 45–48.

Enclosures as Topographies of Vision

1. Camillo Sitte, *Camillo Sitte: The Birth of Modern City Planning, with a Translation of the 1889 Austrian Edition of His "City Planning According to Artistic Principles,"* ed. George R. Collins and Christiane Crasemann Collins (New York: Rizzoli, 1986), 141–42. On Camillo Sitte, see Elbert Peets, "Famous Town Planners: II. Camillo Sitte," *Town Planning Review* 12, no. 4 (December 1927): 249–59; S. D. Adshead, "Camillo Sitte and Le Corbusier," *Town Planning Review* 14, no. 2 (November 1930): 85–94; Rudolf Wittkower, "Camillo Sitte's *Art of Building Cities* in an American Translation," *Town Planning Review* 19, no. 3/4 (Summer 1947): 164–69; Werner Hegemann and Elbert Peets, *The American Vitruvius: An Architects' Handbook of Civic Art*, ed. Alan J. Plattus (New York: Princeton Architectural Press, 1988), 7–27; Mitchell Schwarzer, "The Extremes of Spatial Experience," *AA Files*, no. 57 (2008): 67–73; and Charles C. Bohl and Jean-François Lejeune, *Sitte, Hegemann and the Metropolis: Modern Civic Art and International Exchanges* (London: Routledge, 2009).
2. Regarding the piazza, see, for example, Paul Zucker, *Town and Square from the Agora to the Village Green* (New York: Columbia University Press, 1959); and Eamonn Canniffe, *The Politics of the Piazza: The History and Meaning of the Italian Square* (Aldershot: Ashgate, 2008).
3. Sitte, *Camillo Sitte: The Birth of Modern City Planning*, 152.
4. Sitte, *Camillo Sitte: The Birth of Modern City Planning*, 153.
5. Sitte laments that the plaza no longer occupies a principal role in public life, as it did in the medieval and early modern period: "In those days the main plazas were of primary importance to the life of every city because such a great deal of public life took place in them: today not an open plaza but closed halls would be used for such purposes." Sitte, *Camillo Sitte: The Birth of Modern City Planning*, 143.
6. Sitte, *Camillo Sitte: The Birth of Modern City Planning*, 170–71. On urban enclosure, Norwegian architect Christian Norberg-Schulz states, "The distinctive quality of any man-made place is *enclosure*, and its character and spatial properties are determined by

how it is enclosed. . . . Enclosure primarily means a distinct area which is separated from the surroundings by means of a built boundary." He adds, "The main urban elements are centres and paths. A square obviously functions as a centre and a street as a path. As such they are enclosures; their spatial identity in fact depends upon the presence of relatively continuous lateral boundaries." Christian Norberg-Schulz, *Genius Loci: Towards a Phenomenology of Architecture* (New York: Rizzoli, 1980), 58–59. American architects Robert Venturi, Denise Scott Brown, and Steven Izenour write, "Architects have been bewitched by a single element of the Italian landscape: the piazza. Its traditional, pedestrian-scaled, and intricately enclosed space is easier to like than the spatial sprawl of Route 66 and Los Angeles." Robert Venturi, Denise Scott Brown, and Steven Izenour, *Learning from Las Vegas: The Forgotten Symbolism of Architectural Form* (Cambridge, MA: MIT Press, 1977), 6–7.

7. Sitte, *Camillo Sitte: The Birth of Modern City Planning*, 183.
8. Joshua Holmes, "Building Bridges and Breaking Boundaries: Modernity and Agoraphobia," *Opticon1826* (September 1, 2006): http://dx.doi.org/10.5334/opt.010606.
9. Sitte, *Camillo Sitte: The Birth of Modern City Planning*, 196.
10. John Ruskin, *The Stones of Venice*, vol. 1 (London: George Allen, Sunnyside, Orpington, 1896), 101.
11. On architecture and civic stability, see Edward Muir, *Civic Ritual in Renaissance Venice* (Princeton, NJ: Princeton University Press, 1981), 15.
12. Martin Heidegger, "Building, Dwelling, Thinking," in *Poetry, Language, Thought*, trans. Albert Hofstadter (New York: Harper & Row, 1971), 154. See also Jeff Malpas, *Heidegger's Topology: Being, Place, World* (Cambridge, MA: MIT Press, 2006); and Jeff Malpas, *Heidegger and the Thinking of Place: Explorations in the Topology of Being* (Cambridge, MA: MIT Press, 2012).
13. Sitte, *Camillo Sitte: The Birth of Modern City Planning*, 220. While scholars decry medieval urbanism for an unsystematic engagement with the built environment and a failure to assign any meaningful attention to the architectural onlooker, more recent historiography on the piazza understands city planners as deeply concerned with modalities of vision. For instance, Marvin Trachtenberg concludes that the reshaping of the Florentine piazza brought building in control of its surrounding space by guiding viewing through a coherent system of ordered angles. Areli Marina records planners in communal-age Parma arranging the civic and episcopal squares to produce panoptic views of the city's main monuments. In her study of topographical prints of early modern Rome, Rose Marie San Juan suggests that visual observation fills the represented spaces of the Piazza Navona. She describes the piazza as an urban boundary where vision is kept moving yet contained within prescribed perimeters. See Marvin Trachtenberg, *Dominion of the Eye: Urbanism, Art, and Power in Early Modern Florence* (Cambridge: Cambridge University Press, 1997); Areli Marina, *The Italian Piazza Transformed: Parma in the Communal Age* (University Park, PA: Penn State University Press, 2012); and Rose Marie San Juan, *Rome: A City Out of Print* (Minneapolis: University of Minnesota Press, 2001), 187–217.
14. Hegemann and Peets, *The American Vitruvius*, 9–10.
15. In the late fifteenth century, the French ambassador Philippe de Commynes commented that in Venice, "most of their people are foreigners." Philippe de Commynes, *The Memoirs of Philippe de Commynes*, ed. Samuel Kinser (Columbia: University of South Carolina Press, 1973), 2:493. Regarding Venice's "Others," see

Benjamin Ravid, "How 'Other' Really Was the Jewish Other? The Evidence from Venice," in *Acculturation and Its Discontents: The Italian Jewish Experience Between Exclusion and Inclusion*, ed. David N. Myers (Toronto: University of Toronto Press, 2008), 19–55; Blake de Maria, *Becoming Venetian: Immigrants and the Arts in Early Modern Venice* (New Haven, CT: Yale University Press, 2010); John Jeffries Martin, "Marranos and Nicodemites in Sixteenth-Century Venice," *Journal of Medieval and Early Modern Studies* 41, no. 3 (Fall 2011): 577–99; and E. Natalie Rothman, "Conversion and Convergence in the Venetian-Ottoman Borderlands," *Journal of Medieval and Early Modern Studies* 41, no. 3 (Fall 2011): 601–33.

16. On tolerance in the late medieval and early modern period, see Ole Peter Grell and Bob Scribner, eds., *Tolerance and Intolerance in the European Reformation* (Cambridge: Cambridge University Press, 1996); István Bejczy, "*Tolerantia:* A Medieval Concept," *Journal of the History of Ideas* 58, no. 3 (July 1997): 365–84; John Christian Laursen and Cary J. Nederman, eds., *Beyond the Persecuting Society: Religious Toleration Before the Enlightenment* (Philadelphia: University of Pennsylvania Press, 1998); Cary J. Nederman, *Worlds of Difference: European Discourses of Toleration, c. 1100–c. 1550* (University Park, PA: Penn State University Press, 2000); and Hans Oberdiek, *Tolerance: Between Forbearance and Acceptance* (Lanham, MD: Rowman and Littlefield, 2001). See also Dana E. Katz, *The Jew in the Art of the Italian Renaissance* (Philadelphia: University of Pennsylvania Press, 2008).
17. Regarding the house rules for Germans in the Fondaco dei Tedeschi, see David Chambers and Brian Pullan, eds., *Venice: A Documentary History, 1450–1630* (Toronto: University of Toronto Press, 2001), 328–30.
18. John Jeffries Martin, *Venice's Hidden Enemies: Italian Heretics in a Renaissance City* (Baltimore: Johns Hopkins University Press, 2003), esp. 25–29.
19. See Chambers and Pullan, eds., *Venice: A Documentary History*, 350–52.
20. E. Natalie Rothman, *Brokering Empire: Trans-Imperial Subjects between Venice and Istanbul* (Ithaca, NY: Cornell University Press, 2012), 201.
21. Chambers and Pullan, eds., *Venice: A Documentary History*, 352. See also Benjamin Ravid, "From Geographical Realia to Historiographical Symbol: The Odyssey of the Word *Ghetto*," in *Essential Papers on Jewish Culture in Renaissance and Baroque Italy*, ed. David B. Ruderman (New York: New York University Press, 1992), 380–81.
22. Through the use of the term "Mohammedan Nations," the Cinque Savi alla Mercanzia required Muslims of Turkish and Persian descent to move to the Fondaco dei Turchi. In 1662, the Cinque Savi declared, "There is no doubt, that the commission of the House of the Fondaco was decreed by the Most Excellent Senate for no other purpose but to have the Mohammedan Nations required to live there separately from Christians, as required by public and private utility and the benefit of Religion, as was considered." See Rothman, *Brokering Empire*, 207.
23. As Stefanie Siegmund argues in the context of the Florentine ghetto of 1571, "ghettoization produced – and seems to have been intended to produce – a semi-autonomous community of families in permanent, self-perpetuating residence in a spatially designated location." Stefanie B. Siegmund, *The Medici State and the Ghetto of Florence: The Construction of an Early Modern Jewish Community* (Stanford, CA: Stanford University Press, 2006), 12.

24. On the structural hermeticism of the Venice ghetto, Sanudo writes on March 26, 1516, "Havendo in questi zorni proposto sier Zacaria Dolfin savio dil Consejo in Colegio che li zudei stano mal in la terra, sicome li predicatori predicano le perversità dil Stado vien da questo, e per le sinagoge fano contra la forma di le leze, però è di opinion di mandarli tutti a star in Geto nuovo, ch'è come un castello, e far ponti levadori et serar di muro; habino solo una porta, la qual *etiam* la serano e stagino lì." Marino Sanuto, *I diarii di Marino Sanuto: Dall'autografo Marciano ital. cl. VII codd. CDXIX-CDLXXVII*, ed. Federico Stefani, Nicolò Barozzi, and Guglielmo Berchet, vol. 22 (Venice: Fratelli Visentini, 1888), 72. See also Marin Sanudo, *Venice, Città Excelentissima: Selections from the Renaissance Diaries of Marin Sanudo*, ed. Patricia H. Labalme and Laura Sanguineti White, trans. Linda L. Carroll (Baltimore: Johns Hopkins University Press, 2008), 338.
25. ASVe, Senato, Terra, registro 19, fols. 78r–79r, March 29, 1516. See also Chambers and Pullan, eds., *Venice: A Documentary History*, 339.
26. Ania Loomba, *Shakespeare, Race, and Colonialism* (Oxford: Oxford University Press, 2002), 18.
27. Stuart Hall, "Cultural Identity and Diaspora," in *Identity: Community, Culture, Difference*, ed. Jonathan Rutherford (London: Lawrence & Wishart, 1990), 222. See also Henri Lefebvre, *The Production of Space*, trans. Donald Nicholson-Smith (Oxford: Blackwell, 1991).
28. Benjamin Ravid, "New Light on the Ghetti of Venice," in *Shlomo Simonsohn Jubilee Volume: Studies on the History of the Jews in the Middle Ages and Renaissance Period*, ed. Daniel Carpi et al. (Tel Aviv: Tel Aviv University, 1993), esp. 155–58; and Benjamin Ravid, "Curfew Time in the Ghetto of Venice," in *Medieval and Renaissance Venice*, ed. Ellen E. Kittell and Thomas F. Madden (Urbana: University of Illinois Press, 1999), 257–59. See also Carla Boccato, "Processi ad ebrei nell'archivio degli ufficiali al Cattaver a Venezia," *La rassegna mensile di Israel*, terza serie, 41, no. 3 (March 1975): 166–68.
29. ASVe, Inquisitorato alle Arti, busta 102, fascicolo "Casi tra li Cattaveri con li Cinque Savii sopra le case delli Hebrei," August 3, 1560. See also Ravid, "New Light on the Ghetti of Venice," 155–58; and Ravid, "Curfew Time in the Ghetto of Venice," 257–59.
30. Rothman, *Brokering Empire*, 201.
31. For a history of the geography of vision in early modern Europe, see Renzo Dubbini, *Geography of the Gaze: Urban and Rural Vision in Early Modern Europe*, trans. Lydia G. Cochrane (Chicago: University of Chicago Press, 2002).
32. Beatriz Colomina, "The Split Wall: Domestic Voyeurism," in *Sexuality & Space*, ed. Beatriz Colomina (New York: Princeton Architectural Press, 1992), 83.
33. Colomina, "The Split Wall: Domestic Voyeurism," in *Sexuality & Space*, 82.
34. Laura Gowing, *Domestic Dangers: Women, Words, and Sex in Early Modern London* (Oxford: Clarendon Press, 1996), 97. See also Elizabeth S. Cohen, "Honor and Gender in the Streets of Early Modern Rome," *Journal of Interdisciplinary History* 22, no. 4 (Spring 1992): 597–625.
35. San Juan, *Rome: A City Out of Print*, 34.
36. San Juan, *Rome: A City Out of Print*, 23–55.
37. Leon Battista Alberti's *Della famiglia* (1430s–1440s) clearly states that the balance of power for the family unit was held exclusively by the *pater familias*. Leon

Battista Alberti, *I primi tre libri della famiglia*, ed. Francesco Carlo Pellegrini (Florence: Sansoni, 1946). On Jacob Cats, see, for example, Heidi de Mare, "The Domestic Boundary as Ritual Area in Seventeenth-Century Holland," in *Urban Rituals in Italy and the Netherlands: Historical Contrasts in the Use of Public Space, Architecture, and the Urban Environment*, ed. Heidi de Mare and Anna Vos (Assen: Van Gorcum, 1993), 109–31. Humanist texts and city statutes may have placed women in the home; however, historical evidence demonstrates how women (patrician and peasant, urban and rural) did indeed access the world outside the domestic interior (see Chapter 4). See also, for example, Adrian W. B. Randolph, *Touching Objects: Intimate Experiences of Italian Fifteenth-Century Art* (New Haven, CT: Yale University Press, 2014), esp. 89–90.

38. Alberti allies architecture with the sexuality of its inhabitants. To protect a woman's honor and her husband's bloodline from the dangers that come from contact with the outside world, Alberti instructs women to move away from windows into the most private spaces of their home. There, they should be industrious and see to the affairs of the home. In *Della famiglia*, Alberti cautions women not to "spend all day sitting idly with your elbows on the window sill, like some lazy wives who always hold their sewing in their hands for an excuse, but their sewing never gets done." Leon Battista Alberti, *I libri della famiglia* (*The Family in Renaissance Florence*), trans. Renée Neu Watkins (Columbia: University of South Carolina Press, 1969), 222. "Et per bene potere questo, a te, conviene non tutto il dì sedendo starti otiosa colle gomita in su la finestra, quale fanno alcune mone lentose, quali per suo scusa tengono il cucito in mano che mai viene meno." Alberti, *I primi tre libri della famiglia*, 372. See also Jane Tylus, "Women at the Windows: 'Commedia dell'arte' and Theatrical Practice in Early Modern Italy," *Theatrical Journal* 49, no. 3 (October 1997): 336. Pictorial representation tells another story, as Italian Renaissance portrait painters often situated female patricians near windows. In practice, Renaissance families often positioned their daughters at the window when attempting to attract a future husband. See Patricia Simons, "Women in Frames: The Gaze, the Eye, the Profile in Renaissance Portraiture," *History Workshop: A Journal of Socialist and Feminist Historians* 25 (Spring 1988): 4–30; reprinted in Norma Broude and Mary D. Garrard, eds., *The Expanding Discourse: Feminism and Art History* (New York: Icon Editions, 1992), 38–57; Diane Wolfthal, *Picturing Yiddish: Gender, Identity, and Memory in the Illustrated Yiddish Books of Renaissance Italy* (Leiden: Brill, 2004), 190–96; and Randolph, *Touching Objects*, 69–101.

39. Diane Wolfthal, *In and Out of the Marital Bed: Seeing Sex in Renaissance Europe* (New Haven, CT: Yale University Press, 2010), 75–119. On Renaissance consumption habits, see Evelyn Welch, *Shopping in the Renaissance: Consumer Cultures in Italy, 1400–1600* (New Haven, CT: Yale University Press, 2005).

40. Diane Yvonne Ghirardo, "The Topography of Prostitution in Renaissance Ferrara," *Journal of the Society of Architectural Historians* 60, no. 4 (December 2001): 402.

41. See Dennis Romano, "Gender and the Urban Geography of Renaissance Venice," *Journal of Social History* 23, no. 2 (Winter 1989): 339–53; Edward Muir and Ronald F. E. Weissman, "Social and Symbolic Places in Renaissance Venice and Florence," in *The Power of Place: Bringing Together Geographical and Sociological Imaginations*, ed. John A. Agnew and James S. Duncan (Boston: Unwin Hyman, 1989), 81–103; and Natalie Tomas, "Did Women Have a Space?," in *Renaissance Florence: A Social*

History, ed. Roger J. Crum and John T. Paoletti (New York: Cambridge University Press, 2006), 311–28.

42. In Shakespeare's *The Merchant of Venice*, Jessica, daughter of the Jewish moneylender Shylock, steals away (with her father's riches) under the cover of night disguised as a boy to join her beloved Lorenzo, a Venetian gentile: "Here, catch this casket; it is worth the pains. / I am glad 'tis night, you do not look on me, / For I am much ashamed of my exchange. / But love is blind, and lovers cannot see / The pretty follies that themselves commit; / For if they could, Cupid himself would blush / To see me thus transformèd to a boy." William Shakespeare, *The Merchant of Venice* (II, vi, 33–39).
43. Ghirardo, "The Topography of Prostitution in Renaissance Ferrara," 411.
44. Marilyn Dunn, "Spaces Shaped for Spiritual Perfection: Convent Architecture and Nuns in Early Modern Rome," in *Architecture and the Politics of Gender in Early Modern Europe*, ed. Helen Hills (Aldershot: Ashgate, 2003), 151–76.
45. Enclosure was thought to be necessary to protect the nun from the outside gaze and from her own acts of looking. In the Middle Ages, sight was thought to provide an encouragement to sin. For example, Stephen of Obazine (d. 1158) treated sight in the context of iniquity when writing of the cloistered nuns of Coyroux, "How can one sin . . . when the faculty of vision itself is enclosed?" Jeffrey F. Hamburger, *The Visual and the Visionary: Art and Female Spirituality in Late Medieval Germany* (New York: Zone Books, 1998), 37–38.
46. Helen Hills, *Invisible City: The Architecture of Devotion in Seventeenth-Century Neapolitan Convents* (Oxford: Oxford University Press, 2004); Gianna Pomata and Gabriella Zarri, eds., *I monasteri femminili come centri di cultura fra Rinascimento e Barocco* (Rome: Edizioni di Storia e Letteratura, 2005); Gabriella Zarri, "Venetian Convents and Civic Ritual," in *Arcangela Tarabotti: A Literary Nun in Baroque Venice*, ed. Elissa B. Weaver (Ravenna: Longo, 2006), 37–56; Anne Jacobson Schutte, "The Permeable Cloister?," in *Arcangela Tarabotti: A Literary Nun in Baroque Venice*, ed. Elissa B. Weaver (Ravenna: Longo, 2006), 19–36; and Meredith K. Ray, "Letters and Lace: Arcangela Tarabotti and Convent Culture in *Seicento* Venice," in *Early Modern Women and Transnational Communities of Letters*, ed. Julie D. Campbell and Anne R. Larsen (Farnham: Ashgate, 2009), 45–73.
47. See Schutte, "The Permeable Cloister?," 23–24.
48. Hills, *The Invisible City*, 146–47.
49. Women regularly entered the convent under duress for familial and economic reasons, despite conciliar decrees proscribing forced monachization. Jews similarly entered the ghetto unwillingly, yet in this case with senatorial directives mandating compulsory confinement for all coreligionists. On the enclosure of Jews and monastics in early modern Florence, see Siegmund, *The Medici State and the Ghetto of Florence*, 12–14.
50. Hills, *Invisible City*, 121. In some urban settings, the vertical distinction building engendered required adjustment. As architecture intermingled with the politics of statecraft, tall structures at times were cut short. For instance, by 1200 feudal families in Florence had constructed nearly 200 towers, zoned according to the political allegiances of the prominent Tuscan aristocrats. When the magnate families lost power beginning in 1250, the city passed legislation requiring all towers to be truncated to the maximum height of fifty braccia (approximately twenty-nine

meters). In this Florentine example, the state cut down the ubiquitous towers to symbolize the nobles' political defeat and to mark the skyline with visible signs of the emerging republic. Tim Benton, "The Three Cities Compared: Urbanism," in *Siena, Florence, and Padua: Art, Society, and Religion, 1280–1400*, ed. Diana Norman (New Haven, CT: Yale University Press, 1995), 2:24.

51. Hills, *Invisible City*, 122–23.
52. ASVe, Inquisitorato agli Ebrei, busta 19, October 22, 1603, carta 458r-v. This document also states that a reputable Jewish official would accompany the Christian guard when opening the ghetto in the morning and closing it at night, and each would be furnished with a key that was to be left at the ghetto gates: "Che siano elletti dalli Signori Pressidenti doi guardiani, uno hebreo et uno christiano, di buona fama quali abbino carico di aprire et serare il Ghetto alle hore debite."
53. Regarding the Ghetto Vecchio keys, see also Benjamin Ravid, "The Third Charter of the Jewish Merchants of Venice, 1611: A Case Study in Complex Multifaceted Negotiations," *Jewish Political Studies Review* 6, no. 1/2 (Spring 1994): 83–134. On the key as a symbol of power and control, see Daniel Jütte, *The Strait Gate: Thresholds and Power in Western History* (New Haven, CT: Yale University Press, 2015), esp. 81–133.
54. Ravid, "The Third Charter of the Jewish Merchants of Venice, 1611," 115. On September 25, 1609, the Senate required the Cattaveri to return the guards' keys and to reinstate the ghetto's enforced enclosure so as to prohibit the Jews from leaving the ghetto freely: "sia fatta serrar, et assicurar la clausura del Ghetto Vecchio immediate, et con porte, et con muro, in modo che resti del tutto sicura; et non sia libera per alcun modo agli Hebrei la uscita del Ghetto predetto." ASVe, Senato, Deliberazioni, Terra, filza 192, September 25, 1609. On December 15, 1609, the Senate ruled: "Che la clausura, et custodia delle chiave del Ghetto Vecchio, che è quello dalla parte di Canaregio, continui, et sia commessa al Magistrato dei Cinque Savii, che dal 1541 in quà l'hanno continuamente essercitata." ASVe, Senato, Deliberazioni, Terra, registro 79, carta 146r-v, December 15, 1609; and ASVe, Senato, Deliberazioni, Terra, filza 193, December 15, 1609.
55. Jeremy Bentham, *The Panopticon Writings*, ed. Miran Božovič (London: Verso, 1995); and Michel Foucault, *Discipline and Punish: The Birth of the Prison*, trans. Alan Sheridan (New York: Vintage Books, 1979), esp. 195–228.
56. Hills, *Invisible City*, 145.
57. Hills, *Invisible City*, 137.
58. For Patriarch Lorenzo Priuli and his memorandum on Jews as *nemici domestici*, see ASVe, Senato, Deliberazioni, Terra, filza 141 (m.v.), January 30, 1596. See also Ravid, "Curfew Time in the Ghetto of Venice," 257–59; and Brian Pullan, *Rich and Poor in Renaissance Venice: The Social Institutions of a Catholic State, to 1620* (Cambridge, MA: Harvard University Press, 1971), 557–58.
59. The document specifies, "haver consideratione a quella parte del Ghetto, che risguarda il monasterio delle monache di S. Gironimo perche vi sono alcune finestre che predominano tutto l'horto delle monache, et da quelle gli hebrei parlano et usano atti molti indecenti, onde quelle finestre si dovranno redurle solamente a luce in modo che non habbiano prospetto nel monasterio." ASVe, Senato, Deliberazioni, Terra, filza 141 (m.v.), January 30, 1596.

60. Jutta Gisela Sperling, *Convents and the Body Politic in Late Renaissance Venice* (Chicago: University of Chicago Press, 1999), 158. See also Mary Laven, *Virgins of Venice: Broken Vows and Cloistered Lives in the Renaissance Convent* (New York: Viking, 2003).
61. For other eighteenth-century painted views of Venice's *parlatori*, see Francesco Guardi's *The Parlor of the San Zaccaria Convent* (c. 1746) in Venice's Ca' Rezzonico and Giuseppe de Gobbis's *The Convent Parlor* (c. 1760) at the San Diego Museum of Art.
62. ASVe, Provveditori sopra i Monasteri di Monache, busta 267, fascicolo "Convertide contra Francesco Zachia," September 9, 1625. See also Sperling, *Convents and the Body Politic in Late Renaissance Venice*, 158.
63. "Moisè Coppio hebreo, et hora Christiano d'aparenza, et chiamato Francesco Zachia. . . ." ASVe, Provveditori sopra i Monasteri di Monache, busta 267, fascicolo "Convertide contra Francesco Zachia," September 9, 1625.
64. ASVe, Provveditori sopra i Monasteri di Monache, busta 267, fascicolo "Convertide contra Francesco Zachia," September 9, 1625. Moisè Coppio was the uncle of Sarra Coppio Sulam. Lynn Westwater writes that his confrontations with Christian authorities remained "a constant reminder to the Copio family of the possibility, and the dangers, of conversion." Lynn Lara Westwater, "The Disquieting Voice: Women's Writing and Antifeminism in Seventeenth-Century Venice" (Ph.D. diss., University of Chicago, 2003), 176–77. See also Sarra Copia Sulam, *Jewish Poet and Intellectual in Seventeenth-Century Venice*, ed. and trans. Don Harrán (Chicago: University of Chicago Press, 2009).
65. On the early modern desire to "enclose" female bodies and block women's orifices, see Peter Stallybrass, "Patriarchal Territories: The Body Enclosed," in *Rewriting the Renaissance: The Discourses of Sexual Difference in Early Modern Europe*, ed. Margaret W. Ferguson, Maureen Quilligan, and Nancy J. Vickers (Chicago: University of Chicago Press, 1986), 123–42.
66. Wolfthal, *In and Out of the Marital Bed*, 79. On the Virgin's windows, see also Carla Gottlieb, *The Window in Art: From the Window of God to the Vanity of Man: A Survey of Window Symbolism in Western Painting* (New York: Abaris Books, 1981). On the sexuality of space, see Ghirardo, "The Topography of Prostitution in Renaissance Ferrara," 402–31; and Beatriz Colomina, ed., *Sexuality & Space* (New York: Princeton Architectural Press, 1992).
67. Robert Bonfil, "Change in the Cultural Patterns of a Jewish Society in Crisis: Italian Jewry at the Close of the Sixteenth Century," in *Essential Papers on Jewish Culture in Renaissance and Baroque Italy*, ed. David B. Ruderman (New York: New York University Press, 1992), 410.

Windows as Sites of Visual Disturbance

1. Lisa Lampert, *Gender and Jewish Difference from Paul to Shakespeare* (Philadelphia: University of Pennsylvania Press, 2004), 2.
2. Lampert, *Gender and Jewish Difference from Paul to Shakespeare*, 143. On selected scholarship related to Shakespeare's construction of the Jew, see also Bernard Glassman, *Anti-Semitic Stereotypes without Jews: Images of the Jews in England, 1290–1700* (Detroit, MI: Wayne State University Press, 1975); James Shapiro,

Shakespeare and the Jews (New York: Columbia University Press, 1996); Mary Janell Metzger, "'Now by My Hood, a Gentle and No Jew': Jessica, *The Merchant of Venice*, and the Discourse of Early Modern English Identity," *PMLA* 113, no. 1 (January 1998): 52–63; Ania Loomba, *Shakespeare, Race, and Colonialism* (Oxford: Oxford University Press, 2002); Kenneth Gross, *Shylock Is Shakespeare* (Chicago: University of Chicago Press, 2006); Janet Adelman, *Blood Relations: Christian and Jew in "The Merchant of Venice"* (Chicago: University of Chicago Press, 2008); and Laura Tosi and Shaul Bassi, eds., *Visions of Venice in Shakespeare* (Farnham: Ashgate, 2011).

3. The window evolved as a stage setting within the *commedia dell'arte* tradition that offered the actress a place to negotiate her position within the private and public worlds. According to Jane Tylus, "The theatre of windows introduces female spectatorship onto the stage in such a way as to allow the woman to transform traditional passivity into manipulative action." Jane Tylus, "Women at the Windows: 'Commedia dell'arte' and Theatrical Practice in Early Modern Italy," *Theatre Journal* 49, no. 3 (October 1997): 337.
4. On Shakespeare's windowscape, see, for example, Jill Colaco, "The Window Scenes in 'Romeo and Juliet' and Folk Songs of the Night Visit," *Studies in Philology* 83, no. 2 (Spring 1986): 138–57; and Lena Cowen Orlin, "Women on the Threshold," *Shakespeare Studies* 25 (1997): 50–58. Diane Wolfthal also evokes *Romeo and Juliet* in her study of the window as a space of courtship for both Christians and Jews, writing: "Not only were windows associated generally with the dangers of the outside world, and specifically with female sexuality, but they were also tied to privacy, which was of growing concern at this time." Diane Wolfthal, *Picturing Yiddish: Gender, Identity, and Memory in the Illustrated Yiddish Books of Renaissance Italy* (Leiden: Brill, 2004), 194.
5. Renzo Dubbini writes, "People's gazes crossed, determining a condition of perception that became a cultural, psychological, and moral condition. The window functioned as a space for mediation, diffusion, and exchange." Renzo Dubbini, *Geography of the Gaze: Urban and Rural Vision in Early Modern Europe*, trans. Lydia G. Cochrane (Chicago: University of Chicago Press, 2002), 206.
6. John Ruskin, *The Stones of Venice*, vol. 1: *The Foundations* (London: Smith, Elder and Co., 1858), 174.
7. Although Turks, Africans, and Jews were few in London, theatrical representations of them by Shakespeare, Marlowe, and others are critical to understanding England's relationship with religious, ethnic, and class difference. On England and racial difference, see, for example, Loomba, *Shakespeare, Race, and Colonialism*. On the Venetian eyewitness style and its artists, see Patricia Fortini Brown, *Venetian Narrative Painting in the Age of Carpaccio* (New Haven, CT: Yale University Press, 1988).
8. The word *window* derives from an etymology of "wind" and "eye," suggesting its foundational relationship to ventilation and natural lighting. *Oxford English Dictionary* (Oxford: Oxford University Press, 2000), s.v. "window." See also Ellen Eve Frank, *Literary Architecture: Essays Toward a Tradition: Walter Pater, Gerard Manley Hopkins, Marcel Proust, Henry James* (Berkeley: University of California Press, 1979), 185, 263; Georges Teyssot, "'Water and Gas on All Floors': Notes on the Extraneousness of the Home," *Lotus International* 44 (1984): 90; and Beatriz Colomina, "The Split Wall: Domestic Voyeurism," in *Sexuality & Space*, ed. Beatriz Colomina (New York: Princeton Architectural Press, 1992), 121.

9. Leon Battista Alberti, *On the Art of Building in Ten Books*, trans. Joseph Rykwert, Neil Leach, and Robert Tavernor (Cambridge, MA: MIT Press, 1988), 28. On Alberti and architecture, see Richard Krautheimer, "Alberti and Vitruvius," in *Studies in Early Christian, Medieval, and Renaissance Art* (New York: New York University Press, 1969), 323–32; John Onians, "Alberti and ΦΙΛΑΡΕΤΗ: A Study in Their Sources," *Journal of the Warburg and Courtauld Institutes* 34 (1971): 96–114; Rudolf Wittkower, *Architectural Principles in the Age of Humanism* (New York: W. W. Norton: 1971); Mark Jarzombek, *On Leon Baptista Alberti: His Literary and Aesthetic Theories* (Cambridge, MA: MIT Press, 1989); Vaughan Hart, ed. with Peter Hicks, *Paper Palaces: The Rise of the Renaissance Architectural Treatise* (New Haven, CT: Yale University Press, 1998); Liisa Kanerva, *Defining the Architect in Fifteenth-Century Italy: Exemplary Architects in L. B. Alberti's "De re aedificatoria"* (Helsinki: Suomamalainen Tiedeakatemia, 1998); Anthony Grafton, *Leon Battista Alberti: Master Builder of the Italian Renaissance* (New York: Hill and Wang, 2000); Branko Mitrović, "Aesthetic Formalism in Renaissance Architectural Theory," *Zeitschrift für Kunstgeschichte* 66. Bd., H. 3 (2003): 321–39; and Manfredo Tafuri, *Interpreting the Renaissance: Princes, Cities, Architects*, trans. Daniel Sherer (New Haven, CT: Yale University Press, 2006).
10. Alberti, *On the Art of Building in Ten Books*, 28.
11. Vitruvius, *Vitruvius: Ten Books on Architecture*, ed. Ingrid D. Rowland and Thomas Noble Howe (New York: Cambridge University Press, 1999), 72. On windows and solar energy in the Roman bath, see Edwin Daisley Thatcher, "The Open Rooms of the Terme del Foro at Ostia," *Memoirs of the American Academy in Rome* 24 (1956): 169–264; Fikret Yegül, *Baths and Bathing in Classical Antiquity* (Cambridge, MA: MIT Press, 1992); and James W. Ring, "Windows, Baths, and Solar Energy in the Roman Empire," *American Journal of Archaeology* 100, no. 4 (October 1996): 717–24.
12. Alberti, *On the Art of Building in Ten Books*, 28.
13. Alberti, *On the Art of Building in Ten Books*, 29.
14. Alberti, *On the Art of Building in Ten Books*, 29.
15. Concerning the London Assize of Nuisance, see Diane Shaw, "The Construction of the Private in Medieval London," *Journal of Medieval and Early Modern Studies* 26, no. 3 (Fall 1996): 447–66.
16. Lena Cowen Orlin, *Elizabethan Households: An Anthology* (Seattle: University of Washington Press, 1995), 18. See also Sir John Baker, *Baker and Milsom Sources of English Legal History: Private Law to 1750* (Oxford: Oxford University Press, 2010), 654.
17. Orlin, *Elizabethan Households*, 18; and Baker, *Baker and Milsom Sources of English Legal History*, 655.
18. Laura Gowing, *Domestic Dangers: Women, Words, and Sex in Early Modern London* (Oxford: Clarendon Press, 1996), 97. See also James Grantham Turner, *Libertines and Radicals in Early Modern London: Sexuality, Politics and Literary Culture, 1630–1685* (Cambridge: Cambridge University Press, 2002), 28.
19. For examples of house scorning in the Italian peninsula, which involved throwing excrement, blood, rocks, and ink at house doors and windows, see Elizabeth S. Cohen, "Honor and Gender in the Streets of Early Modern Rome," *Journal of Interdisciplinary History* 22, no. 4 (Spring 1992): 597–625.
20. Dubbini, *Geography of the Gaze*, 192.

21. Nicholas Cooper, *Houses of the Gentry, 1480–1680* (New Haven, CT: Yale University Press, 1999), 129. See also Mark Girouard, *Life in the English Country House: A Social and Architectural History* (New Haven, CT: Yale University Press, 1978).
22. Shaw, "The Construction of the Private in Medieval London," 448.
23. On the idea of community, see Edward Muir, "The Idea of Community in Renaissance Italy," *Renaissance Quarterly* 55, no. 1 (Spring 2002): 1–18; and Edward Muir, "In *Some* Neighbours We Trust: On the Exclusion of Women from the Public in Renaissance Italy," in *Florence and Beyond: Culture, Society and Politics in Renaissance Italy. Essays in Honour of John M. Najemy*, ed. David S. Peterson with Daniel E. Bornstein (Toronto: Centre for Reformation and Renaissance Studies, 2008), 271–89. See also John A. Agnew and James S. Duncan, eds., *The Power of Place: Bringing Together Geographical and Sociological Imaginations* (Boston: Unwin Hyman, 1989); and Alexandra Shepard and Phil Withington, eds., *Communities in Early Modern England: Networks, Place, Rhetoric* (Manchester: Manchester University Press, 2000).
24. Lien Luu, "Natural-Born versus Stranger-Born Subjects: Aliens and Their Status in Elizabethan London," in *Immigrants in Tudor and Early Stuart England*, ed. Nigel Goose and Lien Luu (Brighton: Sussex Academic Press, 2005), 64.
25. Luu, "Natural-Born versus Stranger-Born Subjects," 64.
26. On the Venetian *polis* as a Christian entity, see Guido Ruggiero, "Constructing Civic Morality, Deconstructing the Body: Civic Rituals of Punishment in Renaissance Venice," in *Riti e rituali nelle società medievali*, ed. Jacques Chiffoleau, Lauro Martines, and Agostino Paravicini Bagliani (Spoleto: Centro italiano di studi sull'alto medioevo, 1994), 175–90.
27. ASVe, Inquisitorato alle Arti, busta 102, fascicolo "Casi tra li Cattaveri con li Cinque Savii sopra le case delli Hebrei," July 1541; and ASVe, Inquisitorato agli Ebrei, busta 19, fascicolo "1541," carte 121–22.
28. See Benjamin Arbel, *Trading Nations: Jews and Venetians in the Early Modern Eastern Mediterranean* (Leiden: Brill, 1995); and Joshua Holo, *Byzantine Jewry in the Mediterranean Economy* (Cambridge: Cambridge University Press, 2009).
29. ASVe, Inquisitorato alle Arti, busta 102, fascicolo "Casi tra li Cattaveri con li Cinque Savii sopra le case delli Hebrei," August 3, 1560.
30. On the neighborhood in early modern Venice, see Dennis Romano, *Patricians and Popolani: The Social Foundations of the Venetian Renaissance State* (Baltimore: Johns Hopkins University Press, 1987); Dennis Romano, "Gender and the Urban Geography of Renaissance Venice," *Journal of Social History* 23, no. 2 (Winter 1989): 339–53; Edward Muir and Ronald F. E. Weissman, "Social and Symbolic Places in Renaissance Venice and Florence," in *The Power of Place: Bringing Together Geographical and Sociological Imaginations*, ed. John A. Agnew and James S. Duncan (Boston: Unwin Hyman, 1989), 81–103; and Patricia Fortini Brown, "Not One But Many Separate Cities: Housing Diversity in Sixteenth-Century Venice," in *Home and Homelessness in the Medieval and Renaissance World*, ed. Nicholas Howe (Notre Dame, IN: University of Notre Dame Press, 2004), 13–55; reprinted in *Private Lives in Renaissance Venice: Art, Architecture, and the Family* (New Haven, CT: Yale University Press, 2004), 189–216. See also Mark Girouard, *Cities & People: A Social and Architectural History* (New Haven, CT: Yale University Press, 1985), 100–12.

31. Bronwen Wilson, *The World in Venice: Print, the City, and Early Modern Identity* (Toronto: University of Toronto Press, 2005), 49. See also Juergen Schulz, "Jacopo de' Barbari's View of Venice: Map Making, City Views, and Moralized Geography before the Year 1500," *Art Bulletin* 60, no. 3 (September 1978): 425–74; Lucia Nuti, "The Perspective Plan in the Sixteenth Century: The Invention of a Representational Language," *Art Bulletin* 76, no. 1 (March 1994): 105–28; and Richard Kagan, *Urban Images of the Hispanic World, 1493–1793* (New Haven, CT: Yale University Press, 2000), 22–24.
32. See Marino Sanuto, *I diarii di Marino Sanuto: Dall'autografo Marciano ital. cl. VII codd. CDXIX-CDLXXVII*, ed. Federico Stefani, Nicolò Barozzi, and Guglielmo Berchet, vol. 22 (Venice: Fratelli Visentini, 1888), 72–73; and Marin Sanudo, *Venice, Cità Excelentissima: Selections from the Renaissance Diaries of Marin Sanudo*, ed. Patricia H. Labalme and Laura Sanguineti White, trans. Linda L. Carroll (Baltimore: Johns Hopkins University Press, 2008), 338–39. The Venetian government ultimately eliminated the boat patrol; nevertheless, Christian surveillance remained a permanent feature of ghetto life. See Benjamin Ravid, "The Venetian Government and the Jews," in *The Jews of Early Modern Venice*, ed. Robert C. Davis and Benjamin Ravid (Baltimore: Johns Hopkins University Press, 2001), 10.
33. Shaw, "The Construction of the Private in Medieval London," 447–66.
34. Regarding Venice and the senses, see Jo Wheeler, "Stench in Sixteenth-Century Venice," in *The City and the Senses: Urban Culture Since 1500*, ed. Alexander Cowan and Jill Steward (Aldershot: Ashgate, 2007), 25–38; and Alexander Cowan, "'Not Carrying Out the Vile and Mechanical Arts': Touch as a Measure of Social Distinction in Early Modern Venice," in *The City and the Senses: Urban Culture Since 1500*, ed. Alexander Cowan and Jill Steward (Aldershot: Ashgate, 2007), 39–59. On the social significance of the Florentine soundscape, see Niall Atkinson, *The Noisy Renaissance: Sound, Architecture, and Florentine Urban Life* (University Park, PA: Penn State University Press, 2016).
35. On the relative otherness of Jews and Turks, see Benjamin Ravid, "How 'Other' Really Was the Jewish Other? The Evidence from Venice," in *Acculturation and Its Discontents: The Italian Jewish Experience between Exclusion and Inclusion*, ed. David N. Myers, Massimo Ciavolella, Peter H. Reill, and Geoffrey Symcox (Toronto: University of Toronto Press, 2008), 19–55.
36. Concerning the architecture of the Fondaco dei Turchi, see ASVe, Cinque Savi alla Mercanzia, nuova serie, busta 187, fascicolo 1, May 27, 1621, and copied in ASVe, Cinque Savi alla Mercanzia, nuova serie, busta 187, fascicolo 2, May 27, 1621. See also David Chambers and Brian Pullan, eds., *Venice: A Documentary History, 1450–1630* (Toronto: University of Toronto Press, 2001), 350–52; Deborah Howard, *The Architectural History of Venice* (New Haven, CT: Yale University Press, 2002), 32–34; and Juergen Schulz, *The New Palaces of Medieval Venice* (University Park, PA: Penn State University Press, 2004), 133–63.
37. ASVe, Cinque Savi alla Mercanzia, nuova serie, busta 187, fascicolo 1, May 27, 1621; and Chambers and Pullan, eds., *Venice: A Documentary History*, 350. Venetian administrators [Visdomini] also regulated windows in the Fondaco dei Tedeschi, the warehouse and living quarters for German merchants. Documents from 1366 specify

"che tute le fenestre de le camere del fontego di Todeschi debia esser ferade et alte da le travadure e per oviar molte malicie, le qual per essi se poria cometter e molti Todeschi sia stadi prosumtuoxi, che li a fate molto fenestre averte e bassa senza ferro e senza parola de li visdomini che porave tornar in grandissimo danno del comun: vada la parte che tute le fenestre fate per questo modo debia esser stropade e serade como da prima e che damo avanti non se debia far alguna fenestra in questo modo senza licentia de la signoria in pena de libre xxv." Georg Martin Thomas, *Capitolare dei visdomini del fontego dei todeschi in Venezia / Capitular des deutschen Hauses in Venedig: zum erstenmal bekannt gegeben* (Berlin: A. Asher & Co., 1874), 69–70. As discussed in Chapter 4, the closure of the German merchants' windows served to protect the mercantile economy by architecturally preventing Germans from smuggling wares out of their windows at night.

38. ASVe, Cinque Savi alla Mercanzia, nuova serie, busta 187, fascicolo 1, May 27, 1621; and Chambers and Pullan, eds., *Venice: A Documentary History*, 351.
39. Romano, "Gender and the Urban Geography of Renaissance Venice," 346.
40. ASVe, Compilazione delle Leggi, busta 188, fascicolo 2, fol. 752r–v, January 15, 1619.
41. ASVe, Compilazione delle Leggi, busta 188, fascicolo 2, fol. 752r–v, January 15, 1619.
42. ASVe, Ufficiali al Cattaver, busta 243, registro 3, fol. 97r, April 27, 1588.
43. ASVe, Compilazione delle Leggi, busta 188, fascicolo 2, fols. 726r–727v, November 26, 1614 and December 16, 1614.
44. Sanuto, *I diarii di Marino Sanuto: Dall'autografo Marciano ital. cl. VII codd. CDXIX-CDLXXVII*, vol. 22 (Venice: Fratelli Visentini, 1888), 392. See also Sanudo, *Venice, Cità Excelentissima*, 340–41; and Benjamin Ravid, "Curfew Time in the Ghetto of Venice," in *Medieval and Renaissance Venice*, ed. Ellen E. Kittell and Thomas F. Madden (Urbana: University of Illinois Press, 1999), 244.
45. On Jews and their *altane*, see Carla Boccato, "Licenze per altane concesse ad ebrei del Ghetto di Venezia (sec. XVI-XVII-XVIII)," *La rassegna mensile di Israel, terza serie*, 46, nos. 3–4 (March-April 1980): 106–16.
46. ASVe, Inquisitorato alle Arti, busta 102, fascicolo "Casi tra li Cattaveri con li Cinque Savii sopra le case delli Hebrei," March 28, 1587.
47. ASVe, Inquisitorato alle Arti, busta 102, fascicolo "Casi tra li Cattaveri con li Cinque Savii sopra le case delli Hebrei," December 1604.
48. ASVe, Ufficiali al Cattaver, busta 242, registro 2, "Libro grande dell'Università degli ebrei."
49. David Joshua Malkiel, *A Separate Republic: The Mechanics and Dynamics of Venetian Jewish Self-Government, 1607–1624* (Jerusalem: Magnes Press, Hebrew University, 1991), 154–55. See also Ravid, "Curfew Time in the Ghetto of Venice," 274, no. 126.
50. "Essendo stato fatto comandamento per parte di Signori Cattaveri di fabricar li balconi bassi, che son dalla parte del canale, tanto in Ghetto Novo quanto in Ghetto Vechio, overo metter le feriate, et essendo cosa impossible di farlo per causa della sanità delli habitanti in quelli lochi." ASVe, Ufficiali al Cattaver, busta 242, registro 2, fols. 169v-170r. See also Malkiel, *Separate Republic*, 155, 514.
51. Ravid, "Curfew Time in the Ghetto of Venice," 239.
52. Hubert Damisch, *Skyline: The Narcissistic City* (Stanford, CA: Stanford University Press, 2001), 14.

53. See Elizabeth Grosz, *Architecture from the Outside: Essays on Virtual and Real Space* (Cambridge, MA: MIT Press, 2001), 65.
54. For Patriarch Lorenzo Priuli and his memorandum on Jews, see ASVe, Senato, Deliberazioni, Terra, filza 141 (m.v.), January 30, 1596. See also Ravid, "Curfew Time in the Ghetto of Venice," 257–59; and Brian Pullan, *Rich and Poor in Renaissance Venice: The Social Institutions of a Catholic State, to 1620* (Cambridge, MA: Harvard University Press, 1971), 557–58.
55. ASVe, Senato, Terra, filza 276, April 20 and April 23, 1625.
56. Sanuto, *I diarii di Marino Sanuto: Dall'autografo Marciano ital. cl. VII codd. CDXIX-CDLXXVII*, vol. 20 (Venice: Fratelli Visentini, 1887), 98; and Sanudo, *Venice, Città Excelentissima*, 337.
57. Ruggiero, "Constructing Civic Morality, Deconstructing the Body," 182. See also Miri Rubin, *Gentile Tales: The Narrative Assault on Late Medieval Jews* (New Haven, CT: Yale University Press, 1999); and Kenneth Stow, *Jewish Dogs: An Image and Its Interpreters, Continuity in the Catholic-Jewish Encounter* (Stanford, CA: Stanford University Press, 2006), 133–57.
58. Amnon Linder, *The Jews in the Legal Sources of the Early Middle Ages* (Detroit, MI: Wayne State University Press, 1997), 471. For a twelfth-century papal edict requiring Jews to close their windows, see Shlomo Simonsohn, *The Apostolic See and the Jews: Documents, 492–1404* (Toronto: Pontifical Institute of Mediaeval Studies, 1988), 50.
59. According to Camille, "The Host can be described as the single most important image to Christians from the middle of the thirteenth century onward, perhaps even overtaking veneration of the cross." Michael Camille, *The Gothic Idol: Ideology and Image-Making in Medieval Art* (Cambridge: Cambridge University Press, 1989), 215. See also Miri Rubin, *Corpus Christi: The Eucharist in Late Medieval Culture* (Cambridge: Cambridge University Press, 1991).
60. The proclamations (*gride*) state: "Per observatione de li ordeni et bone consuetudine introducte in questa nostra citade per li nostri Illustrissimi Signori progenitori circa il stare serato de li hebrei quali volendoli immitare in honore de la passione de christo lo Illustrissimo Signor nostro Marchese de Mantua etc. fa fare publica crida et commandomento che tutti li hebrei habitante in questa sua citade et dominio debbano stare chiusi et serati in casa tutta la septimana sancta." Archivio di Stato di Mantova, Archivio Gonzaga, busta 2038–39, fascicolo 9, fol. 5, March 17, 1497. *Gride* restricting the Jews during Holy Week are repeated throughout busta 2038–39. See Dana E. Katz, *The Jew in the Art of the Italian Renaissance* (Philadelphia: University of Pennsylvania Press, 2008), 40–68.
61. "Siano tenuti essi hebrei star in casa la Zobia Santa fino il Sabato Santo da una campana all'altra secondo li consueto, et li Rettori de i luoghi siano tenuti à far far le cride che non siano molestati sotto le pene consuete." For example, see ASVe, Compilazione delle Leggi, busta 188, fascicolo 2, fol. 422r, April 2, 1566. See also Giovanni Battista Gallicciolli, *Delle memorie venete antiche, profane ed ecclesiastiche* (Venice: Domenico Fracasso, 1795) 2:313–314, section 955. This stipulation was repeated regularly in the Jews' charters of sojourn.
62. See ASVe, Senato, Deliberazioni, Terra, filza 141 (m.v.), January 30, 1596.
63. Rubin, *Gentile Tales*.
64. Stow, *Jewish Dogs*, 149.
65. Stow, *Jewish Dogs*, 150.

66. Stow, *Jewish Dogs*, 150.
67. Ariel Toaff, *Love, Work, and Death: Jewish Life in Medieval Umbria*, trans. Judith Landry (London: Littman Library of Jewish Civilization, 1996), 181. On the seasonal stoning of Jews' homes, see also Cecil Roth, "The Eastertide Stoning of the Jews and Its Liturgical Echoes," *Jewish Quarterly Review*, New Series, 35, no. 4 (April 1945): 361–70.
68. See Rosemary Radford Ruether, "The *Adversus Judaeos* Tradition in the Church Fathers: The Exegesis of Christian Anti-Judaism," in *Essential Papers on Judaism and Christianity in Conflict: From Late Antiquity to the Reformation*, ed. Jeremy Cohen (New York: New York University Press, 1991), 174–89. On Christian sight and Jewish blindness, see Sara Lipton, "'The Sweet Lean of His Head': Writing about Looking at the Crucifix in the High Middle Ages," *Speculum* 80, no. 4 (October 2005): esp. 1179–82; and Sara Lipton, *Dark Mirror: The Medieval Origins of Anti-Jewish Iconography* (New York: Metropolitan Books, 2014).
69. On the ritualized violence of Holy Week, see, for example, David Nirenberg, *Communities of Violence: Persecution of Minorities in the Middle Ages* (Princeton, NJ: Princeton University Press, 1996), esp. 200–30.

Walls as Boundaries of the Night

1. Walter Benjamin, *Illuminations*, ed. Hannah Arendt, trans. Harry Zohn (New York: Schocken Books, 1968), 240.
2. Katherine Fischer Taylor, "Architecture's Place in Art History: Art or Adjunct?," *Art Bulletin* 83, no. 2 (June 2001): 342.
3. Elizabeth D. Harvey, ed., *Sensible Flesh: On Touch in Early Modern Culture* (Philadelphia: University of Pennsylvania Press, 2003), 2. See also Sander Gilman, *Inscribing the Other* (Lincoln: University of Nebraska Press, 1991), 29–49.
4. Georg Simmel, "Brücke und Tür," *Das Individuum und die Freiheit. Essais* (Berlin: Klaus Wagenbach, 1984), 7–11; and Georg Simmel, "Bridge and Door," in *Rethinking Architecture: A Reader in Cultural Theory*, ed. Neil Leach (New York: Routledge, 1997), 66–69.
5. W. J. T. Mitchell, "Christo's *Gates* and Gilo's Wall," *Critical Inquiry* 32, no. 4 (Summer 2006): 587.
6. ASVe, Consiglio di Dieci, Deliberazioni miste, registro 14 (1450–1454), fol. 18r, December 16, 1450. See also Elisabeth Pavan, "Recherches sur la nuit vénitienne à la fin du Moyen Âge," *Journal of Medieval History* 7, no. 4 (December 1981): 346.
7. On the evening after Christmas, the doge visited the island of San Giorgio Maggiore. After crossing the lagoon on a bridge of boats, he, accompanied by members of government, entered the Church of San Giorgio Maggiore to venerate the relic of Saint Stephen. In 1829, Giustina Renier Michiel, niece to the penultimate doge of Venice, observed how the lights of the nocturnal ceremony produced a magical effect: "Veniva egli preceduto da certe barche co' lumi, appositamente dal Governo destinate, e seguito da innumerabili barchette di ogni maniera, fornite anch'esse di fanali, che tutte insieme coprivano lo spazio che avvi fra S. Marco e l'Isola di S. Giorgio Maggiore. Illuminavano questo spazio a dritta e a manca certi fuochi piantati sull'acqua, chiamati *ludri*, composti di corda bene impeciata, che

mandavano anche da lungi un vivacissimo splendore, il quale riflettuto nell'acqua produceva un effetto magico." Giustina Renier Michiel, *Origine delle feste veneziane* (Milan: Annali universali delle scienze e dell'industria, 1829), II:33–34. In 1659, Englishman Francis Mortoft wrote a travelogue entry describing the night of Good Friday, "About 8 a clocke at night was about 4 or 500 candles set on the windowes in the Place, which gave such a light that it seemd as if the place were on fire, when these Torches were lighted came multitudes of People in procession in the same manner as the former. It is a wonder to thinke what a multitude of torches were lighted this night, there being People in procession in all quarters of the Citty." Francis Mortoft, *Francis Mortoft: His Book, Being His Travels Through France and Italy, 1658–1659*, ed. Malcolm Letts (London: Hakluyt Society, 1925), 183. See also Åsa Boholm, *Venetian Worlds: Nobility and the Cultural Construction of Society* (Gothenburg: Institute for Advanced Studies in Social Anthropology, 1993), 90. On Venetian feast culture, see Giuseppe Tassini, *Feste, spettacoli, divertimenti, e piaceri degli antichi veneziani* (Venice: Filippi, 1961); Bianca Tamassia Mazzarotto, *Le feste veneziane: I giochi popolari, le cerimonie religiose e di governo* (Florence: Sansoni, 1980); Edward Muir, *Civic Ritual in Renaissance Venice* (Princeton, NJ: Princeton University Press, 1981); and Susanne Tichy, *Et vene la mumaria: Studien zur venezianischen Festkultur der Renaissance* (Munich: Scaneg, 1997).

8. The Feast of the Redeemer began in Venice in 1577 to mark the end of the plague, with subsequent celebrations scheduled annually on the third Sunday of July. In 1576, the Senate pledged to erect a votive church dedicated to Christ the Redeemer, commissioning Andrea Palladio in 1577 to execute the work on the island of the Giudecca. Patriarch Giovanni Trevisan laid the cornerstone of the church on May 3, 1577, and the church was completed in 1592. See Francesco Basaldella, *La festa del Redentore: Storica festa nazionale veneziana* (Venice: Quaderni di cultura giudecchina, 2000); Deborah Howard, "Venice between East and West: Marc'Antonio Barbaro and Palladio's Church of the Redentore," *Journal of the Society of Architectural Historians* 62, no. 3 (September 2003): 306–25; Tracy Elizabeth Cooper, *Palladio's Venice: Architecture and Society in a Renaissance Republic* (New Haven, CT: Yale University Press, 2005), 228–57; and Deborah Howard and Laura Moretti, *Sound and Space in Renaissance Venice: Architecture, Music, Acoustics* (New Haven, CT: Yale University Press, 2009), 114–28.
9. W. Carew Hazlitt, *The Venetian Republic: Its Rise, Its Growth, and Its Fall, 421–1797* (London: A. and C. Black, 1900), 2:737.
10. Julia Mary Cartwright Ady, *Beatrice d'Este, Duchess of Milan, 1475–1497: A Study of the Renaissance* (London: J. M. Dent, 1903), 201.
11. Cartwright Ady, *Beatrice d'Este*, 201. See also Tichy, *Et vene la mumaria*, 45–62; and Paul Hills, "Titian's Fire: Pyrotechnics and Representations in Sixteenth-Century Venice," *Oxford Art Journal* 30, no. 2 (2007), esp. 12.
12. ASVe, Senato, Terra, registro 19, fols. 78r–79r, March 29, 1516. See also David Chambers and Brian Pullan, eds., *Venice: A Documentary History, 1450–1630* (Toronto: University of Toronto Press, 2001), 338–39.
13. A. Roger Ekirch, *At Day's Close: Night in Times Past* (New York: W. W. Norton, 2005), 8.
14. The Senate adjusted the Jews' curfew to accommodate the change in season. Benjamin Ravid explains, "Already in December 1516, some nine months after

the establishment of the Ghetto Nuovo, at the request of the Jews the Senate extended the time of closing slightly, from sunset until the first hour of the night in summer and the second hour of the night in winter (presumably a necessary extra concession since it became darker considerably earlier in winter), and these provisions were subsequently extended very slightly by administrative rulings." Benjamin Ravid, "Curfew Time in the Ghetto of Venice," in *Medieval and Renaissance Venice*, ed. Ellen E. Kittell and Thomas F. Madden (Urbana: University of Illinois Press, 1999), 241; reprinted in *Studies on the Jews of Venice, 1382–1797* (Aldershot: Ashgate, 2003).

15. On night in the medieval and early modern periods, see Jean Verdon, *La nuit au Moyen Âge* (Paris: Perrin, 1994); Jean Verdon, "Recherches sur la société religieuse et la nuit au Moyen Âge," in *Les prélats, l'Église et la société, XIe-XVe siècles: Hommage à Bernard Guillemain*, ed. Françoise Bériac (Bordeaux: Université Michel de Montaigne, 1994), 327–36; Bryan D. Palmer, *Cultures of Darkness: Night Travels in the Histories of Transgression* (New York: Monthly Review Press, 2000); Ekirch, *At Day's Close*; and Craig Koslofsky, *Evening's Empire: A History of the Night in Early Modern Europe* (Cambridge: Cambridge University Press, 2011). See also Wolfgang Schivelbusch, *Disenchanted Night: The Industrialization of Life in the Nineteenth Century* (Berkeley: University of California Press, 1988).
16. On the presence of Jews in Uccello's Corpus Domini predella, see Marilyn Aronberg Lavin, "The Altar of Corpus Domini in Urbino: Paolo Uccello, Joos Van Ghent, Piero della Francesca," *Art Bulletin* 49, no. 1 (March 1967): 1–24; Catherine Gallagher and Stephen Greenblatt, *Practicing New Historicism* (Chicago: University of Chicago Press, 2000), 75–109; and Dana E. Katz, *The Jew in the Art of the Italian Renaissance* (Philadelphia: University of Pennsylvania Press, 2008), 16–39.
17. Regarding the alleged ritual murder of Simon of Trent, see R. Po-chia Hsia, *The Myth of Ritual Murder: Jews and Magic in Reformation Germany* (New Haven, CT: Yale University Press, 1988); Anna Esposito and Diego Quaglioni, *Processi contro gli ebrei di Trento (1475–1478): I processi del 1475* (Padua: CEDAM, 1990); Iginio Rogger and Marco Bellabarba, eds., *Il principe vescovo Johannes Hinderbach (1465–1486) fra tardo Medioevo e Umanesimo* (Bologna: Edizioni Dehoniane, 1992); R. Po-chia Hsia, *Trent 1475: Stories of a Ritual Murder Trial* (New Haven, CT: Yale University Press, 1992); Wolfgang Treue, *Der Trienter Judenprozeß: Voraussetzungen, Abläufe, Auswirkungen, 1475–1588* (Hannover: Hahnsche Buchhandlung, 1996); Gianni Gentilini, *Pasqua 1475: Antigiudaismo e lotta alle eresie, il caso di Simonino* (Milan: Medusa, 2007); and Katz, *The Jew in the Art of the Italian Renaissance*, 119–57.
18. Bereshit – Genesis 1:5.
19. Elliott Horowitz, "Coffee, Coffeehouses, and the Nocturnal Rituals of Early Modern Jewry," *AJS Review* 14, no. 1 (Spring 1989): 17–46. In his analysis of Jewish confraternities in the ghetto of early modern Rome, Kenneth Stow notes, "Through the introduction of coffee in their gatherings, with caffeine's well-known effects, these confraternities managed to shift the hour of often mystical and spiritually unfettered devotions from morning to night. Night, the time of enforced enclosure in the Ghetto, was being turned into a time of liberation. Thus the enclosure in the Ghetto became a liberating space." Kenneth R. Stow, *Theater of Acculturation: The Roman Ghetto in the Sixteenth Century* (Seattle: University of Washington Press, 2001), 105.

20. Moses Maimonides, *Hilchot de'ot: The Laws of Personality Development; and, Hilchot Talmud Torah: The Laws of Torah Study* (New York: Moznaim, 1989), 206–07. See also Raymond L. Weiss, *Maimonides' Ethics: The Encounter of Philosophic and Religious Morality* (Chicago: University of Chicago Press, 1991), 118.
21. Maimonides, *Hilchot de'ot and Hilchot Talmud*, 206–07.
22. Elliott Horowitz, "The Eve of the Circumcision: A Chapter in the History of Jewish Nightlife," *Journal of Social History* 23, no. 1 (Autumn 1989): 45–69.
23. Horowitz, "The Eve of the Circumcision," 58.
24. Regarding the Signori di Notte, see Hazlitt, *The Venetian Republic*, 516–18; Guido Ruggiero, "The Cooperation of Physicians and the State in the Control of Violence in Renaissance Venice," *Journal of the History of Medicine and Allied Sciences* 33, no. 2 (April 1978): 156–66; Guido Ruggiero, *Violence in Early Renaissance Venice* (New Brunswick, NJ: Rutgers University Press, 1980), 27–29; Pavan, "Recherches sur la nuit venitienne à la fin du Moyen Âge," 339–56; Guido Ruggiero, *The Boundaries of Eros: Sex Crime and Sexuality in Renaissance Venice* (New York: Oxford University Press, 1985), 40; Michael Rocke, *Forbidden Friendships: Homosexuality and Male Culture in Renaissance Florence* (New York: Oxford University Press, 1996), esp. chapter 2; Stanley Chojnacki, *Women and Men in Renaissance Venice: Twelve Essays on Patrician Society* (Baltimore: Johns Hopkins University Press, 2000), 35; Louis Crompton, *Homosexuality & Civilization* (Cambridge, MA: Belknap Press of Harvard University Press, 2003), 247–49; and Alan M. Stahl, "Coin and Punishment in Medieval Venice," in *Law and the Illicit in Medieval Europe*, ed. Ruth Mazo Karras, Joel Kaye, and E. Ann Matter (Philadelphia: University of Pennsylvania Press, 2008), 164–79.
25. See ASVe, Signori di Notte al Civil and Signori di Notte al Criminal.
26. For example, ASVe, Signori di Notte al Criminal, busta 13, July 1653, fascicolo "SS.ri de Notte al Criminal contro Capi dell'arte dei Strazzaroli degli'Ebrei"; and August 19, 1766, fascicolo "Indolenza di Donna Nicoletta Grillo Libo Duchessa di Massa e Carrara contro Maria Tedesca e Isach Coen."
27. Palmer, *Cultures of Darkness*, 17–18.
28. Leon Modena, *The Autobiography of a Seventeenth-Century Venetian Rabbi: Leon Modena's Life of Judah*, ed. Mark R. Cohen (Princeton, NJ: Princeton University Press, 1988), 5–6.
29. For a description of the event involving Hercule Turco and the Jews of Mantua, see Archivio di Stato di Mantova, Archivio Gonzaga (AG), busta 2440, fol. 638, September 17, 1491; AG, busta 2440, fol. 561, September 18, 1491; and AG, busta 2904, libro 139, fol. 69, September 30, 1491. On Hercule (Ercole) Turco, see also David Chambers and Trevor Dean, *Clean Hands and Rough Justice: An Investigating Magistrate in Renaissance Italy* (Ann Arbor: University of Michigan Press, 1997), 236–38.
30. On the Jews of early modern Mantua, see Shlomo Simonsohn, *History of the Jews in the Duchy of Mantua* (Jerusalem: Kiryath Sepher, 1977); Katz, *The Jew in the Art of the Italian Renaissance*, 40–68; and Luigi Carnevali, *Il ghetto di Mantova* (Bologna: Arnaldo Forni, 2009). In early seventeenth-century Modena, an eyewitness claimed that local Jews had blasphemed Christ in order to replicate an alleged Mantuan abuse. Barbara Rubbiano accused Modenese Jews of recreating the Passion of Christ in their homes while uttering loudly: "hang the man," "hit the man," "the man is

dead," "kill the man." The terrors of the night contributed to this tale, as the Jews purportedly committed this Eastertide act of blasphemy on the night of Holy Thursday. See Kenneth R. Stow, *Jewish Dogs: An Image and Its Interpreters, Continuity in the Catholic-Jewish Encounter* (Stanford, CA: Stanford University Press, 2006), 68; and Katherine Aron-Beller, *Jews on Trial: The Papal Inquisition in Modena, 1598–1638* (Manchester: Manchester University Press, 2011), 191–218.

31. See Katz, *The Jew in the Art of the Italian Renaissance.*
32. The first inventions in street lighting came in the seventeenth century with the use of candles and oil lamps that were housed in glass lanterns. European cities, however, did not consistently illuminate their streets until 1700 when Amsterdam, Paris, Turin, London, and Copenhagen, as well as cities throughout the Holy Roman Empire, brought more reliable techniques to the urban night. Koslofsky, *Evening's Empire*, 1–18.
33. Koslofsky, *Evening's Empire*, 133.
34. See Thomas V. Cohen, "The Case of the Mysterious Coil of Rope: Street Life and Jewish Persona in Rome in the Middle of the Sixteenth Century," *Sixteenth Century Journal* 19, no. 2 (Summer 1988): 211.
35. Chambers and Pullan, eds., *Venice: A Documentary History*, 339.
36. ASVe, Collegio Notatorio, registro 24, fols. 176v-177v, July 20, 1541: "Che alla bocca del campedello del Ghetto vecchio dalla banda di Canareglio, che discorre verso il rio, dove è il pozzo, sia tirato uno muro di conveniente altezza, che si congionga con i muri a parte destra, et sinistra, nel qual muro sia fatta una porta per l'entrar, et uscir, il qual muro continovar etiam debba fino a i confini di detto Ghetto per traverso recto tramite talche detta parte, si a banda destra, come sinistra sia serrata con muro, ne li sia altro esito verso la banda di Canareglio, salvo la porta, ut supra dechiarita"; and ASVe, Inquisitorato alle Arti, busta 102, fascicolo "Casi tra li Cattaveri con li Cinque Savii sopra le case delli Hebrei," fols. 12r–15v. See also Giovanni Battista Gallicciolli, *Delle memorie venete antiche, profane ed ecclesiastiche* (Venice: Domenico Fracasso, 1795) 2:309–310, section 946. For a full transcription of the archival document, see Benjamin Ravid, "The Religious, Economic and Social Background and Context of the Establishment of the Ghetti of Venice," in *Gli ebrei e Venezia: Secoli XIV–XVIII*, ed. Gaetano Cozzi (Milan: Edizioni Comunità, 1987), esp. 251–52.
37. ASVe, Inquisitorato alle Arti, busta 102, fascicolo "Casi tra li Cattaveri con li Cinque Savii sopra le case delli Hebrei," fols. 21r–24v, August 3, 1560.
38. ASVe, Compilazione delle Leggi, busta 189, March 3, 1633.
39. ASVe, Ufficiali al Cattaver, busta 278, June 14, 1758.
40. Richard Sennett, "The Open City," *Urban Age* (November 2006): 3.
41. As quoted in Stephen J. Milner, "The Florentine Piazza della Signoria as Practiced Place," in *Renaissance Florence: A Social History*, ed. Roger J. Crum and John T. Paoletti (New York: Cambridge University Press, 2006), 83.
42. See Edward Muir, "In *Some* Neighbours We Trust: On the Exclusion of Women from the Public in Renaissance Italy," in *Florence and Beyond: Culture, Society and Politics in Renaissance Italy. Essays in Honour of John M. Najemy*, ed. David S. Peterson with Daniel E. Bornstein (Toronto: Centre for Reformation and Renaissance Studies, 2008), 283. On community formation, Elizabeth Grosz writes: "Communities, which make language, culture, and thus architecture their modes

of existence and expression, come into being not through the recognition, generation, or establishment of common interests, values, and needs, and the establishment of universal, neutral laws and conventions that bind and enforce them (as social contractarians proclaim), but through the remainders they cast out, the figures they reject, the terms that they consider unassimilable, that they attempt to sacrifice, revile, and expel. There are many names for this unassimilable residue: the other, the abject, the scapegoat, the marginalized, the destitute, the refugee, the dying, etc." Elizabeth Grosz, *Architecture from the Outside: Essays on Virtual and Real Space* (Cambridge, MA: MIT Press, 2001), 152.

43. David Jacoby posits that the Jews residing in Candia during the Byzantine period most likely selected the location of the Judaica, along the seawall on the Bay of Dermata (or, "Bay of Hides"), because the Jews themselves played an important role in the tanning industry. In Byzantium, he suggests, Jewish residential segregation in Candia (Greek Chandax) was voluntary. Segregation became compulsory in the early fourteenth century under Venetian rule. By 1423, Venetian authorities prohibited Jews from acquiring real estate outside the Judaica and compelled the Jews to sell any property previously purchased. David Jacoby, "Jews and Christians in Venetian Crete: Segregation, Interaction, and Conflict," in *Interstizi: Culture ebraico-cristiane a Venezia e nei suoi domini dal medioevo all'età moderna*, ed. Uwe Israel, Robert Jütte, and Reinhold C. Mueller (Rome: Edizioni di storia e letteratura, 2010), 248–61.

44. Maria Georgopoulou, "Mapping Religious and Ethnic Identities in the Venetian Colonial Empire," *Journal of Medieval and Early Modern Studies* 26, no. 3 (1996), 482. See also Joshua Starr, "Jewish Life in Crete Under the Rule of Venice," *Proceedings of the American Academy for Jewish Research* 12 (1942): 59–114; Zvi Ankori, "From *Zudecha* to *Yahudi Mahallesi*: The Jewish Quarter of Candia in the Seventeenth Century," in *Salo Wittmayer Baron Jubilee Volume*, ed. Saul Lieberman, 3 vols. (Jerusalem: American Academy for Jewish Research, 1974), 1:85; David Jacoby, "Venice and the Venetian Jews in the Eastern Mediterranean," in *Gli ebrei e Venezia: Secoli XIV-XVIII*, ed. Gaetano Cozzi (Milan: Edizioni di Comunità, 1987), 29–58; and Maria Georgopoulou, *Venice's Mediterranean Colonies: Architecture and Urbanism* (Cambridge: Cambridge University Press, 2001), 192–210.

45. ASVe, Duca di Candia, busta 32, Memoriali, fascicolo 44/4, fols. 334v-35r (July 8, 1450). I would like to thank Sonia Sabnis for translating this document. See also Georgopoulou, "Mapping Religious and Ethnic Identities in the Venetian Colonial Empire," 483.

46. ASVe, Duca di Candia, busta 32, Memoriali, fascicolo 44/4, fols. 334v-35r (July 8, 1450).

47. Jacoby, "Venice and the Venetian Jews in the Eastern Mediterranean," 37. Georgopoulou too notes, "The Judaica of Candia may very well have functioned as a model for the ghetto of Venice." Georgopoulou, "Mapping Religious and Ethnic Identities in the Venetian Colonial Empire," 487.

48. Mark Wigley, "Untitled: The Housing of Gender," in *Sexuality & Space*, ed. Beatriz Colomina (New York: Princeton Architectural Press, 1992), 338.

49. Resmiye Alpar Atun and Naciye Doratli, "Walls in Cities: A Conceptual Approach to the Walls of Nicosia," *Geopolitics* 14, no. 1 (2009): 109.

50. Leon Battista Alberti, *On the Art of Building in Ten Books*, trans. Joseph Rykwert, Neil Leach, and Robert Tavernor (Cambridge, MA: MIT Press, 1988), 118. Alberti advocated for the construction of city walls but cautioned that their presence would not prevent enemies from attacking: "For our part, when we think of the power that the walls offer for the safety and freedom of citizens against better-placed and more numerous enemies, we will side neither with those who want their city to be defencelessly naked nor with those who put all their hopes in the structure of the walls. . . . This being so, who would deny the need to add guard upon guard, and defense upon defense." Alberti, *On the Art of Building in Ten Books*, 102.
51. On the evolution of the wall, see Lewis Mumford, *The City in History: Its Origins, Its Transformations, and Its Prospects* (New York: Harcourt, Brace & World, 1961), esp. 63–66.
52. Pirenne writes, "It is impossible to imagine a town existing at that era without walls. It was an attribute by which towns were distinguished from villages." Henri Pirenne, *Medieval Cities: Their Origins and the Revival of Trade*, trans. Frank D. Halsey (Garden City, NY: Doubleday, 1956), 107. See also Simon Pepper, "Siege Law, Siege Ritual, and the Symbolism of City Walls in Renaissance Europe," in *City Walls: The Urban Enceinte in Global Perspective*, ed. James D. Tracy (New York: Cambridge University Press, 2000), 573–604.
53. Garry Wills writes that Venice's "fragility was the paradoxical source of its stability over time." Garry Wills, *Venice, Lion City: The Religion of Empire* (New York: Simon & Schuster, 2001), 11.
54. Benjamin Ravid, "All Ghettos Were Jewish Quarters but Not All Jewish Quarters Were Ghettos," in *The Frankfurt "Judengasse": Jewish Life in an Early Modern German City*, ed. Fritz Backhaus, Gisela Engel, Robert Liberles, and Margarete Schlüter (London: Vallentine Mitchell, 2010), 5–22.
55. On Venice's ghetto skylines, see Dana E. Katz, "'Clamber Not You Up to the Casements': On Ghetto Views and Viewing," *Jewish History* 24, no. 2 (June 2010): 127–53; and Dana E. Katz, "The Ghetto and the Gaze in Early Modern Venice," in *Judaism and Christian Art: Aesthetic Anxieties from the Catacombs to Colonialism*, ed. Herbert L. Kessler and David Nirenberg (Philadelphia: University of Pennsylvania Press, 2011), 233–62.
56. Henri Lefebvre, *The Production of Space*, trans. Donald Nicholson-Smith (Oxford: Blackwell, 1991), 87. Sennett similarly writes, "walls functioned much like cell membranes, both porous and resistant. That dual quality of the membrane is, I believe, an important principle for visualising more modern living urban forms. Whenever we construct a barrier, we have to equally make the barrier porous; the distinction between inside and outside has to be breachable, if not ambiguous." Sennett, "The Open City," 3. Moreover, Robert Venturi defines "architecture as the wall between the inside and the outside. . . . And by recognizing the difference between the inside and the outside, architecture opens the door once again to an urbanistic point of view." Robert Venturi, *Complexity and Contradiction in Architecture* (New York: Museum of Modern Art, 2002), 86.
57. See Michel de Certeau, *The Practice of Everyday Life*, trans. Steven Rendall (Berkeley: University of California Press, 1984), 126.
58. This analysis was informed in part by my spatial study of Renaissance Mantua. See Dana E. Katz, "Spatial Stories: Mantua and the Painted Jew," in *Rabbi Judah Moscato*

and the Jewish Intellectual World of Mantua in the 16th-17th Centuries, ed. Giuseppe Veltri and Gianfranco Miletto (Leiden: Brill, 2012), 199–225.

59. "Ils demeurent tous-ensemble en un lieu enfermé de hautes murailles, dont le circuit ne touche aux maisons de la ville, & sont là dedans reserrez comme en un cloistre pour estre separez d'avec les Chrestiens. . . . A Venize on l'appelle il *Guetto*." Nicolas Audeber, *Le voyage et observations de plusieurs choses diverses qui se peuvent remarquer en Italie* (Paris: Gervais Clouzier, 1656), 123. See also Sarra Copia Sulam, *Jewish Poet and Intellectual in Seventeenth-Century Venice: The Works of Sarra Copia Sulam in Verse and Prose, along with Writings of Her Contemporaries in Her Praise, Condemnation, or Defense*, ed. and trans. Don Harrán (Chicago: University of Chicago Press, 2009), 9.

60. Regarding Jewish doctors, Sanudo writes on July 29, 1516: "Many Jewish doctors are living in the Ghetto who are likely to be called during the night to treat the sick living outside the Ghetto and who sometimes will stay out very late for some consultation. In order that they not run afoul of the law for this reason, let it be law that each time these doctors go out at night to tend to the sick or remain out late for a consultation, they must inform our guards in writing of the details of where they have been, who the sick persons are, and what consultation they attended. The guards are obligated to present the written information the following day to our Cataveri, on pain of losing their job and spending six months in prison and paying fifty lire de pizoli to our Cataveri. The officials must immediately make diligent inquiries concerning whether the said doctors were in the stated places; if they find that it is not true, they must punish the doctors according to the provisions of the law passed by this council on March 29 of the present year." Marino Sanuto, *I diarii di Marino Sanuto: Dall'autografo Marciano ital. cl. VII codd. CDXIX-CDLXXVII*, ed. Federico Stefani, Nicolò Barozzi, and Guglielmo Berchet, vol. 22 (Venice: Fratelli Visentini, 1888), 392. See also Marin Sanudo, *Venice, Città Excelentissima: Selections from the Renaissance Diaries of Marin Sanudo*, ed. Patricia H. Labalme and Laura Sanguineti White, trans. Linda L. Carroll (Baltimore: Johns Hopkins University Press, 2008), 340–41; and Ravid, "Curfew Time in the Ghetto of Venice," 243.

61. Documents from 1366 specify that the Visdomini regulated window apertures: "che tute le fenestre de le camere del fontego di Todeschi debia esser ferade et alte da le travadure e per oviar molte malicie, le qual per essi se poria cometter e molti Todeschi sia stadi si prosumtuoxi, che li a fate molto fenestre averte e bassa senza ferro e senza parola de li visdomini che porave tornar in grandissimo danno del comun: vada la parte che tute le fenestre fate per questo modo debia esser stropade e serade como da prima e che damo avanti non se debia far alguna fenestra in questo modo senza licentia de la signoria in pena de libre xxv." Georg Martin Thomas, *Capitolare dei visdomini del Fontego dei Todeschi in Venezia / Capitular des deutschen Hauses in Venedig: zum erstenmal bekannt gegeben* (Berlin: A. Asher & Co., 1874), 69–70.

62. Sennett, *Flesh and Stone*, 228. On the Fondaco dei Tedeschi, see also Thomas, *Capitolare dei visdomini del fontego dei todeschi in Venezia / Capitular des deutschen Hauses in Venedig*; Henry Simonsfeld, *Der Fondaco dei Tedeschi in Venedig und die deutsch-venetianischen Handelsbeziehungen* (Stuttgart: Cotta, 1887); and J. Wesley Hoffmann, "The Fondaco Dei Tedeschi: The Medium of Venetian-German Trade," *Journal of Political Economy* 40, no. 2 (April 1932): 244–52.

63. Ekirch, *At Day's Close*, 93.
64. See, for example, ASVe, Compilazione delle Leggi, busta 187, Ebraica Stamperia Ebrei, fascicolo 1, fol. 296, January 18, 1767: "Li Custodi Cristiani suddetti, o sian Guardiani Deputati alle Porte de Ghetti, quali sono tenuti abitare giorno, e notte, ivi senza famiglia, dovranno aver l'incarico di portar al Loro Eccellentissimo Magistrato le loro esatte riferte in scritto di qualunque contraffazione venisse commessa, e ciò settimanalmente, con descrivere in esse relazioni tutti li Ebrei, che entrassero, & uscissero di notte, conotando l'ora precisa, il numero delle sere, il Nome, Cognome, & Abitazione de medesimi per le opportune deliberazioni."
65. Cary Howie, *Claustrophilia: The Erotics of Enclosure in Medieval Literature* (New York: Palgrave Macmillan, 2007), 7.
66. Franco Mormando, *The Preacher's Demons: Bernardino of Siena and the Social Underworld of Early Renaissance Italy* (Chicago: University of Chicago Press, 1999), 170.
67. For Patriarch Lorenzo Priuli and his memorandum on Jews, see ASVe, Senato, Deliberazioni, Terra, filza 141 (m.v.), January 30, 1596.
68. See, for example, the *condotte* found in the following archival sources: ASVe, Deliberazioni, Senato, Terra, filza 141 m.v., January 30, 1596; and ASVe, Compilazione delli Leggi, busta 187, Ebraica Stamperia Ebrei, fascicolo 1, fol. 296, January 11, 1767. On Christians entering the ghetto after nightfall, see Ravid, "Curfew Time in the Ghetto of Venice," 251–53.
69. On Marquardus de Susannis and the *De Iudaeis et aliis infidelibus*, see Kenneth R. Stow, *Catholic Thought and Papal Jewry Policy, 1555–1593* (New York: Jewish Theological Seminary of America, 1977).
70. Stow, *Catholic Thought and Papal Jewry Policy*, 90.
71. Stow, *Catholic Thought and Papal Jewry Policy*, 100.
72. On the sartorial restrictions placed on the Jews of Venice, see Benjamin Ravid, "From Yellow to Red: On the Distinguishing Head-covering of the Jews of Venice," *Jewish History* 6, nos. 1–2 (1992): 179–210; reprinted in *Studies on the Jews of Venice, 1382–1797* (Aldershot: Ashgate, 2003).
73. Robert Chazan, *Medieval Stereotypes and Modern Antisemitism* (Berkeley: University of California Press, 1997), 100.
74. Stow, *Catholic Thought and Papal Jewry Policy*, 107.
75. Stow, *Catholic Thought and Papal Jewry Policy*, 106.
76. ASVe, Compilazione delle Leggi, busta 188, fascicolo 1, fol. 85r–86r, July 19, 1424. Giovanni Battista Gallicciolli chronicles this law, "Ma prima che si confermasse e ampliasse, il Consiglio di XL adi 19 Luglio dello stesso anno 1424, dovette con severo Decreto ovviare a un altro disordine, che fino dal secolo antecedente commettevano gli Ebrei domiciliati in Venezia, o nello Stato. Fu dunque posto e preso a tutti voti di quel Consiglio, che se *Repertus fuerit aliquis Judæus cum aliqua muliere Christiana, aut probatum fuerit jacuisse cum ea; si fuerit de loco publico Rivoalti, cadat in pœnam de libris 500, & stare debeat menses sex in uno carcere inferiori: si vero mulier non fuerit de ipso loco publico Rivoalti, stare debeat uno anno in uno carcere inferiori, & solvere libras 500.*" Giovanni Battista Gallicciolli, *Delle memorie venete antiche profane ed ecclesiastiche* (Venice: Domenico Fracasso, 1795) 2:291–292, section 907. See also Benjamin Ravid, "The Legal Status of the Jews in Venice to 1509," *Proceedings of the American Academy for Jewish Research* 54 (1987): 185–87.

77. Ravid, "The Legal Status of the Jews in Venice to 1509," 186.
78. For more on the consequences of sexual relationships between Christians and Jews, see Brian Pullan, *The Jews of Europe and the Inquisition of Venice, 1550–1670* (London: I. B. Tauris, 1983), 79–80.
79. Sennett, *Flesh and Stone*, 225–27.
80. According to the chronicles of Marin Sanudo dated April 6, 1515, Jewish doctors threatened the health of the civic body when committing immoral acts with Christian woman. Sanudo writes, "The preacher at the Frari, Fra Giovan Maria di Arezzo, thunders ... against doctors, especially Master Lazaro. He has made Christian women become dissolute and has frequented Christian women, and no measures have been taken" (*à fato disperder christiane, usato con christiane et nulla di provision si fa*). Sanuto, *I diarii di Marino Sanuto: Dall'autografo Marciano ital. cl. VII codd. CDXIX-CDLXXVII*, ed. Federico Stefani, Nicolò Barozzi, and Guglielmo Berchet, vol. 20 (Venice: Fratelli Visentini, 1887), 98. See also Sanudo, *Venice, Cità Excelentissima*, ed. Labalme and Sanguineti White, 338; and Riccardo Calimani, *The Ghetto of Venice*, trans. Katherine Silberblatt Wolfthal (Milan: Arnoldo Mondadori, 1995), 32.
81. See ASVe, Provveditori alla Sanità, busta 2, Capitolare I (1485–1574), fol. 43; and ASVe, Consiglio di Dieci, Comune, registro 5, 1529, fol. 116v. See also Benjamin Ravid, "New Light on the Ghetti of Venice," in *Shlomo Simonsohn Jubilee Volume: Studies on the History of the Jews in the Middle Ages and Renaissance Period*, ed. Daniel Carpi et al. (Tel Aviv: Tel Aviv University, Faculty of Humanities, 1993); and Lisa Pon's forthcoming work on the lazzaretto and ghetto.
82. ASVe, Ufficiali al Cattaver, busta 247, fol. 196r, December 16, 1630; and see Ravid, "Curfew Time in the Ghetto of Venice," 240.
83. Fear of the Jews' sexuality permeated early modern Europe. According to Christian theologians and anatomists, the sexual dangers of Jews derived from their distinct biology. For instance, Jewish women were thought to have enhanced libidos that triggered their uncontrollable attraction to Christian men, whereas the unusual sexual proclivities of Jewish men stemmed from the belief that they menstruate. See Willis Johnson, "The Myth of Jewish Male Menses," *Journal of Medieval History* 24, no. 3 (1998): 273–95; David S. Katz, "Shylock's Gender: Jewish Male Menstruation in Early Modern England," *Review of English Studies* 50, no. 200 (November 1999): 440–62; and Irven M. Resnick, "Medieval Roots of the Myth of Jewish Male Menses," *Harvard Theological Review* 93, no. 3 (July 2000): 241–63. See also Amy Neff and Anne Derbes, "'This Unnatural Flow': Bleeding Demons in the *Supplicationes variae*, the Arena Chapel, and Notre-Dame des Fontaines, La Brigue," in *Anathēmata Heortika: Studies in Honor of Thomas F. Mathews*, ed. Joseph D. Alchermes, Helen C. Evans, and Thelma K. Thomas (Mainz: Philipp von Zabern, 2009), 247–55.
84. On Jessica's willful female sexuality, see Lisa Lampert, *Gender and Jewish Difference from Paul to Shakespeare* (Philadelphia: University of Pennsylvania Press, 2004), 138–67. On the seductive powers of Synagoga, see Sara Lipton, "The Temple Is My Body: Gender, Carnality, and Synagoga in the *Bible Moralisée*," in *Imagining the Self, Imagining the Other: Visual Representation and Jewish-Christian Dynamics in the Middle Ages and Early Modern Period*, ed. Eva Frojmovic (Leiden: Brill, 2002), 129–63.
85. Lipton, "The Temple Is My Body," 135.

86. Thomas Coryat, *Coryat's Crudities* (Glasgow: James MacLehose, 1905), 1:372–73.
87. John Evelyn, *The Diary of John Evelyn*, ed. E. S. De Beer (Oxford: Clarendon Press, 1955), 2:477.
88. In his book *Venetian Life* (first published in 1866), American author William Dean Howells documents his encounter with Jewish women in a chapter entitled "The Ghetto and the Jews of Venice:" "They [Jewish women] are sometimes, also, very pretty; and I have seen one Jewish lady who might have stepped out of the sacred page, down from the patriarchal age, and been known for Rebecca, with her oriental grace, and delicate, sensitive, high-bred look and bearing." William Dean Howells, *Venetian Life* (Boston, MA: Houghton, Mifflin & Company, 1907), 191.
89. On the sexual politics of segregation, see David Nirenberg, "Conversion, Sex, and Segregation: Jews and Christians in Medieval Spain," *American Historical Review* 107, no. 4 (October 2002): 1065–93.
90. Elizabeth Grosz, "Bodies-Cities," in *Sexuality & Space*, ed. Beatriz Colomina (New York: Princeton Architectural Press, 1992), 242.
91. Vitruvius writes, "No temple can have any compositional system without symmetry and proportion, unless, as it were, it has an exact system of correspondence to the likeness of a well-formed human being." He continues, "Therefore, if it is agreed that from the limbs of the human body number was discovered, and also the fact that a correspondence of dimension exists among individual elements and the appearance of the entire body in each of its parts, then it is left for us to recognize that the ancients, who also established the houses of the immortal gods, ordered the elements of those works so that, in both their shape and their symmetries, fitting dimensions of separate elements and of the work as a whole might be created." Vitruvius, *Vitruvius: Ten Books on Architecture*, trans. Ingrid D. Rowland and Thomas Noble Howe (New York: Cambridge University Press, 1999), 47–48. See also Diane Agrest, "Architecture from Without: Body, Logic, and Sex," in *Gender Space Architecture: An Interdisciplinary Introduction*, ed. Jane Rendell, Barbara Penner, and Iain Borden (London: Routledge, 2000), 358–70; and George Dodds and Robert Tavernor, eds., *Body and Building: Essays on the Changing Relation of Body and Architecture* (Cambridge, MA: MIT Press, 2002). For Pallasmaa's phenomenological insights on architecture, see Juhani Pallasmaa, *The Eyes of the Skin: Architecture and the Senses* (Chichester: John Wiley & Sons, 2005), 40.
92. For an analysis of boundaries, see Brian Massumi, *The Politics of Everyday Fear* (Minneapolis: University of Minnesota Press, 1993), esp. 27; and Grosz, *Architecture from the Outside*, esp. 65.
93. On Rachel Hebrea Cantarina, see ASVe, Compilazione delle Leggi, busta 188, fascicolo 2, fol. 660, September 16, 1609. See also ASVe, Compilazione delle Leggi, busta 188, fascicolo 2, fol. 666, January 1, 1609; ASVe, Ufficiali al Cattaver, busta 247, registro 8, fol. 77v, January 21, 1609; and ASVe, Ufficiali al Cattaver, busta 246, registro 7, fol. 45v, June 26, 1613.
94. Ravid, "Curfew Time in the Ghetto of Venice," 247.
95. Koslofsky, *Evening's Empire*, 189. See also Paul Griffiths, "Meanings of Nightwalking in Early Modern England," *Seventeenth Century* 13, no. 2 (Autumn 1998): 212–38.

96. "Colui che tiene la Piazza, sempre è vincente della Città," Giovanni Cavalcanti, *Istorie fiorentine*, vol. I (Florence: Tipografia all'insegna di Dante, 1838), libro X, capitolo VIII, 577.
97. See Dennis Romano, "Gender and the Urban Geography of Renaissance Venice," *Journal of Social History* 23, no. 2 (Winter 1989), 352.
98. Muir, "In *Some* Neighbours We Trust," 271–89.
99. Judith C. Brown, "A Woman's Place Was in the Home: Women's Work in Renaissance Tuscany," in *Rewriting the Renaissance: The Discourses of Sexual Difference in Early Modern Europe*, ed. Margaret W. Ferguson, Maureen Quilligan, and Nancy J. Vickers (Chicago: University of Chicago Press, 1986), 206–24; and Wills, *Venice, Lion City*, 157.
100. On women's relationship with the public, see also Romano, "Gender and the Urban Geography of Renaissance Venice," 339–53; Robert C. Davis, "The Geography of Gender in the Renaissance," in *Gender and Society in Renaissance Italy*, ed. Judith C. Brown and Robert C. Davis (London: Longman, 1998), 19–38; Sharon Strocchia, "Gender and the Rites of Honor in Italian Renaissance Cities," in *Gender and Society in Renaissance Italy*, ed. Judith C. Brown and Robert C. Davis (London: Longman, 1998), 39–60; Christiane Klapisch-Zuber, "Les femmes dans les espaces publics de la ville italienne (XIVe-XVe siècles)," in *Anthropologie de la ville médiévale*, ed. Michal Tymowski (Warsaw: Wydawnictwo DiG, 1999), 83–90; and Natalie Tomas, "Did Women Have a Space?" in *Renaissance Florence: A Social History*, ed. Roger J. Crum and John T. Paoletti (New York: Cambridge University Press, 2006), 311–28.
101. Pier Cesare Ioly Zorattini, *Processi del S. Uffizio di Venezia contro ebrei e giudaizzanti, 1682–1734* (Florence: Leo S. Olschki, 1994), XII:114. I would like to thank Lisa Pon for sharing this reference with me.
102. ASVe, Senato, Deliberazioni, Terra, filza 141 (m.v.), January 30, 1596.
103. ASVe, Ufficiali al Cattaver, busta 128, fascicolo "1715," July 15, 1715 through September 11, 1715; and ASVe, Ufficiali al Cattaver, busta 128, fascicolo "1717," September 22, 1717. For further examples, see Carla Boccato, "Processi ad ebrei nell'archivio degli ufficiali al Cattaver a Venezia," *La rassegna mensile di Israel*, terza serie, 41, no. 3 (March 1975): 175; and Pier Cesare Ioly Zorattini, "Jews, Crypto-Jews, and the Inquisition," in *The Jews of Early Modern Venice*, ed. Robert C. Davis and Benjamin Ravid (Baltimore: Johns Hopkins University Press, 2001), 101.
104. Beatriz Colomina, "Introduction," in *Sexuality & Space*, ed. Beatriz Colomina (New York: Princeton Architectural Press, 1992), iii.
105. Niccolò Machiavelli, *The Prince*, chapter 18, in *Selected Political Writings*, ed. and trans. David Wootton (Indianapolis, IN: Hackett, 1994), 55. "Li uomini in universale iudicano più alli occhi che alle mani, perché tocca a vedere a ognuno, a sentire a pochi. Ognuno vede quello che tu pari, pochi sentono quello che tu se'." Niccolò Machiavelli, *Il principe e altri scritti minori*, ed. Michele Scherillo (Milan: Ulrico Hoepli, 1924), 183.
106. In the Western tradition, sight evolved as the most privileged of the senses. In the allegorized cave of Plato's *Republic*, for example, true sight emanates from the powers of the mind where knowledge and memory reside. Vision, Plato insists, refers to the images of the mind transmitted through the eyes. Aristotle further

complicated the ancient affinity for sight in *De anima* in which he famously wrote that sight is the noblest of the senses, while touch maintains the lowest (and most basic) position. Indeed, the separation of sight from the other senses – what Martin Jay calls "ocularcentrism" – dominated Greek culture and the subsequent traditions in Western philosophy. See Martin Jay, *Downcast Eyes: The Denigration of Vision in Twentieth-Century French Thought* (Berkeley: University of California Press, 1993).

Conclusion

1. Richard Lassels, *The Voyage of Italy, or A Compleat Journey through Italy in Two Parts* (Paris: Vincent du Moutier, 1670), 422–23.
2. The title page of *The Voyage of Italy* presents Lassels's pedagogical preparation for the book: "Richard Lassels, Gent. who Travelled through Italy Five times, as Tutor to several of the English Nobility and Gentry." On Richard Lassels and Venice's emblematic role in the Grand Tour, see Bruce Redford, *Venice & the Grand Tour* (New Haven, CT: Yale University Press, 1996). See also Richard Lassels, *The Grand Tour and the Great Rebellion: Richard Lassels and "The Voyage of Italy" in the Seventeenth Century*, ed. Edward Chaney (Geneva: Slatkine, 1985).
3. Lassels, *The Voyage of Italy*, "A Preface to the Reader, Concerning Travelling," n.p.
4. John Stoye writes that Grand Tour itineraries rarely varied among the different travelers. In particular, seventeenth-century English tourists would visit: "the Piazza, the Clock, the Treasury, the Cathedral, all of St. Mark; the Ducal Palace, the Arsenal, the Palazzo Grimani, the statue of Bartolomeo Colleoni; the islands of S. Giorgio Maggiore, S. Cristoforo and S. Michele with their ecclesiastical buildings; the Ghetto; and the glassworks of Murano." John Stoye, *English Travellers Abroad, 1604–1667: Their Influence in English Society and Politics* (New York: Octagon Books, 1968), 193.
5. See John Julius Norwich, ed., *A Traveller's Companion to Venice* (New York: Interlink Books, 2002).
6. Benjamin Ravid, "Christian Travelers in the Ghetto of Venice: Some Preliminary Observations," in *Studies on the Jews of Venice, 1382–1797* (Aldershot: Ashgate, 2003), 111–50; and Norwich, ed., *A Traveller's Companion to Venice*, esp. 206–15.
7. Simon Worrall's interview of Shaul Bassi, *Smithsonian Journeys Quarterly* (November 6, 2015), www.smithsonianmag.com/travel/venice-ghetto-jews-italy-anniversary-shaul-bassi-180956867/?no-ist. See also Shaul Bassi, "Re-imagining the Ghetto: Introduction to the Forum 'The Ghetto as a Victorian Text,'" *Partial Answers: Journal of Literature and the History of Ideas* 13, no. 1 (January 2015): 74.
8. Henry James makes several allusions to the Jew as peddler in *Italian Hours*. See Henry James, *Italian Hours*, ed. John Auchard (University Park, PA: Penn State University Press, 1992), 38, 210, 257. On Henry James and the Jews, see Eli Ben-Joseph, *Aesthetic Persuasion: Henry James, the Jews, and Race* (Lanham, MD: University Press of America, 1996); Jonathan Freedman, *The Temple of Culture: Assimilation and Anti-Semitism in Literary Anglo-America* (Oxford: Oxford University Press, 2000), 117–209; and Gert Buelens, *Henry James and the "Aliens": In Possession of the American Scene* (Amsterdam: Rodopi, 2002). On John Ruskin and Henry James,

see, for example, Michael O'Neill, Mark Sandy, and Sarah Wootton, eds., *Venice and the Cultural Imagination: "This Strange Dream upon the Water"* (London: Pickering & Chatto, 2012).

9. Riccardo Calimani, *The Ghetto of Venice*, trans. Katherine Silberblatt Wolfthal (Milan: Arnoldo Mondadori, 1995), 252. See also Simon Levis Sullam and Fabio Brusò, *Il Ghetto. Piazza Barche* (Padua: Il Poligrafo, 2008), 14–16.
10. After Venice was ceded to the newly emerging Kingdom of Italy in 1866, Jews received total emancipation.
11. Calimani, *The Ghetto of Venice*, 257–67.
12. Rodney D. Olsen, *Dancing in Chains: The Youth of William Dean Howells* (New York: New York University Press, 1991), 218–44. See also James Leslie Woodress, *Howells & Italy* (Durham, NC: Duke University Press, 1952), esp. 3–66; and Susan Goodman and Carl Dawson, *William Dean Howells: A Writer's Life* (Berkeley: University of California Press, 2005), 72–99.
13. Goodman and Dawson, *William Dean Howells: A Writer's Life*, 97. In *Italian Journeys*, William Dean Howells references the ghetto of Ferrara. For example, he writes: "We . . . walked down by the side of the Duomo toward the Ghetto, which is not so foul as one could wish a Ghetto to be." William Dean Howells, *Italian Journeys: From Venice to Naples and Beyond* (London: I. B. Tauris, 2011), 12.
14. William Dean Howells, *Venetian Life* (Boston: Houghton, Mifflin, & Co., 1907), 189.
15. Howells, *Venetian Life*, 189. See also Shaul Bassi and Alberto Toso Fei, *Shakespeare in Venice: Luoghi, personaggi e incanti di una città che va in scena* (Treviso: Elzeviro, 2007), 152.
16. Howells, *Venetian Life*, 193.
17. Howells, *Venetian Life*, 190.
18. Howells, *Venetian Life*, 193.
19. On place and memory, see Pierre Nora, *Realms of Memory: Rethinking the French Past*, trans. Lawrence D. Kritzman, 3 vols. (New York: Columbia University Press, 1996–1998); and Edward S. Casey, *Remembering: A Phenomenological Study* (Bloomington: Indiana University Press, 2000), esp. 181–215.
20. Howells, *Venetian Life*, 199.
21. On Jews, art, and memory, see James E. Young, *At Memory's Edge: After-Images of the Holocaust in Contemporary Art and Architecture* (New Haven, CT: Yale University Press, 2000).

BIBLIOGRAPHY

Archives

Archivio di Stato di Mantova
  Archivio Gonzaga
Archivio di Stato di Venezia
  Cinque Savi alla Mercanzia
  Collegio Notatorio
  Compilazione delle Leggi
  Consiglio di Dieci
  Duca di Candia
  Inquisitorato agli Ebrei
  Inquisitorato alle Arti
  Provveditori alla Sanità
  Provveditori sopra i Monasteri di Monache
  Senato, Mar
  Senato, Terra
  Signori di Notte al Civil
  Signori di Notte al Criminal
  Ufficiali al Cattaver

Primary Sources

Alberti, Leon Battista. *De re aedificatoria libri decem*. Edited by Eberhard Tappe. Argentorati: M. Iacobus Cammerlander Moguntinus, 1541.

I primi tre libri della famiglia. Edited by Francesco Carlo Pellegrini. Florence: Sansoni, 1946.

I libri della famiglia (The Family in Renaissance Florence). Translated by Renée Neu Watkins. Columbia: University of South Carolina Press, 1969.

On the Art of Building in Ten Books. Translated by Joseph Rykwert, Neil Leach, and Robert Tavernor. Cambridge, MA: MIT Press, 1988.

Azeglio, Massimo d'. *Dell'emancipazione civile degl'Israeliti*. Florence: F. Le Monnier, 1848.

Bentham, Jeremy. *The Panopticon Writings*. Edited by Miran Božovič. London: Verso, 1995.

Canale, Martino da. *Les Estoires de Venise: Cronaca veneziana in lingua francese dalle origini al 1275*. Edited by Alberto Limentani. Florence: Leo S. Olschki, 1972.

Cavalcanti, Giovanni. *Istorie fiorentine*. Vol. 1. Florence: Tipografia all'insegna di Dante, 1838.

Chambers, David, and Brian Pullan, eds. *Venice: A Documentary History, 1450–1630*. Toronto: University of Toronto Press, 2001.

Commynes, Philippe de. *The Memoirs of Philippe de Commynes*. Edited by Samuel Kinser. Translated by Isabelle Cazeaux. Vol. 2. Columbia: University of South Carolina Press, 1973.

Coryat, Thomas. *Coryat's Crudities*. Vol. 1. Glasgow: James MacLehose and Sons, 1905.

Esposito, Anna, and Diego Quaglioni. *Processi contro gli ebrei di Trento (1475–1478): I processi del 1475*. Padua: CEDAM, 1990.

Evelyn, John. *The Diary of John Evelyn*. Edited by E. S. De Beer. Vol. 2. Oxford: Clarendon Press, 1955.

Gallicciolli, Giovanni Battista. *Delle memorie venete antiche, profane ed ecclesiastiche*. Vol. 2. Venice: Domenico Fracasso, 1795.

Gregorovius, Ferdinand. *The Ghetto and the Jews of Rome*. Translated by Moses Hadas. New York: Schocken, 1966.

Howells, William Dean. *Venetian Life*. Boston: Houghton, Mifflin & Company, 1907.

Italian Journeys: From Venice to Naples and Beyond. London: I. B. Tauris, 2011.

Ioly Zorattini, Pier Cesare. *Processi del S. Uffizio di Venezia contro ebrei e giudaizzanti, 1682–1734*. Vol. 12. Florence: Leo S. Olschki, 1994.

James, Henry. *Italian Hours*. Edited by John Auchard. University Park, PA: Penn State University Press, 1992.

Lapini, Agostino. *Diario fiorentino di Agostino Lapini dal 252 al 1596*. Edited by Giuseppe Odoardo Corazzini. Florence: G. C. Sansoni, 1900.

Lassels, Richard. *The Voyage of Italy, or A Compleat Journey through Italy in Two Parts*. Paris: Vincent du Moutier, 1670.

The Grand Tour and the Great Rebellion: Richard Lassels and "The Voyage of Italy" in the Seventeenth Century. Edited by Edward Chaney. Geneva: Slatkine, 1985.

Machiavelli, Niccolò. *Il principe e altri scritti minori*. Edited by Michele Scherillo. Milan: Ulrico Hoepli, 1924.

The Prince. In *Selected Political Writings*. Edited and translated by David Wootton. Indianapolis, IN: Hackett, 1994.

Maimonides, Moses. *Hilchot de'ot: The Laws of Personality Development; and, Hilchot Talmud Torah: The Laws of Torah Study*. New York: Moznaim, 1989.

Modena, Leon. *The Autobiography of a Seventeenth-Century Venetian Rabbi: Leon Modena's "Life of Judah."* Edited and translated by Mark R. Cohen. Princeton, NJ: Princeton University Press, 1988.

Mortoft, Francis. *Francis Mortoft: His Book, Being His Travels Through France and Italy, 1658–1659*. Edited by Malcolm Letts. London: Hakluyt Society, 1925.

Palladio, Andrea. *I quattro libri dell'architettura*. Venice: Domenico de' Franceschi, 1570.

The Four Books on Architecture. Translated by Robert Tavernor and Richard Schofield. Cambridge, MA: MIT Press, 1997.

Pallasmaa, Juhani. *The Eyes of the Skin: Architecture and the Senses*. Chichester: John Wiley & Sons, 2005.

Petrarca, Francesco. *Letters from Petrarch*. Translated by Morris Bishop. Bloomington: Indiana University Press, 1966.

Renier Michiel, Giustina. *Origine delle feste veneziane*. Milan: Annali universali delle scienze e dell'industria, 1829.
Rilke, Rainer Maria. *Geschichten vom lieben Gott*. Wiesbaden: Insel, 1955.
Stories of God. Translated by Michael H. Kohn. Boston: Shambhala, 2003.
Ruskin, John. *The Stones of Venice*. Vol. 1. London: George Allen, Sunnyside, Orpington, 1896.
Sansovino, Francesco. *Venetia, citta nobilissima et singolare, descritta in XIIII. libri*. Venice: Iacomo Sansovino, 1581.
Sanudo, Marin. *Venice, Città Excelentissima: Selections from the Renaissance Diaries of Marin Sanudo*. Edited by Patricia H. Labalme and Laura Sanguineti White. Translated by Linda L. Carroll. Baltimore: Johns Hopkins University Press, 2008.
Sanuto, Marino. *I diarii di Marino Sanuto, MCCCCXCVI-MDXXXIII: Dall'autografo Marciano ital. cl. VII codd. CDXIX-CDLXXVII*. Edited by Federico Stefani, Nicolò Barozzi, and Guglielmo Berchet. Vols. 20 and 22. Venice: Fratelli Visentini, 1887–1888.
Shakespeare, William. *The Merchant of Venice*. Edited by A. R. Braunmuller. New York: Penguin, 2000.
Sitte, Camillo. *Camillo Sitte: The Birth of Modern City Planning, with a Translation of the 1889 Austrian Edition of His "City Planning According to Artistic Principles."* Edited by George R. Collins and Christiane Crasemann Collins. New York: Rizzoli, 1986.
Sulam, Sarra Copia. *Jewish Poet and Intellectual in Seventeenth-Century Venice*. Edited and translated by Don Harrán. Chicago: University of Chicago Press, 2009.
Thomas, Georg Martin. *Capitolare dei visdomini del fontego dei todeschi in Venezia / Capitular des deutschen Hauses in Venedig: zum erstenmal bekannt gegeben*. Berlin: A. Asher & Co., 1874.
Thomas, William. *The History of Italy (1549)*. Edited by George B. Parks. Ithaca, NY: Cornell University Press, 1963.
Vasi, Giuseppe. *Delle magnificenze di Roma antica e moderna: Libro II, Le piazze principali di Roma con obelischi, colonne, ed altri ornamenti*. Rome: Stamperia di Apollo, presso gli Eredi Barbiellini, 1752.
Vitruvius. *Vitruvius: Ten Books on Architecture*. Edited by Ingrid D. Rowland and Thomas Noble Howe. New York: Cambridge University Press, 1999.

Secondary Sources

Ackerman, James S., and Myra Nan Rosenfeld. "Social Stratification in Renaissance Urban Planning." In *Urban Life in the Renaissance*. Edited by Susan Zimmerman and Ronald F. E. Weissman. Newark: University of Delaware Press, 1989.
Adelman, Howard E. "Leon Modena: The Autobiography and the Man." In *The Autobiography of a Seventeenth-Century Venetian Rabbi: Leon Modena's "Life of Judah."* Edited and translated by Mark R. Cohen. Princeton, NJ: Princeton University Press, 1988.
"Jewish Women and Family Life, Inside and Outside the Ghetto." In *The Jews of Early Modern Venice*. Edited by Robert C. Davis and Benjamin Ravid. Baltimore: Johns Hopkins University Press, 2001.
Adelman, Janet. *Blood Relations: Christian and Jew in "The Merchant of Venice."* Chicago: University of Chicago Press, 2008.

Adshead, S. D. "Camillo Sitte and Le Corbusier." *Town Planning Review* 14, no. 2 (November 1930): 85–94.

Ady, Julia Mary Cartwright. *Beatrice d'Este, Duchess of Milan, 1475–1497: A Study of the Renaissance*. London, J. M. Dent, 1903.

Agnew, John A., and James S. Duncan, eds. *The Power of Place: Bringing Together Geographical and Sociological Imaginations*. Boston: Unwin Hyman, 1989.

Agrest, Diane. "Architecture From Without: Body, Logic, and Sex." In *Gender Space Architecture: An Interdisciplinary Introduction*. Edited by Jane Rendell, Barbara Penner, and Iain Borden. London: Routledge, 2000.

Alpers, Svetlana, Emily Apter, Carol Armstrong, et al. "Visual Culture Questionnaire," *October* 77 (Summer 1996): 25–70.

Ankori, Zvi. "From *Zudecha* to *Yahudi Mahallesi*: The Jewish Quarter of Candia in the Seventeenth Century." In *Salo Wittmayer Baron Jubilee Volume*. Edited by Saul Lieberman. 3 vols. Jerusalem: American Academy for Jewish Research, 1974.

Arbel, Benjamin. *Trading Nations: Jews and Venetians in the Early Modern Eastern Mediterranean*. Leiden: Brill, 1995.

"Venice's Maritime Empire in the Early Modern Period." In *A Companion to Venetian History, 1400–1797*. Edited by Eric R. Dursteler. Leiden: Brill, 2013.

Aron-Beller, Katherine. *Jews on Trial: The Papal Inquisition in Modena, 1598–1638*. New York: Manchester University Press, 2011.

Ascarelli, Giovanni, Daniela Di Castro, et al., eds. *Il Tempio Maggiore di Roma: Nel centenario dell'inaugurazione della Sinagoga, 1904–2004*. Turin: Allemandi, 2004.

Atkinson, Niall. *The Noisy Renaissance: Sound, Architecture, and Florentine Urban Life*. University Park, PA: Penn State University Press, 2016.

Atun, Resmiye Alpar, and Naciye Doratli. "Walls in Cities: A Conceptual Approach to the Walls of Nicosia." *Geopolitics* 14, no. 1 (2009): 108–34.

Backhaus, Fritz. "The Jewish Ghetto in Frankfurt." In *The Life and Times of N. M. Rothschild, 1777–1836*. Edited by Victor Gray and Melanie Aspey. London: N. M. Rothschild & Sons, 1998.

Backhaus, Fritz, Gisela Engel, et al., eds. *The Frankfurt "Judengasse": Jewish Life in an Early Modern German City*. London: Vallentine Mitchell, 2010.

Baker, Sir John. *Baker and Milsom Sources of English Legal History: Private Law to 1750*. Oxford: Oxford University Press, 2010.

Basaldella, Francesco. *La festa del Redentore: Storica festa nazionale veneziana*. Venice: Quaderni di cultura giudecchina, 2000.

Bassi, Shaul. "Re-imagining the Ghetto: Introduction to the Forum 'The Ghetto as a Victorian Text.'" *Partial Answers: Journal of Literature and the History of Ideas* 13, no. 1 (January 2015): 73–78.

Bassi, Shaul, and Alberto Toso Fei. *Shakespeare in Venice: Luoghi, personaggi e incanti di una città che va in scena*. Treviso: Elzeviro, 2007.

Baxandall, Michael. *Painting and Experience in Fifteenth-Century Italy: A Primer in the Social History of Pictorial Style*. Oxford: Clarendon Press, 1972.

Bejczy, István. "Tolerantia: A Medieval Concept." *Journal of the History of Ideas* 58, no. 3 (July 1997): 365–84.

Bemporad, Dora Liscia. "Jewish Ceremonial Art in the Era of the City States and the Ghettos." In *Gardens and Ghettos: The Art of Jewish Life in Italy*. Edited by Vivian B. Mann. Berkeley: University of California Press, 1989.

Benjamin, Walter. *Illuminations*. Edited by Hannah Arendt. Translated by Harry Zohn. New York: Schocken, 1968.

Ben-Joseph, Eli. *Aesthetic Persuasion: Henry James, the Jews, and Race*. Lanham, MD: University Press of America, 1996.

Benton, Tim. "The Three Cities Compared: Urbanism." In *Siena, Florence, and Padua: Art, Society, and Religion, 1280–1400*. Edited by Diana Norman. Vol. 2. New Haven, CT: Yale University Press, 1995.

Berger, David. "'Cum Nimis Absurdum' and the Conversion of the Jews." *Jewish Quarterly Review* 70, no. 1 (July 1979): 41–49.

Boccato, Carla. "Processi ad ebrei nell'archivio degli ufficiali al Cattaver a Venezia." *La rassegna mensile di Israel*, terza serie, 41, no. 3 (March 1975): 164–80.

"Licenze per altane concesse ad ebrei del Ghetto di Venezia (sec. XVI-XVII- XVIII)." *La rassegna mensile di Israel*, terza serie, 46, nos. 3–4 (March-April 1980): 106–16.

Boes, Maria. "Jews in the Criminal-Justice System of Early Modern Germany." *Journal of Interdisciplinary History* 30, no. 3 (Winter 1999): 407–35.

Bohl, Charles C., and Jean-François Lejeune. *Sitte, Hegemann and the Metropolis: Modern Civic Art and International Exchanges*. London: Routledge, 2009.

Boholm, Åsa. *Venetian Worlds: Nobility and the Cultural Construction of Society*. Gothenburg: Institute for Advanced Studies in Social Anthropology, 1993.

Bonfil, Robert. "Change in the Cultural Patterns of a Jewish Society in Crisis: Italian Jewry at the Close of the Sixteenth Century." In *Essential Papers on Jewish Culture in Renaissance and Baroque Italy*. Edited by David B. Ruderman. New York: New York University Press, 1992.

Jewish Life in Renaissance Italy. Translated by Anthony Oldcorn. Berkeley: University of California Press, 1994.

Botticini, Maristella. "A Tale of 'Benevolent' Governments: Private Credit Markets, Public Finance, and the Role of Jewish Lenders in Medieval and Renaissance Italy." *Journal of Economic History* 60, no. 1 (March 2000): 164–89.

Bourke, Eoin. "The Frankfurt Judengasse in Eyewitness Accounts from the Seventeenth to the Nineteenth Century." In *Ghetto Writing: Traditional and Eastern Jewry in German-Jewish Literature from Heine to Hilsenrath*. Edited by Anne Fuchs and Florian Krobb. Columbia, SC: Camden House, 1999.

Bouwsma, William J. "The Politics of Commynes." *Journal of Modern History* 23, no. 4 (December 1951): 315–28.

Brackett, John K. "The Florentine Onestà and the Control of Prostitution, 1403–1680." *Sixteenth Century Journal* 24, no. 2 (Summer 1993): 273–300.

Brandes, Francesca, ed. *Venice and Environs: Jewish Itineraries, Places, History, and Art*. Venice: Marsilio, 1997.

Bristol, Katharine G. "The Pruitt-Igoe Myth." *Journal of Architectural Education* 44, no. 3 (May 1991): 163–71.

Brown, Judith C. "A Woman's Place Was in the Home: Women's Work in Renaissance Tuscany." In *Rewriting the Renaissance: The Discourses of Sexual Difference in Early Modern Europe*. Edited by Margaret W. Ferguson, Maureen Quilligan, and Nancy J. Vickers. Chicago: University of Chicago Press, 1986.

Brown, Patricia Fortini. "Not One But Many Separate Cities: Housing Diversity in Sixteenth-Century Venice." In *Home and Homelessness in the Medieval and*

Renaissance World. Edited by Nicholas Howe. Notre Dame, IN: University of Notre Dame Press, 2004.

Private Lives in Renaissance Venice: Art, Architecture, and the Family. New Haven, CT: Yale University Press, 2004.

Brucker, Gene. *The Society of Renaissance Florence: A Documentary Study.* New York: Harper & Row, 1971.

Renaissance Florence. Berkeley: University of California Press, 1983.

Bryson, Norman. *Vision and Painting: The Logic of the Gaze.* New Haven, CT: Yale University Press, 1983.

Bryson, Norman, Michael Ann Holly, and Keith Moxey, eds. *Visual Theory: Painting and Interpretation.* Cambridge: Polity Press, 1991.

Buelens, Gert. *Henry James and the "Aliens": In Possession of the American Scene.* Amsterdam: Rodopi, 2002.

Calabi, Donatella. "Il ghetto e la città." In *La città degli ebrei: Il ghetto di Venezia, architettura e urbanistica.* Edited by Ennio Concina, Ugo Camerino, and Donatella Calabi. Venice: Albrizzi, 1991.

"Gli stranieri e la città." In *Storia di Venezia. Dalle origini alla caduta della Serenissima.* Edited by Gino Benzoni and Antonio Menniti Ippolito. 14 vols. Rome: Istituto della Enciclopedia Italiana, 1991–2002. Vol. 5: *Il Rinascimento. Società ed economia.* Edited by Alberto Tenenti and Ugo Tucci, 1996.

"The 'City of the Jews.'" In *The Jews of Early Modern Venice.* Edited by Robert C. Davis and Benjamin Ravid. Baltimore: Johns Hopkins University Press, 2001.

Venezia e il ghetto: Cinquecento anni del "recinto degli ebrei." Turin: Bollati Boringhieri, 2016.

Calimani, Riccardo. *The Ghetto of Venice.* Translated by Katherine Silberblatt Wolfthal. Milan: Arnoldo Mondadori, 1995.

Camille, Michael. *The Gothic Idol: Ideology and Image-Making in Medieval Art.* Cambridge: Cambridge University Press, 1989.

Image on the Edge: The Margins of Medieval Art. London: Reaktion, 1992.

Camporesi, Piero. *The Incorruptible Flesh: Bodily Mutation and Mortification in Religion and Folklore.* Translated by Tania Croft-Murray. Cambridge: Cambridge University Press, 1988.

Canniffe, Eamonn. *The Politics of the Piazza: The History and Meaning of the Italian Square.* Aldershot: Ashgate, 2008.

Carnevali, Luigi. *Il ghetto di Mantova.* Bologna: Arnaldo Forni, 2009.

Casey, Edward S. *Remembering: A Phenomenological Study.* Bloomington: Indiana University Press, 2000.

Cassuto, David. "The Scuola Grande Tedesca in the Venice Ghetto." *Journal of Jewish Art* 3–4 (1977): 40–57.

Cassuto, Umberto. "I più antichi capitoli del ghetto di Firenze." *Rivista israelitica* 9 (1912): 203–11.

Gli ebrei a Firenze nell'età del Rinascimento. Florence: Galetti e Cocci, 1918.

"La famille des Médicis et les Juifs." *Revue des études juives* 76 (1923): 132–45.

Certeau, Michel de. *The Practice of Everyday Life.* Translated by Steven Rendall. Berkeley: University of California Press, 1984.

Chambers, David, and Trevor Dean. *Clean Hands and Rough Justice: An Investigating Magistrate in Renaissance Italy.* Ann Arbor: University of Michigan Press, 1997.

Chazan, Robert. *Medieval Stereotypes and Modern Antisemitism*. Berkeley: University of California Press, 1997.

Chojnacki, Stanley. *Women and Men in Renaissance Venice: Twelve Essays on Patrician Society*. Baltimore: Johns Hopkins University Press, 2000.

Ciscato, Antonio. *Gli ebrei in Padova (1300–1800): Monografia storica documentata*. Bologna: Forni, 1967.

Clark, Stuart. *Vanities of the Eye: Vision in Early Modern European Culture*. Oxford: Oxford University Press, 2007.

Cohen, Adam S. "La Haggadah multi-sensorielle." *Cahiers de civilisation médiévale* 55 (2012): 521–39.

Cohen, Elizabeth S. "Honor and Gender in the Streets of Early Modern Rome." *Journal of Interdisciplinary History* 22, no. 4 (Spring 1992): 597–625.

Cohen, Thomas V. "The Case of the Mysterious Coil of Rope: Street Life and Jewish Persona in Rome in the Middle of the Sixteenth Century." *Sixteenth Century Journal* 19, no. 2 (Summer 1988): 209–21.

Colaco, Jill. "The Window Scenes in 'Romeo and Juliet' and Folk Songs of the Night Visit." *Studies in Philology* 83, no. 2 (Spring 1986): 138–57.

Colomina, Beatriz, ed. *Sexuality & Space*. New York: Princeton Architectural Press, 1992.

"Introduction." In *Sexuality & Space*. Edited by Beatriz Colomina. New York: Princeton Architectural Press, 1992.

"The Split Wall: Domestic Voyeurism." In *Sexuality & Space*. Edited by Beatriz Colomina. New York: Princeton Architectural Press, 1992.

Concina, Ennio. "Owners, Houses, Functions: New Research on the Origins of the Venetian Ghetto." *Mediterranean Historical Review* 6, no. 2 (December 1991): 180–89.

Storia dell'architettura di Venezia: Dal VII al XX secolo. Milan: Electa, 1995.

A History of Venetian Architecture. Translated by Judith Landry. Cambridge: Cambridge University Press, 1998.

Concina, Ennio, Ugo Camerino, and Donatella Calabi. *La città degli ebrei: Il ghetto di Venezia, architettura e urbanistica*. Venice: Albrizzi, 1991.

Cooper, Nicholas. *Houses of the Gentry, 1480–1680*. New Haven, CT: Yale University Press, 1999.

Cooper, Tracy Elizabeth. *Palladio's Venice: Architecture and Society in a Renaissance Republic*. New Haven, CT: Yale University Press, 2005.

Cooperman, Bernard D. "Ethnicity and Institution Building among Jews in Early Modern Rome." *AJS Review* 30, no. 1 (April 2006): 119–45.

Cosgrove, Denis. *Geography & Vision: Seeing, Imagining and Representing the World*. London: I. B. Tauris, 2008.

Cowan, Alexander. "'Not Carrying Out the Vile and Mechanical Arts': Touch as a Measure of Social Distinction in Early Modern Venice." In *The City and the Senses: Urban Culture Since 1500*. Edited by Alexander Cowan and Jill Steward. Aldershot: Ashgate, 2007.

Crary, Jonathan. *Techniques of the Observer: On Vision and Modernity in the Nineteenth Century*. Cambridge, MA: MIT Press, 1990.

Crompton, Louis. *Homosexuality & Civilization*. Cambridge, MA: Belknap Press of Harvard University Press, 2003.

Curiel, Roberta, and Bernard Dov Cooperman. *The Venetian Ghetto*. New York: Rizzoli, 1990.

Damisch, Hubert. *Skyline: The Narcissistic City*. Stanford, CA: Stanford University Press, 2001.

Davis, Robert C. "The Geography of Gender in the Renaissance." In *Gender and Society in Renaissance Italy*. Edited by Judith C. Brown and Robert C. Davis. London: Longman, 1998.

"Introduction." In *The Jews of Early Modern Venice*. Edited by Robert C. Davis and Benjamin Ravid. Baltimore: Johns Hopkins University Press, 2001.

Debenedetti-Stow, Sandra. "The Etymology of 'Ghetto': New Evidence from Rome." *Jewish History* 6, no. 1–2, The Frank Talmage Memorial Volume (1992): 79–85.

Deleuze, Gilles. *Foucault*. Translated by Seán Hand. Minneapolis: University of Minnesota Press, 1988.

Dodds, George, and Robert Tavernor, eds. *Body and Building: Essays on the Changing Relation of Body and Architecture*. Cambridge, MA: MIT Press, 2002.

Dubbini, Renzo. *Geography of the Gaze: Urban and Rural Vision in Early Modern Europe*. Translated by Lydia G. Cochrane. Chicago: University of Chicago Press, 2002.

Dunn, Marilyn. "Spaces Shaped for Spiritual Perfection: Convent Architecture and Nuns in Early Modern Rome." In *Architecture and the Politics of Gender in Early Modern Europe*. Edited by Helen Hills. Aldershot: Ashgate, 2003.

Dursteler, Eric R., ed. *A Companion to Venetian History, 1400–1797*. Leiden: Brill, 2013.

Ekirch, A. Roger. *At Day's Close: Night in Times Past*. New York: W. W. Norton, 2005.

Elkins, James. *Visual Studies: A Skeptical Introduction*. New York: Routledge, 2003.

Elsner, Jaś. *Roman Eyes: Visuality and Subjectivity in Art & Text*. Princeton, NJ: Princeton University Press, 2007.

Encyclopaedia Judaica. Edited by Fred Skolnik and Michael Berenbaum. Detroit, MI: Macmillan, 2007.

Fedalto, Giorgio. "Le minoranze straniere a Venezia tra politica e legislazione." In *Venezia: Centro di mediazione tra oriente e occidente, secoli XV-XVI: Aspetti e problemi*. Edited by Hans-Georg Beck, Manoussos Manoussacas, and Agostino Pertusi. Florence: L. S. Olschki, 1977.

"Stranieri a Venezia e a Padova." *Storia della cultura veneta*. Edited by Girolamo Arnaldi and Manlio Pastore Stocchi. Vicenza: Neri Pozza, 1980. Vol. 3/I: *Dal primo Quattrocento al Concilio di Trento*, 1980.

"Stranieri a Venezia e a Padova, 1550–1700." *Storia della cultura veneta*. Edited by Girolamo Arnaldi and Manlio Pastore Stocchi. Vicenza: Neri Pozza, 1984. Vol. 4/II: *Dalla Controriforma alla fine della Repubblica. Il Seicento*, 1984.

Fenlon, Iain. *The Ceremonial City: History, Memory and Myth in Renaissance Venice*. New Haven, CT: Yale University Press, 2007.

Finlay, Robert. "The Foundation of the Ghetto: Venice, the Jews, and the War of the League of Cambrai." *Proceedings of the American Philosophical Society* 126, no. 2 (April 8, 1982), 140–54.

Fiorani, Francesca. *The Marvel of Maps: Art, Cartography and Politics in Renaissance Italy*. New Haven, CT: Yale University Press, 2005.

Folin, Marco. *Rappresentare la città: Topografie urbane nell'Italia di antico regime*. Reggio Emilia: Diabasis, 2010.

Fortis, Umberto. *The Ghetto on the Lagoon: A Guide to the History and Art of the Venetian Ghetto, 1516–1797*. Translated by Roberto Matteoda. Venice: Storti, 1988.

Foster, Hal, ed. *Vision and Visuality*. Seattle, WA: Bay Press, 1988.

Foucault, Michel. *Discipline and Punish: The Birth of the Prison.* Translated by Alan Sheridan. New York: Vintage Books, 1979.

Francesconi, Federica. "From Ghetto to Emancipation: The Role of Moisè Formiggini." *Jewish History* 24, no. 3/4 (2010): 331–54.

"Dangerous Readings in Early Modern Modena: Negotiating Jewish Culture in an Italian Key." In *The Hebrew Book in Early Modern Italy*. Edited by Joseph Hacker and Adam Shear. Philadelphia: University of Pennsylvania Press, 2011.

Frank, Ellen Eve. *Literary Architecture: Essays Toward a Tradition: Walter Pater, Gerard Manley Hopkins, Marcel Proust, Henry James*. Berkeley: University of California Press, 1979.

Freedman, Jonathan. *The Temple of Culture: Assimilation and Anti-Semitism in Literary Anglo-America*. Oxford: Oxford University Press, 2000.

Gallagher, Catherine, and Stephen Greenblatt. *Practicing New Historicism*. Chicago: University of Chicago Press, 2000.

Geanakoplos, Deno John. *Greek Scholars in Venice: Studies in the Dissemination of Greek Learning from Byzantium to Western Europe*. Cambridge, MA: Harvard University Press, 1962.

Gentilini, Gianni. *Pasqua 1475: Antigiudaismo e lotta alle eresie, il caso di Simonino*. Milan: Medusa, 2007.

Georgopoulou, Maria. "Mapping Religious and Ethnic Identities in the Venetian Colonial Empire." *Journal of Medieval and Early Modern Studies* 26, no. 3 (Fall 1996): 467–96.

Venice's Mediterranean Colonies: Architecture and Urbanism. Cambridge: Cambridge University Press, 2001.

Ghirardo, Diane Yvonne. "The Topography of Prostitution in Renaissance Ferrara." *Journal of the Society of Architectural Historians* 60, no. 4 (December 2001): 402–31.

Gianighian, Giorgio. "Building a Renaissance Double House in Venice." *Architectural Research Quarterly* 8, nos. 3–4 (December 2004): 299–312.

"Building Castelforte." *Architectural Research Quarterly* 9, no. 1 (March 2005): 51–68.

Gianighian, Giorgio, and Paola Pavanini. *Dietro i palazzi: Tre secoli di architettura minore a Venezia, 1492–1803*. Venice: Arsenale, 1984.

Gilbert, Allan H. *Machiavelli's "Prince" and Its Forerunners: "The Prince" as a Typical Book "De regimine principum."* Durham, NC: Duke University Press, 1938.

Gilbert, Felix. "The Humanist Concept of the Prince and *The Prince* of Machiavelli." *Journal of Modern History* 11, no. 4 (December 1939): 449–83.

Gilman, Sander. *Inscribing the Other*. Lincoln: University of Nebraska Press, 1991.

Girouard, Mark. *Life in the English Country House: A Social and Architectural History*. New Haven, CT: Yale University Press, 1978.

Cities & People: A Social and Architectural History. New Haven, CT: Yale University Press, 1985.

Glassman, Bernard. *Anti-Semitic Stereotypes without Jews: Images of the Jews in England, 1290–1700*. Detroit, MI: Wayne State University Press, 1975.

Goodman, Susan, and Carl Dawson. *William Dean Howells: A Writer's Life*. Berkeley: University of California Press, 2005.

Gowing, Laura. *Domestic Dangers: Women, Words, and Sex in Early Modern London*. Oxford: Clarendon Press, 1996.

Goy, Richard J. *Venetian Vernacular Architecture: Traditional Housing in the Venetian Lagoon*. Cambridge: Cambridge University Press, 1989.

Venice: The City and Its Architecture. London: Phaidon, 1997.
Grafton, Anthony. *Leon Battista Alberti: Master Builder of the Italian Renaissance*. New York: Hill and Wang, 2000.
Grell, Ole Peter, and Bob Scribner, eds. *Tolerance and Intolerance in the European Reformation*. Cambridge: Cambridge University Press, 1996.
Griffiths, Paul. "Meanings of Nightwalking in Early Modern England." *Seventeenth Century* 13, no. 2 (Autumn 1998): 212–38.
Gross, Kenneth. *Shylock Is Shakespeare*. Chicago: University of Chicago Press, 2006.
Grosz, Elizabeth. "Bodies-Cities." In *Sexuality & Space*. Edited by Beatriz Colomina. New York: Princeton Architectural Press, 1992.
Architecture from the Outside: Essays on Virtual and Real Space. Cambridge, MA: MIT Press, 2001.
Guarini, Elena Fasano. "Center and Periphery." *Journal of Modern History* 67, supplement: "The Origins of the State in Italy, 1300–1600" (December 1995): S74–S96.
Habermas, Jürgen. *The Structural Transformation of the Public Sphere: An Inquiry into a Category of Bourgeois Society*. Translated by Thomas Burger and Frederick Lawrence. Cambridge, MA: MIT Press, 1989.
Hall, Stuart. "Cultural Identity and Diaspora." In *Identity: Community, Culture, Difference*. Edited by Jonathan Rutherford. London: Lawrence & Wishart, 1990.
Hamburger, Jeffrey F. *The Visual and the Visionary: Art and Female Spirituality in Late Medieval Germany*. New York: Zone Books, 1998.
Harris, Dianne, and D. Fairchild Ruggles, eds. *Sites Unseen: Landscape and Vision*. Pittsburgh, PA: University of Pittsburgh Press, 2007.
Harris, Jonathan. *Greek Emigres in the West, 1400–1520*. Camberley: Porphyrogenitus, 1995.
Hart, Vaughan, ed., with Peter Hicks. *Paper Palaces: The Rise of the Renaissance Architectural Treatise*. New Haven, CT: Yale University Press, 1998.
Harvey, Elizabeth D., ed. *Sensible Flesh: On Touch in Early Modern Culture*. Philadelphia: University of Pennsylvania Press, 2003.
Hasan-Rokem, Galit, and Alan Dundes, eds. *The Wandering Jew: Essays in the Interpretation of a Christian Legend*. Bloomington: Indiana University Press, 1986.
Haverkamp, Alfred. "The Jewish Quarters in German Towns during the Late Middle Ages." In *In and Out of the Ghetto: Jewish-Gentile Relations in Late Medieval and Early Modern Germany*. Edited by R. Po-chia Hsia and Hartmut Lehmann. Cambridge: Cambridge University Press, 1995.
Hazlitt, W. Carew. *The Venetian Republic: Its Rise, Its Growth, and Its Fall, 421–1797*. London: A. and C. Black, 1900.
Hegemann, Werner, and Elbert Peets. *The American Vitruvius: An Architects' Handbook of Civic Art*. Edited by Alan J. Plattus. New York: Princeton Architectural Press, 1988.
Heidegger, Martin. "Building, Dwelling, Thinking." In *Poetry, Language, Thought*. Translated by Albert Hofstadter. New York: Harper & Row, 1971.
Hills, Helen. *Invisible City: The Architecture of Devotion in Seventeenth-Century Neapolitan Convents*. Oxford: Oxford University Press, 2004.
Hills, Paul. "Titian's Fire: Pyrotechnics and Representations in Sixteenth-Century Venice." *Oxford Art Journal* 30, no. 2 (2007): 187–204.
Hoffmann, J. Wesley. "The Fondaco Dei Tedeschi: The Medium of Venetian-German Trade." *Journal of Political Economy* 40, no. 2 (April 1932): 244–52.

Holmes, Joshua. "Building Bridges and Breaking Boundaries: Modernity and Agoraphobia." *Opticon1826* (September 1, 2006): http://pdfsr.com/pdf/building-bridges-and-breaking-boundaries-modernity-and-agoraphobia.

Holo, Joshua. *Byzantine Jewry in the Mediterranean Economy*. Cambridge: Cambridge University Press, 2009.

Horowitz, Elliott. "The Eve of the Circumcision: A Chapter in the History of Jewish Nightlife." *Journal of Social History* 23, no. 1 (Autumn 1989): 45–69.

"Coffee, Coffeehouses, and the Nocturnal Rituals of Early Modern Jewry." *AJS Review* 14, no. 1 (Spring 1989): 17–46.

Howard, Deborah. *Venice & the East: The Impact of the Islamic World on Venetian Architecture, 1100–1500*. New Haven, CT: Yale University Press, 2000.

The Architectural History of Venice. New Haven, CT: Yale University Press, 2002.

"Venice between East and West: Marc'Antonio Barbaro and Palladio's Church of the Redentore." *Journal of the Society of Architectural Historians* 62, no. 3 (September 2003): 306–25.

Howard, Deborah, and Laura Moretti. *Sound and Space in Renaissance Venice: Architecture, Music, Acoustics*. New Haven, CT: Yale University Press, 2009.

Howie, Cary. *Claustrophilia: The Erotics of Enclosure in Medieval Literature*. New York: Palgrave Macmillan, 2007.

Hsia, R. Po-chia. *The Myth of Ritual Murder: Jews and Magic in Reformation Germany*. New Haven, CT: Yale University Press, 1988.

Trent 1475: Stories of a Ritual Murder Trial. New Haven, CT: Yale University Press, 1992.

"The Usurious Jew: Economic Structure and Religious Representations in an Anti-Semitic Discourse." In *In and Out of the Ghetto: Jewish-Gentile Relations in Late Medieval and Early Modern Germany*. Edited by R. Po-chia Hsia and Hartmut Lehmann. Cambridge: Cambridge University Press, 1995.

Hughes, Diane Owen. "Distinguishing Signs: Ear-Rings, Jews and Franciscan Rhetoric in the Italian Renaissance City." *Past & Present* 112 (August 1986): 3–59.

Hunt, John Dixon. "The Garden in the City of Venice: Epitome of State and Site." *Studies in the History of Gardens and Designed Landscapes* 19, no. 1 (March 1999): 46–61.

The Venetian City Garden: Place, Typology, and Perception. Basel: Birkhäuser, 2009.

Ioly Zorattini, Pier Cesare. "Jews, Crypto-Jews, and the Inquisition." In *The Jews of Early Modern Venice*. Edited by Robert C. Davis and Benjamin Ravid. Baltimore: Johns Hopkins University Press, 2001.

Jacoby, David. "Venice and the Venetian Jews in the Eastern Mediterranean." In *Gli ebrei e Venezia: Secoli XIV-XVIII*. Edited by Gaetano Cozzi. Milan: Edizioni di Comunità, 1987.

"Jews and Christians in Venetian Crete: Segregation, Interaction, and Conflict." In *Interstizi: Culture ebraico-cristiane a Venezia e nei suoi domini dal medioevo all'età moderna*. Edited by Uwe Israel, Robert Jütte, and Reinhold C. Mueller. Rome: Edizioni di storia e letteratura, 2010.

Jarzombek, Mark. *On Leon Baptista Alberti: His Literary and Aesthetic Theories*. Cambridge, MA: MIT Press, 1989.

Jay, Martin. *Downcast Eyes: The Denigration of Vision in Twentieth-Century French Thought*. Berkeley: University of California Press, 1993.

Jencks, Charles A. *The Language of Post-Modern Architecture*. New York: Rizzoli, 1984.

Jenks, Chris, ed. *Visual Culture*. London: Routledge, 1995.

Johnson, Willis. "The Myth of Jewish Male Menses." *Journal of Medieval History* 24, no. 3 (1998): 273–95.

Jütte, Daniel. *The Strait Gate: Thresholds and Power in Western History*. New Haven, CT: Yale University Press, 2015.

Kagan, Richard. *Urban Images of the Hispanic World, 1493–1793*. New Haven, CT: Yale University Press, 2000.

Kanerva, Liisa. *Defining the Architect in Fifteenth-Century Italy: Exemplary Architects in L. B. Alberti's "De re aedificatoria."* Helsinki: Suomamalainen Tiedeakatemia, 1998.

Katz, Dana E. "Painting and the Politics of Persecution: Representing the Jew in Fifteenth-Century Mantua." *Art History* 23, no. 4 (November 2000): 475–95.

The Jew in the Art of the Italian Renaissance. Philadelphia: University of Pennsylvania Press, 2008.

"'Clamber Not You Up to the Casements': On Ghetto Views and Viewing." *Jewish History* 24, no. 2 (June 2010): 127–53.

"The Ghetto and the Gaze in Early Modern Venice." In *Judaism and Christian Art: Aesthetic Anxieties from the Catacombs to Colonialism*. Edited by Herbert L. Kessler and David Nirenberg. Philadelphia: University of Pennsylvania Press, 2011.

"Spatial Stories: Mantua and the Painted Jew." In *Rabbi Judah Moscato and the Jewish Intellectual World of Mantua in the 16th-17th Centuries*. Edited by Giuseppe Veltri and Gianfranco Miletto. Leiden: Brill, 2012.

"Sensing the City: Night in the Venetian Ghetto." In *Sensational Religion: Sensory Cultures in Material Practice*. Edited by Sally M. Promey. New Haven, CT: Yale University Press, 2014.

Katz, David S. "Shylock's Gender: Jewish Male Menstruation in Early Modern England." *Review of English Studies* 50, no. 200 (November 1999): 440–62.

Kaye, Joel. *Economy and Nature in the Fourteenth Century: Money, Market Exchange, and the Emergence of Scientific Thought*. Cambridge: Cambridge University Press, 1998.

Klapisch-Zuber, Christiane. "Les femmes dans les espaces publics de la ville italienne (XIVe-XVe siècles)." In *Anthropologie de la ville médiévale*. Edited by Michal Tymowski. Warsaw: Wydawnictwo DiG, 1999.

Koslofsky, Craig. *Evening's Empire: A History of the Night in Early Modern Europe*. Cambridge: Cambridge University Press, 2011.

Krautheimer, Richard. "Alberti and Vitruvius." In *Studies in Early Christian, Medieval, and Renaissance Art*. New York: New York University Press, 1969.

Krinsky, Carol Herselle. *Synagogues of Europe: Architecture, History, Meaning*. Cambridge, MA: MIT Press, 1985.

Lacan, Jacques. "Of the Gaze as *Objet petit a*." In *The Four Fundamental Concepts of Psycho-Analysis*. Edited by Jacques-Alain Miller. Translated by Alan Sheridan. New York: W. W. Norton, 1978.

Lampert, Lisa. *Gender and Jewish Difference from Paul to Shakespeare*. Philadelphia: University of Pennsylvania Press, 2004.

Laursen, John Christian, and Cary J. Nederman, eds. *Beyond the Persecuting Society: Religious Toleration Before the Enlightenment*. Philadelphia: University of Pennsylvania Press, 1998.

Laven, Mary. *Virgins of Venice: Broken Vows and Cloistered Lives in the Renaissance Convent*. New York: Viking, 2003.

Lavin, Marilyn Aronberg. "The Altar of Corpus Domini in Urbino: Paolo Uccello, Joos Van Ghent, Piero della Francesca." *Art Bulletin* 49, no. 1 (March 1967): 1–24.

Lefebvre, Henri. *The Production of Space*. Translated by Donald Nicholson-Smith. Oxford: Blackwell, 1991.

Le Goff, Jacques. *Your Money or Your Life: Economy and Religion in the Middle Ages*. New York: Zone Books, 1988.

Lerner, L. Scott. "Narrating over the Ghetto of Rome." *Jewish Social Studies*, New Series, 8, no. 2/3 (Winter-Spring 2002): 1–38.

Levis Sullam, Simon, and Fabio Brusò. *Il Ghetto. Piazza Barche*. Padua: Il Poligrafo, 2008.

Lieberman, Ralph. *Renaissance Architecture in Venice, 1450–1540*. New York: Abbeville, 1982.

Linder, Amnon. *The Jews in the Legal Sources of the Early Middle Ages*. Detroit, MI: Wayne State University Press, 1997.

Lipton, Sara. *Images of Intolerance: The Representation of Jews and Judaism in the "Bible moralisée."* Berkeley: University of California Press, 1999.

"The Temple Is My Body: Gender, Carnality, and Synagoga in the *Bible Moralisée*." In *Imagining the Self, Imagining the Other: Visual Representation and Jewish-Christian Dynamics in the Middle Ages and Early Modern Period*. Edited by Eva Frojmovic. Leiden: Brill, 2002.

"'The Sweet Lean of His Head': Writing about Looking at the Crucifix in the High Middle Ages." *Speculum* 80, no. 4 (October 2005): 1172–1208.

Dark Mirror: The Medieval Origins of Anti-Jewish Iconography. New York: Metropolitan Books, 2014.

Loomba, Ania. *Shakespeare, Race, and Colonialism*. Oxford: Oxford University Press, 2002.

Luu, Lien. "Natural-Born versus Stranger-Born Subjects: Aliens and Their Status in Elizabethan London." In *Immigrants in Tudor and Early Stuart England*. Edited by Nigel Goose and Lien Luu. Brighton: Sussex Academic Press, 2005.

Lyotard, Jean-François. *Heidegger and "the jews."* Translated by Andreas Michel and Mark S. Roberts. Minneapolis: University of Minnesota Press, 1990.

Malkiel, Joshua. *A Separate Republic: The Mechanics and Dynamics of Venetian Jewish Self-Government, 1607–1624*. Jerusalem: Magnes Press, Hebrew University, 1991.

Malpas, Jeff. *Heidegger's Topology: Being, Place, World*. Cambridge, MA: MIT Press, 2006.

Heidegger and the Thinking of Place: Explorations in the Topology of Being. Cambridge, MA: MIT Press, 2012.

Mann, Vivian B., ed. *Gardens and Ghettos: The Art of Jewish Life in Italy*. Berkeley: University of California Press, 1989.

Mare, Heidi de. "The Domestic Boundary as Ritual Area in Seventeenth-Century Holland." In *Urban Rituals in Italy and the Netherlands: Historical Contrasts in the Use of Public Space, Architecture, and the Urban Environment*. Edited by Heidi de Mare and Anna Vos. Assen: Van Gorcum, 1993.

Maria, Blake de. "The Patron for Pordenone's Frescos on Palazzo Talenti d'Anna, Venice." *Burlington Magazine* 146, no. 1217 (August 2004): 548–49.

Becoming Venetian: Immigrants and the Arts in Early Modern Venice. New Haven, CT: Yale University Press, 2010.

Marin, Louis. *Utopics: Spatial Play*. Translated by Robert A. Vollrath. Atlantic Highlands, NJ: Humanities Press, 1984.

Marina, Areli. *The Italian Piazza Transformed: Parma in the Communal Age*. University Park, PA: Penn State University Press, 2012.

Martin, John Jeffries. *Venice's Hidden Enemies: Italian Heretics in a Renaissance City*. Baltimore: Johns Hopkins University Press, 2003.

"Marranos and Nicodemites in Sixteenth-Century Venice." *Journal of Medieval and Early Modern Studies* 41, no. 3 (Fall 2011): 577–99.

Massumi, Brian. *The Politics of Everyday Fear*. Minneapolis: University of Minnesota Press, 1993.

McAndrew, John. *Venetian Architecture of the Early Renaissance*. Cambridge, MA: MIT Press, 1980.

Metzger, Mary Janell. "'Now by My Hood, a Gentle and No Jew': Jessica, *The Merchant of Venice*, and the Discourse of Early Modern English Identity." *PMLA* 113, no. 1 (January 1998): 52–63.

Migliau, Bice. "Le vicende dell'edificio delle Cinque Scole." In *Roma capitale, 1870–1911. Architettura e urbanistica: Uso e trasformazione della città storica*. Edited by Giorgio Ciucci and Vanna Fraticelli. Venice: Marsilio, 1984.

Milano, Attilio. *Il ghetto di Roma: Illustrazioni storiche*. Roma: Staderini, 1964.

Miller, Naomi. *Mapping the City: The Language and Culture of Cartography in the Renaissance*. London: Continuum, 2003.

Milner, Stephen J. "The Florentine Piazza della Signoria as Practiced Place." In *Renaissance Florence: A Social History*. Edited by Roger J. Crum and John T. Paoletti. New York: Cambridge University Press, 2006.

Mirzoeff, Nicholas. *The Right to Look: A Counterhistory of Visuality*. Durham, NC: Duke University Press, 2011.

Mirzoeff, Nicholas, ed. *The Visual Culture Reader*. London: Routledge, 2013.

Mitchell, W. J. T. "Showing Seeing: A Critique of Visual Culture." *Journal of Visual Culture* 1, no. 2 (August 2002): 165–81.

"Christo's *Gates* and Gilo's Wall." *Critical Inquiry* 32, no. 4 (Summer 2006): 587–601.

"There Are No Visual Media." In *The Visual Culture Reader*. Edited by Nicholas Mirzoeff. London: Routledge, 2013.

Mitrović, Branko. "Aesthetic Formalism in Renaissance Architectural Theory." *Zeitschrift für Kunstgeschichte* 66. Bd., H. 3 (2003): 321–39.

Mormando, Franco. *The Preacher's Demons: Bernardino of Siena and the Social Underworld of Early Renaissance Italy*. Chicago: University of Chicago Press, 1999.

Mueller, Reinhold C. "Aspects of Venetian Sovereignty in Medieval and Renaissance Dalmatia." In *Quattrocento Adriatico: Fifteenth-Century Art of the Adriatic Rim*. Edited by Charles Dempsey. Bologna: Nuova Alfa, 1996.

Immigrazione e cittadinanza nella Venezia medievale. Rome: Viella, 2010.

Muir, Edward. "Images of Power: Art and Pageantry in Renaissance Venice." *American Historical Review* 84, no. 1 (February 1979): 16–52.

Civic Ritual in Renaissance Venice. Princeton, NJ: Princeton University Press, 1981.

"The Idea of Community in Renaissance Italy." *Renaissance Quarterly* 55, no. 1 (Spring 2002): 1–18.

"In *Some* Neighbours We Trust: On the Exclusion of Women from the Public in Renaissance Italy." In *Florence and Beyond: Culture, Society and Politics in Renaissance Italy. Essays in Honour of John M. Najemy*. Edited by David S. Peterson with Daniel E. Bornstein. Toronto: Centre for Reformation and Renaissance Studies, 2008.

Muir, Edward, and Ronald F. E. Weissman. "Social and Symbolic Places in Renaissance Venice and Florence." In *The Power of Place: Bringing Together Geographical and Sociological Imaginations*. Edited by John A. Agnew and James S. Duncan. Boston: Unwin Hyman, 1989.

Mumford, Lewis. *The City in History: Its Origins, Its Transformations, and Its Prospects*. New York: Harcourt, Brace & World, 1961.

Natali, Ettore. *Il ghetto di Roma*. Vol. 1. Rome: Stabilimento Tipografico della Tribuna, 1887.

Nederman, Cary J. *Worlds of Difference: European Discourses of Toleration, c. 1100–c. 1550*. University Park, PA: Penn State University Press, 2000.

Neff, Amy, and Anne Derbes. "'This Unnatural Flow': Bleeding Demons in the *Supplicationes variae*, the Arena Chapel, and Notre-Dame des Fontaines, La Brigue." In *Anathēmata Heortika: Studies in Honor of Thomas F. Mathews*. Edited by Joseph D. Alchermes, Helen C. Evans, and Thelma K. Thomas. Mainz: Philipp von Zabern, 2009.

Nelson, Benjamin. *The Idea of Usury: From Tribal Brotherhood to Universal Otherhood*. Princeton, NJ: Princeton University Press, 1949.

Nelson, Robert, ed. *Visuality Before and Beyond the Renaissance: Seeing as Others Saw*. Cambridge: Cambridge University Press, 2000.

Nirenberg, David. *Communities of Violence: Persecution of Minorities in the Middle Ages*. Princeton, NJ: Princeton University Press, 1996.

"Conversion, Sex, and Segregation: Jews and Christians in Medieval Spain." *American Historical Review* 107, no. 4 (October 2002): 1065–93.

Noonan, John. *The Scholastic Analysis of Usury*. Cambridge, MA: Harvard University Press, 1957.

Nora, Pierre. *Realms of Memory: Rethinking the French Past*. Translated by Lawrence D. Kritzman. 3 vols. New York: Columbia University Press, 1996–1998.

Norberg-Schulz, Christian. *Genius Loci: Towards a Phenomenology of Architecture*. New York: Rizzoli, 1980.

Norwich, John Julius, ed. *A Traveller's Companion to Venice*. New York: Interlink Books, 2002.

Nuti, Lucia. "The Perspective Plan in the Sixteenth Century: The Invention of a Representational Language." *Art Bulletin* 76, no. 1 (March 1994): 105–28.

"Mapping Places: Chorography and Vision in the Renaissance." In *Mappings*. Edited by Denis Cosgrove. London: Reaktion, 1999.

Oberdiek, Hans. *Tolerance: Between Forbearance and Acceptance*. Lanham, MD: Rowman and Littlefield, 2001.

O'Connell, Monique. *Men of Empire: Power and Negotiation in Venice's Maritime State*. Baltimore: Johns Hopkins University Press, 2009.

Olsen, Rodney D. *Dancing in Chains: The Youth of William Dean Howells*. New York: New York University Press, 1991.

O'Neill, Michael, Mark Sandy, and Sarah Wootton, eds. *Venice and the Cultural Imagination: "This Strange Dream upon the Water."* London: Pickering & Chatto, 2012.

Onians, John. "Alberti and ΦΙΛΑΡΕΤΗ: A Study in Their Sources." *Journal of the Warburg and Courtauld Institutes* 34 (1971): 96–114.

Orlin, Lena Cowen. *Elizabethan Households: An Anthology*. Seattle: University of Washington Press, 1995.

"Women on the Threshold." *Shakespeare Studies* 25 (1997): 50–58.

Palmer, Bryan D. *Cultures of Darkness: Night Travels in the Histories of Transgression*. New York: Monthly Review Press, 2000.

Pavan, Elisabeth. "Recherches sur la nuit vénitienne à la fin du Moyen Âge." *Journal of Medieval History* 7, no. 4 (December 1981): 339–56.

Pavanini, Paola. "Abitazioni popolari e borghesi nella Venezia cinquecentesca." *Studi veneziani* 5 (1981): 63–126.

Payne, Alina A. *The Architectural Treatise in the Italian Renaissance: Architectural Invention, Ornament, and Literary Culture*. Cambridge: Cambridge University Press, 1999.

Peets, Elbert. "Famous Town Planners: II. Camillo Sitte." *Town Planning Review* 12, no. 4 (December 1927): 249–59.

Pepper, Simon. "Siege Law, Siege Ritual, and the Symbolism of City Walls in Renaissance Europe." In *City Walls: The Urban Enceinte in Global Perspective*. Edited by James D. Tracy. New York: Cambridge University Press, 2000.

Pirenne, Henri. *Medieval Cities: Their Origins and the Revival of Trade*. Translated by Frank D. Halsey. Garden City, NY: Doubleday, 1956.

Pomata, Gianna, and Gabriella Zarri, eds. *I monasteri femminili come centri di cultura fra Rinascimento e Barocco*. Rome: Edizioni di Storia e Letteratura, 2005.

Pullan, Brian. *Rich and Poor in Renaissance Venice: The Social Institutions of a Catholic State, to 1620*. Cambridge, MA: Harvard University Press, 1971.

The Jews of Europe and the Inquisition of Venice, 1550–1670. London: I. B. Tauris, 1997.

Racheli, Alberto M. "La demolitzione e ricostruzione del quartiere del Ghetto (1885–1911)." In *Roma capitale, 1870–1911. Architettura e urbanistica: Uso e trasformazione della città storica*. Edited by Giorgio Ciucci and Vanna Fraticelli. Venice: Marsilio, 1984.

Randolph, Adrian W. B. "Renaissance Genderscapes." In *Structures and Subjectivities: Attending to Early Modern Women*. Edited by Adele F. Seeff and Joan Hartman. Newark: University of Delaware Press, 2007.

Touching Objects: Intimate Experiences of Italian Fifteenth-Century Art. New Haven, CT: Yale University Press, 2014.

Ravid, Benjamin. "The Jewish Mercantile Settlement of Twelfth and Thirteenth Century Venice: Reality or Conjecture?" *AJS Review* 2 (1977): 201–25.

"The Legal Status of the Jews in Venice to 1509." *Proceedings of the American Academy for Jewish Research* 54 (1987): 169–202.

"The Religious, Economic, and Social Background and Context of the Establishment of the Ghetti of Venice." In *Gli ebrei e Venezia: Secoli XIV-XVIII*. Edited by Gaetano Cozzi. Milan: Edizioni Comunità, 1987.

"From Geographical Realia to Historiographical Symbol: The Odyssey of the Word Ghetto." In *Essential Papers on Jewish Culture in Renaissance and Baroque Italy*. Edited by David B. Ruderman. New York: New York University Press, 1992.

"From Yellow to Red: On the Distinguishing Head-Covering of the Jews of Venice." *Jewish History* 6, nos. 1–2, The Frank Talmage Memorial Volume (1992): 179–210.

"New Light on the Ghetti of Venice." In *Shlomo Simonsohn Jubilee Volume: Studies on the History of the Jews in the Middle Ages and Renaissance Period*. Edited by Daniel Carpi et al. Tel Aviv: Tel Aviv University, 1993.

"The Third Charter of the Jewish Merchants of Venice, 1611: A Case Study in Complex Multifaceted Negotiations." *Jewish Political Studies Review* 6, no. 1/2 (Spring 1994): 83–134.

"The Minotto Family and an Unapproved Construction Project in the Ghetto Vecchio of Venice, 1608–1609." In *Daniel Carpi Jubilee Volume*. Edited by Minna Rozen, Anita Shapira, and Dina Porat. Tel Aviv: Tel Aviv University, 1996.

"Curfew Time in the Ghetto of Venice." In *Medieval and Renaissance Venice*. Edited by Ellen E. Kittell and Thomas F. Madden. Urbana: University of Illinois Press, 1999.

"Between the Myth of Venice and the Lachrymose Conception of Jewish History: The Case of the Jews of Venice." In *The Jews of Italy: Memory and Identity*. Edited by Bernard Dov Cooperman and Barbara Garvin. Potomac: University Press of Maryland, 2000.

"The Venetian Government and the Jews." In *The Jews of Early Modern Venice*. Edited by Robert C. Davis and Benjamin Ravid. Baltimore: Johns Hopkins University Press, 2001.

"An Introduction to the Charters of the Jewish Merchants of Venice." In *The Mediterranean and the Jews: Society, Culture and Economy in Early Modern Times*. Edited by Elliott Horowitz and Moises Orfali. Ramat-Gan: Bar-Ilan University Press, 2002.

Studies on the Jews of Venice, 1382–1797. Aldershot: Ashgate, 2003.

"How 'Other' Really Was the Jewish Other? The Evidence from Venice." In *Acculturation and Its Discontents: The Italian Jewish Experience Between Exclusion and Inclusion*. Edited by David N. Myers. Toronto: University of Toronto Press, 2008.

"All Ghettos Were Jewish Quarters but Not All Jewish Quarters Were Ghettos." In *The Frankfurt "Judengasse": Jewish Life in an Early Modern German City*. Edited by Fritz Backhaus, Gisela Engel, Robert Liberles, and Margarete Schlüter. London: Vallentine Mitchell, 2010.

"Venice and Its Minorities." In *A Companion to Venetian History, 1400–1797*. Edited by Eric R. Dursteler. Leiden: Brill, 2013.

Ray, Meredith K. "Letters and Lace: Arcangela Tarabotti and Convent Culture in *Seicento* Venice." In *Early Modern Women and Transnational Communities of Letters*. Edited by Julie D. Campbell and Anne R. Larsen. Farnham: Ashgate, 2009.

Redford, Bruce. *Venice & the Grand Tour*. New Haven, CT: Yale University Press, 1996.

Reill, Dominique Kirchner. *Nationalists Who Feared the Nation: Adriatic Multi-Nationalism in Habsburg Dalmatia, Trieste, and Venice*. Stanford, CA: Stanford University Press, 2012.

Resnick, Irven M. "Medieval Roots of the Myth of Jewish Male Menses." *Harvard Theological Review* 93, no. 3 (July 2000): 241–63.

Ring, James W. "Windows, Baths, and Solar Energy in the Roman Empire." *American Journal of Archaeology* 100, no. 4 (October 1996): 717–24.

Rocke, Michael. *Forbidden Friendships: Homosexuality and Male Culture in Renaissance Florence*. New York: Oxford University Press, 1996.

Rogger, Iginio, and Marco Bellabarba, eds. *Il principe vescovo Johannes Hinderbach (1465–1486) fra tardo Medioevo e Umanesimo*. Bologna: Edizioni Dehoniane, 1992.

Romano, Dennis. *Patricians and Popolani: The Social Foundations of the Venetian Renaissance State*. Baltimore: Johns Hopkins University Press, 1987.

"Gender and the Urban Geography of Renaissance Venice." *Journal of Social History* 23, no. 2 (Winter 1989): 339–53.

Rosand, David. *Myths of Venice: The Figuration of a State*. Chapel Hill: University of North Carolina Press, 2001.

Roth, Cecil. "The Eastertide Stoning of the Jews and Its Liturgical Echoes." *Jewish Quarterly Review*, New Series, 35, no. 4 (April 1945): 361–70.

History of the Jews in Venice. New York: Schocken, 1958.

Rothman, E. Natalie. "Conversion and Convergence in the Venetian-Ottoman Borderlands." *Journal of Medieval and Early Modern Studies* 41, no. 3 (Fall 2011): 601–33.

Brokering Empire: Trans-Imperial Subjects between Venice and Istanbul. Ithaca, NY: Cornell University Press, 2012.

Rubin, Miri. *Corpus Christi: The Eucharist in Late Medieval Culture*. Cambridge, MA: Cambridge University Press, 1991.

Gentile Tales: The Narrative Assault on Late Medieval Jews. New Haven, CT: Yale University Press, 1999.

Ruderman, David B. "The Cultural Significance of the Ghetto in Jewish History." In *From Ghetto to Emancipation: Historical and Contemporary Reconsiderations of the Jewish Community*. Edited by David N. Myers and William V. Rowe. Scranton, PA: University of Scranton Press, 1997.

Ruether, Rosemary Radford. "The *Adversus Judaeos* Tradition in the Church Fathers: The Exegesis of Christian Anti-Judaism." In *Essential Papers on Judaism and Christianity in Conflict: From Late Antiquity to the Reformation*. Edited by Jeremy Cohen. New York: New York University Press, 1991.

Ruggiero, Guido. "The Cooperation of Physicians and the State in the Control of Violence in Renaissance Venice." *Journal of the History of Medicine and Allied Sciences* 33, no. 2 (April 1978): 156–66.

Violence in Early Renaissance Venice. New Brunswick, NJ: Rutgers University Press, 1980.

The Boundaries of Eros: Sex Crime and Sexuality in Renaissance Venice. New York: Oxford University Press, 1985.

"Constructing Civic Morality, Deconstructing the Body: Civic Rituals of Punishment in Renaissance Venice." In *Riti e rituali nelle società medievali*. Edited by Jacques Chiffoleau, Lauro Martines, and Agostino Paravicini Bagliani. Spoleto: Centro italiano di studi sull'alto medioevo, 1994.

Sacerdoti, Annie. *The Guide to Jewish Italy*. Translated by David Kerr. New York: Rizzoli, 2004.

San Juan, Rose Marie. *Rome: A City Out of Print*. Minneapolis: University of Minnesota Press, 2001.

Schivelbusch, Wolfgang. *Disenchanted Night: The Industrialization of Life in the Nineteenth Century*. Berkeley: University of California Press, 1988.

Schuder, Rosemarie, and Rudolf Hirsch. *Der gelbe Fleck: Wurzeln und Wirkungen des Judenhasses in der deutschen Geschichte: Essays*. Cologne: Röderberg im Pahl-Rugenstein, 1988.

Schulz, Juergen. "The Printed Plans and Panoramic Views of Venice (1486–1797)." In *Saggi e memorie di storia dell'arte*. Vol. 7. Florence: Leo S. Olschki, 1970.

"Jacopo de' Barbari's View of Venice: Map Making, City Views, and Moralized Geography before the Year 1500." *Art Bulletin* 60, no. 3 (September 1978): 425–74.

The New Palaces of Medieval Venice. University Park, PA: Penn State University Press, 2004.

Schutte, Anne Jacobson. "The Permeable Cloister?" In *Arcangela Tarabotti: A Literary Nun in Baroque Venice*. Edited by Elissa B. Weaver. Ravenna: Longo, 2006.

Schwarzer, Mitchell. "The Extremes of Spatial Experience." *AA Files*, no. 57 (2008): 67–73.

Sennett, Richard. *Flesh and Stone: The Body and the City in Western Civilization*. New York: W. W. Norton, 1994.

"The Open City." *Urban Age* (November 2006): 1–5.

Shapiro, James. *Shakespeare and the Jews*. New York: Columbia University Press, 1996.

Shaw, Diane. "The Construction of the Private in Medieval London." *Journal of Medieval and Early Modern Studies* 26, no. 3 (Fall 1996): 447–66.

Shepard, Alexandra, and Phil Withington, eds. *Communities in Early Modern England: Networks, Place, Rhetoric*. Manchester: Manchester University Press, 2000.

Siegmund, Stefanie B. *The Medici State and the Ghetto of Florence: The Construction of an Early Modern Jewish Community*. Stanford, CA: Stanford University Press, 2006.

Simmel, Georg. "Brücke und Tür." *Das Individuum und die Freiheit. Essais*. Berlin: Klaus Wagenbach, 1984.

"Bridge and Door." In *Rethinking Architecture: A Reader in Cultural Theory*. Edited by Neil Leach. New York: Routledge, 1997.

Simons, Patricia. "Women in Frames: The Gaze, the Eye, the Profile in Renaissance Portraiture." *History Workshop: A Journal of Socialist and Feminist Historians* 25 (Spring 1988): 4–30. Reprinted in *The Expanding Discourse: Feminism and Art History*. Edited by Norma Broude and Mary D. Garrard. New York: Icon Editions, 1992.

Simonsfeld, Henry. *Der Fondaco dei Tedeschi in Venedig und die deutsch-venetianischen Handelsbeziehungen*. Stuttgart: Cotta, 1887.

Simonsohn, Shlomo. *History of the Jews in the Duchy of Mantua*. Jerusalem: Kiryath Sepher, 1977.

The Apostolic See and the Jews: Documents, 492–1404. Toronto: Pontifical Institute of Mediaeval Studies, 1988.

Skinner, Quentin. *The Foundations of Modern Political Thought*. Vol. 1. Cambridge: Cambridge University Press, 1978.

Sperling, Jutta Gisela. *Convents and the Body Politic in Late Renaissance Venice*. Chicago: University of Chicago Press, 1999.

Stacey, Peter. *Roman Monarchy and the Renaissance Prince*. Cambridge: Cambridge University Press, 2007.

Stahl, Alan M. "Coin and Punishment in Medieval Venice." In *Law and the Illicit in Medieval Europe*. Edited by Ruth Mazo Karras, Joel Kaye, and E. Ann Matter. Philadelphia: University of Pennsylvania Press, 2008.

Stallybrass, Peter. "Patriarchal Territories: The Body Enclosed." In *Rewriting the Renaissance: The Discourses of Sexual Difference in Early Modern Europe*. Edited by Margaret W. Ferguson, Maureen Quilligan, and Nancy J. Vickers. Chicago: University of Chicago Press, 1986.

Starr, Joshua. "Jewish Life in Crete Under the Rule of Venice." *Proceedings of the American Academy for Jewish Research* 12 (1942): 59–114.

Stiefel, Barry. *Jews and the Renaissance of Synagogue Architecture, 1450–1730*. London: Pickering & Chatto, 2014.

Stow, Kenneth. *Catholic Thought and Papal Jewry Policy, 1555–1593*. New York: Jewish Theological Seminary of America, 1977.

"The Proper Meaning of 'Cum Nimis Absurdum.'" *Jewish Quarterly Review* 71, no. 4 (April 1981): 251–52.

"Hatred of the Jews or Love of the Church: Papal Policy Toward the Jews in the Middle Ages." In *Antisemitism Through the Ages*. Edited by Shmuel Almog. Translated by Nathan H. Reisner. Oxford: Pergamon Press, 1988.

"The Consciousness of Closure: Roman Jewry and Its *Ghet*." In *Essential Papers on Jewish Culture in Renaissance and Baroque Italy*. Edited by David B. Ruderman. New York: New York University Press, 1992.

"Ethnic Rivalry or Melting Pot: The Edot in the Roman Ghetto." *Judaism* 41, no. 3 (Summer 1992): 286–96.

"Sanctity and the Construction of Space: The Roman Ghetto as Sacred Space." In *Jewish Assimilation, Acculturation, and Accommodation: Past Traditions, Current Issues, and Future Prospects*. Edited by Menachem Mor. Lanham, MD: University Press of America, 1992.

"A Tale of Uncertainties: Converts in the Roman Ghetto." In *Shlomo Simonsohn Jubilee Volume: Studies on the History of the Jews in the Middle Ages and Renaissance Period*. Edited by Daniel Carpi et al. Tel Aviv: Tel Aviv University, 1993.

"Marriages Are Made in Heaven: Marriage and the Individual in the Roman Jewish Ghetto." *Renaissance Quarterly* 48, no. 3 (Autumn 1995): 445–91.

Theater of Acculturation: The Roman Ghetto in the Sixteenth Century. Seattle: University of Washington Press, 2001.

Jewish Dogs: An Image and Its Interpreters, Continuity in the Catholic-Jewish Encounter. Stanford, CA: Stanford University Press, 2006.

Jewish Life in Early Modern Rome: Challenge, Conversion, and Private Life. Aldershot: Ashgate, 2007.

Stoye, John. *English Travellers Abroad, 1604–1667: Their Influence in English Society and Politics*. New York: Octagon Books, 1968.

Strocchia, Sharon. "Gender and the Rites of Honor in Italian Renaissance Cities." In *Gender and Society in Renaissance Italy*. Edited by Judith C. Brown and Robert C. Davis. London: Longman, 1998.

"Theaters of Everyday Life." In *Renaissance Florence: A Social History*. Edited by Roger J. Crum and John T. Paoletti. New York: Cambridge University Press, 2006.

Sturken, Marita, and Lisa Cartwright. *Practices of Looking: An Introduction to Visual Culture*. Oxford: Oxford University Press, 2001.

Tafuri, Manfredo. *Interpreting the Renaissance: Princes, Cities, Architects*. Translated by Daniel Sherer. New Haven, CT: Yale University Press, 2006.

Tamassia Mazzarotto, Bianca. *Le feste veneziane: I giochi popolari, le cerimonie religiose e di governo*. Florence: Sansoni, 1980.

Tassini, Giuseppe. *Feste, spettacoli, divertimenti, e piaceri degli antichi veneziani*. Venice: Filippi, 1961.

Taylor, Katherine Fischer. "Architecture's Place in Art History: Art or Adjunct?" *Art Bulletin* 83, no. 2 (June 2001): 342–46.

Terpstra, Nicholas. *Lost Girls: Sex and Death in Renaissance Florence*. Baltimore: Johns Hopkins University Press, 2010.

Teyssot, Georges. "'Water and Gas on All Floors': Notes on the Extraneousness of the Home." *Lotus International* 44 (1984): 82–93.

Thatcher, Edwin Daisley. "The Open Rooms of the Terme del Foro at Ostia." *Memoirs of the American Academy in Rome* 24 (1956): 169–264.

Tichy, Susanne. *Et vene la mumaria: Studien zur venezianischen Festkultur der Renaissance.* Munich: Scaneg, 1997.

Toaff, Ariel. *Love, Work, and Death: Jewish Life in Medieval Umbria.* Translated by Judith Landry. London: Littman Library of Jewish Civilization, 1996.

Tomas, Natalie. "Did Women Have a Space?" In *Renaissance Florence: A Social History.* Edited by Roger J. Crum and John T. Paoletti. New York: Cambridge University Press, 2006.

Tosi, Laura, and Shaul Bassi, eds. *Visions of Venice in Shakespeare.* Farnham: Ashgate, 2011.

Trachtenberg, Marvin. *Dominion of the Eye: Urbanism, Art, and Power in Early Modern Florence.* Cambridge: Cambridge University of Press, 1997.

Treue, Wolfgang. *Der Trienter Judenprozeß: Voraussetzungen, Abläufe, Auswirkungen, 1475–1588.* Hannover: Hahnsche Buchhandlung, 1996.

Trexler, Richard C. "La prostitution florentine au XVe siècle: Patronages et clientèles." *Annales. Économies, Sociétés, Civilisations* 36, no. 6 (1981): 983–1015.

Trincanato, Egle R. *Venezia minore.* Milan: Edizioni del Milione, 1948.

Turner, James Grantham. *Libertines and Radicals in Early Modern London: Sexuality, Politics and Literary Culture, 1630–1685.* Cambridge: Cambridge University Press, 2002.

Tylus, Jane. "Women at the Windows: 'Commedia dell'arte' and Theatrical Practice in Early Modern Italy." *Theatre Journal* 49, no. 3 (October 1997): 323–42.

Venkatesh, Sudhir Alladi. *American Project: The Rise and Fall of a Modern Ghetto.* Cambridge, MA: Harvard University Press, 2000.

Venturi, Robert. *Complexity and Contradiction in Architecture.* New York: Museum of Modern Art, 2002.

Venturi, Robert, Denise Scott Brown, and Steven Izenour. *Learning from Las Vegas: The Forgotten Symbolism of Architectural Form.* Cambridge, MA: MIT Press, 1977.

Verdon, Jean. *La nuit au Moyen Âge.* Paris: Perrin, 1994.

"Recherches sur la société religieuse et la nuit au Moyen Âge." In *Les prélats, l'Église et la société, XIe-XVe siècles: Hommage à Bernard Guillemain.* Edited by Françoise Bériac. Bordeaux: Université Michel de Montaigne, 1994.

Wamers, Egon, and Markus Grossbach. *Die Judengasse in Frankfurt am Main: Ergebnisse der archäologischen Untersuchungen am Börneplatz.* Stuttgart: Jan Thorbecke, 2000.

Weiss, Raymond L. *Maimonides' Ethics: The Encounter of Philosophic and Religious Morality.* Chicago: University of Chicago Press, 1991.

Welch, Evelyn. *Shopping in the Renaissance: Consumer Cultures in Italy, 1400–1600.* New Haven, CT: Yale University Press, 2005.

Westwater, Lynn Lara. "The Disquieting Voice: Women's Writing and Antifeminism in Seventeenth-Century Venice." Ph.D. diss., University of Chicago, 2003.

Wharton, Annabel, ed. "Maps of Authority: Conflict in the Medieval & Early Modern Urban Landscape." Special Issue: *Journal of Medieval and Early Modern Studies* 26, no. 3 (Fall 1996).

Wheeler, Jo. "Stench in Sixteenth-Century Venice." In *The City and the Senses: Urban Culture Since 1500.* Edited by Alexander Cowan and Jill Steward. Aldershot: Ashgate, 2007.

Wigley, Mark. "Untitled: The Housing of Gender." In *Sexuality & Space*. Edited by Beatriz Colomina. New York: Princeton Architectural Press, 1992.

Wills, Garry. *Venice, Lion City: The Religion of Empire*. New York: Simon & Schuster, 2001.

Wilson, Bronwen. *The World in Venice: Print, the City, and Early Modern Identity*. Toronto: University of Toronto Press, 2005.

Wittkower, Rudolf. "Camillo Sitte's Art of Building Cities in an American Translation." *Town Planning Review* 19, no. 3/4 (Summer 1947): 164–69.

Architectural Principles in the Age of Humanism. New York: W. W. Norton: 1971.

Wolff, Larry. "Venice and the Slavs of Dalmatia: The Drama of the Adriatic Empire in the Venetian Enlightenment." *Slavic Review* 56, no. 3 (Autumn 1997): 428–55.

"The Enlightened Anthropology of Friendship in Venetian Dalmatia: Primitive Ferocity and Ritual Fraternity among the Morlacchi." *Eighteenth-Century Studies* 32, no. 2 (Winter 1998/99): 157–78.

Venice and the Slavs: The Discovery of Dalmatia in the Age of Enlightenment. Stanford, CA: Stanford University Press, 2001.

Wolfthal, Diane. *Picturing Yiddish: Gender, Identity, and Memory in the Illustrated Yiddish Books of Renaissance Italy*. Leiden: Brill, 2004.

In and Out of the Marital Bed: Seeing Sex in Renaissance Europe. New Haven, CT: Yale University Press, 2010.

Woodress, James Leslie. *Howells & Italy*. Durham, NC: Duke University Press, 1952.

Worrall, Simon. Interview of Shaul Bassi. *Smithsonian Journeys Quarterly* (November 6, 2015): www.smithsonianmag.com/travel/venice-ghetto-jews-italy-anniversary-shaul-bassi-180956867/?no-ist.

Yegül, Fikret. *Baths and Bathing in Classical Antiquity*. Cambridge, MA: MIT Press, 1992.

Young, James E. *At Memory's Edge: After-Images of the Holocaust in Contemporary Art and Architecture*. New Haven, CT: Yale University Press, 2000.

Zarri, Gabriella. "Venetian Convents and Civic Ritual." In *Arcangela Tarabotti: A Literary Nun in Baroque Venice*. Edited by Elissa B. Weaver. Ravenna: Longo, 2006.

Žižek, Slavoj. *Looking Awry: An Introduction to Jacques Lacan through Popular Culture*. Cambridge, MA: MIT Press, 1991.

Zucker, Paul. *Town and Square from the Agora to the Village Green*. New York: Columbia University Press, 1959.

INDEX

Page numbers in italics refer to figures.